Elias Cornelius Boudinot

Elias Cornelius Boudinot

A Life on the Cherokee Border

JAMES W. PARINS

University of Nebraska Press   Lincoln and London

All photographs are courtesy of the
Archives and Manuscripts Division
of the Oklahoma Historical Society

Library of Congress Cataloging-in-
Publication Data
Parins, James W.
Elias Cornelius Boudinot: a life on
the Cherokee border / James W. Parins.
p.   cm.—(American Indian lives)
Includes bibliographical references and index.
ISBN-13: 978-0-8032-3752-0 (hardcover: alk. paper)
ISBN-10: 0-8032-3752-9 (hardcover: alk. paper)
1. Boudinot, Elias C. (Elias Cornelius), 1835–1890.
2. Indian Territory—Biography.   3. Racially
mixed people—Oklahoma—Biography.
4. Cherokee Indians—Biography.
5. Cherokee Indians—Government relations.
I. Title.   II. Series.
F697.B753   2006
973.3'092—dc22
2005013460

For Marylyn

Contents

Illustrations

Acknowledgments

The Arkansas Humanities Council and the Office of Research and Sponsored Programs at the University of Arkansas at Little Rock were generous in their support for this project. The staff at the following institutions were also very helpful: Ottenheimer Library and Archives; Western History Collections, University of Oklahoma; Chicago Historical Society; Oklahoma State Historical Society; Missouri Historical Society; Arkansas History Commission; Gilcrease Museum Library; Federal Records Center, Fort Worth; Division of Manuscripts, Library of Congress; Kansas Historical Society; Newberry Library; St. Louis Mercantile Library Association; Union Pacific Archives; Fort Smith Public Library; Mullins Library Archives, University of Arkansas, Fayetteville; American Native Press Archives, University of Arkansas at Little Rock.

I would also like to thank the following individuals: Bill Welge of the Oklahoma State Historical Society; Helen Davis, a historian of the Boudinot family; Jack Baker of the Trail of Tears Association; LaVonne Ruoff; Marylyn Jackson Parins; and my longtime friend, collaborator, and colleague, Daniel F. Littlefield Jr.

Elias Cornelius Boudinot

Background and Boyhood

An examination of Elias Cornelius Boudinot's life is important if only for the light it sheds on Cherokee history. Boudinot was a leading figure in a turbulent era of that nation, one in which the tribe was forced from their traditional homeland by white encroachment to a new world west of the Mississippi, a country they eventually lost to the inexorable advance of Manifest Destiny. Much as his father had been embroiled in the controversy over Cherokee removal in the eastern Cherokee Nation, Elias Cornelius Boudinot was intimately involved in the events that led to the demise of the Cherokee Nation in the West. From early on the younger Boudinot predicted the outcome of the struggle between the Native American nations of Indian Territory and the amalgam of economic, social, and political forces that buffeted them.

Perhaps more importantly, Boudinot's life is also worth viewing from the perspective of the twenty-first century, a time in which Native Americans' problems have not changed. The struggles of Boudinot's day—over sovereignty, taxation, citizenship, treaty rights, tribal factionalism, and the exploitation of Native American natural and economic resources—continue in our own. During his lifetime, Boudinot was enmeshed in major events that influenced these issues. For much of his life, for example, he advocated the dissolution of tribal sovereignty in Indian Territory and championed a territorial government. Sovereignty remains a major issue today in Native Americans' dealings with local, state, and federal governments. Further, he favored the extinction of tribal titles to land, to be replaced by individual allotments for Native Americans. Many of the arguments in that controversy recur in twenty-first-century discussions of tribal termination. In what was probably the first "Indian smoke shop" case, Boudinot was involved in one of the most important tax disputes between federal and state governments and American Indians. In response to charges by white competitors that he had an unfair advantage, his tobacco factory in the Cherokee Nation was closed for selling untaxed goods to people in surrounding states. In addition, he was a figure in various tribal citizenship disputes involving both Cherokees and their former black slaves while at the same time he lobbied in Washington to make all Native Americans U.S. citizens. Citizenship has continued to be a hotly debated issue in many Indian nations to the present. Boudinot was a principal in a Cherokee factional struggle that can be traced to the present day. As a leader of the Ridge-Boudinot-Watie party, he waged relentless war against the Ross faction; the Boudinot/Ross dichotomy is mirrored in many "progressive" versus "conservative" tribal disputes today. Boudinot, like his father, was involved with treaty making for a time, but by about 1870 he had come to believe that all the treaties signed by the federal government and the Native nations were not worth the paper they were written on, a stand that reverberates today in Indian Country as Native Americans fight to preserve their rights. Finally, this Cherokee orator, editor, lawyer, and lobbyist was also an inveterate businessman, involved in numerous schemes to extract wealth from the land, minerals, and markets of Indian Territory. Boudinot drove the first railroad spike in the Territory, initiated a "colonization" effort in the tribally owned Cherokee Outlet, and was instrumental in opening what is now Oklahoma to white settlement. Today, of course, economic considerations are at the heart of many controversies involving Natives and the larger society, from fisheries in the Northwest to mining in the Southwest to grazing rights in the Great Plains.

Over the years, the question of Cornelius Boudinot's reputation has been problematic. At his funeral, for example, speaker after speaker stood before a packed and distinguished audience in Judge Isaac Parker's ornate courtroom to praise the deceased.[1] Later, in the early twentieth century, various proposals were offered to name an Oklahoma town and a county in honor of Boudinot.[2] This is in stark contrast to a period of his life when he was warned to stay out of the Cherokee Nation on pain of death. More than a hundred years after Boudinot's death, the Sons of the Confederacy named its Sallisaw, Oklahoma, chapter after him and plans to erect a monument over his grave in Fort Smith.[3] But the controversy over whether Boudinot was a greedy charlatan or a patriotic visionary continues.

Elias Cornelius Boudinot was born into an important Cherokee family at his Nation's capital, New Echota, in present-day Georgia. His father, the well-educated Elias Boudinot (Gallegina, or Buck Watie), even as a young man was regarded as a leader in the Nation and as a person who would help his people resist the increasing encroachment of white settlers. The elder Boudinot was the son of David Watie (Oo-watie) and the nephew of Major Ridge, a man prominent in Cherokee affairs. In 1818, David Watie and Major Ridge made a decision that had far-reaching implications for their sons and for the Cherokee Nation: they chose to enroll their sons in the American Board of Commissioners for Foreign Missions (ABCFM) school in Cornwall, Connecticut.

Longtime advocates of education, Watie and Ridge had earlier arranged schooling for their children in local schools provided by white missionaries. They saw the whites' schools as important for the advancement of not only their own families but the entire Nation. Missionaries had conducted schools in the Cherokee Nation in parts of what are now North Carolina, Georgia, and Tennessee since April or May 1801, when Abraham Steiner and Gottlieb Byhan started a Moravian mission and school at Spring Place, in present-day Georgia. In 1805 John Gambold and his wife arrived at the mission, bringing new enthusiasm and energy to the school. In 1803 Gideon Blackburn had opened a Presbyterian mission and school near the Hiwassee River, having secured approval for his enterprise from the federal government, the principal chiefs of the Nation, and Colonel Return J. Meigs, the American agent to the Cherokees. John and Nancy Ridge attended the Spring Place school in 1810, with Buck Watie joining them in the following year. The children did well under the Gambolds' tutelage, but in 1815 Major Ridge and his wife, Susanna (Sehoya), decided to withdraw their children because young John was ailing with a "scrofulous" hip. The Ridges hired an itinerant teacher to teach the Ridge and Watie children at home, but the experiment failed when the new schoolmaster turned out to be an incompetent drunk. After three months, Buck Watie returned to Spring Place, taking his brother Stand with him. The Ridge children, however, were sent to Cyrus Kingsbury's new Brainerd School on Chickamauga Creek in Tennessee, some sixty miles from their home.

During this period, the federal government was pressing the Cherokees to remove to western Arkansas, where land taken from the Osages had been set aside for them. Cherokee leaders, among them Major Ridge, offered a proposal in the form of a petition asking the government to provide more aid to education in the Nation. The carefully prepared proposal documented the need for the aid and also showed that the Cherokees were sincere in their efforts to accept white civilization. The strategy of depicting themselves as civilized—or at least well on the road to civilization—was an important part of the Cherokees' defense against forced removal and the encroachment of white settlers into the Nation. Just as the petition was being drafted, an agent from the ABCFM, one Elias Cornelius, arrived in the area.

Cornelius was impressed by the Cherokees' plan, so much so that he asked the Cherokee National Council for permission to expand ABCFM efforts among their people. As part of this initiative, he proposed to enroll promising Cherokee students in the new ABCFM boarding school at Cornwall. The school, established as a means of educating "foreign youth," had already enrolled one Abnaki, two Chinese, two Malays, one Bengali, one Hindu, several Hawaiians, two Marquesans, and three white Americans. The school's founders were now seeking to add representatives from southern Native American groups. Cornelius invited Buck Watie, John Ridge, and Leonard Hicks, son of the Cherokee assistant principal chief, to travel with him to Connecticut so they could assess the suitability of the school. Accordingly, they set out in May 1818, stopping at Monticello to meet Thomas Jefferson and at Washington to greet President Monroe. In addition, Cornelius introduced the boys to Elias Boudinot, president of the American Bible Society and former president of the Continental Congress. The elder statesman took an interest in Buck Watie and urged the Cherokee to adopt his name. When the young man entered Cornwall School, he did so as Elias Boudinot, the name by which he was known for the rest of his life.

A contingent of Cherokee students including John Ridge, John Vann, and David Steiner (Darcheechee) left for Connecticut in September 1818, arriving in late November. They were joined later by Elias Boudinot. The new students did well at their studies, which consisted of Latin, natural science, geography, history, surveying, and rhetoric. In addition, the students received "instruction" in agriculture, a large part of which involved working on the school farm, and religious training, a staple in any mission school. Cornwall's headmaster, Rev. Herman Daggett, identified Ridge and Boudinot as his best students.[4]

Although Ridge was doing well at his studies, his health was not improving. As the lymphatic condition of his hip worsened, he was moved out of the school's attic dormitory into a private home and put under the care of Mrs. John Northrup and her fourteen-year-old daughter, Sarah Bird. Ridge slowly regained his health, but as he did so it became apparent to everyone that the Cherokee and the younger of his nurses had fallen in love. Sarah's family reacted by sending her to stay with her grandmother in New Haven. Undaunted, John wrote to his parents asking for permission to marry Sarah, but his mother, after consulting the missionaries at Brainerd, refused to give her consent. Ridge persisted, however, and his parents reluctantly gave in to his wishes. With one hurdle cleared, he proposed to Sarah, but found her family clearly opposed to the union; Sarah's parents, perhaps hoping that a separation would cool off the relationship, suggested that Ridge return to his people in the South, regain his health fully, then return to pursue his suit if he was still so inclined. Accordingly, he left Cornwall at the end of the summer of 1822 and did not return until December the following year. When he arrived he found the Northrups reconciled to the idea of the marriage, but now opposition was forthcoming from other sources: the couple was denounced by area newspapers and castigated on racial grounds by members of the clergy. A published denunciation of the marriage quoted some outraged Cornwallians as saying that "the girl ought to be whipped, the Indian hung, and the mother drown'd." [5] Apparently, many Cornwall citizens did not want one of their white daughters carried off by an Indian, no matter how civilized he was. The ceremony took place on January 27, 1824, but the couple was forced to leave Cornwall immediately because they were in danger of being mobbed. John and Sarah Bird Northrup Ridge headed south to take up residence in the Cherokee Nation.

The controversy did not end with the pair's departure, however. Isaiah Bunce, editor of the *Litchfield Eagle* and longtime opponent of the mission school, made sure that the controversy was kept alive. Announcing that Sarah Bird had "made herself a *squaw*" and had been taken "into the wilderness among savages," he denounced "intermarriages" with Indians and blacks.[6] He went on to blame the situation on supporters of the school, many of whom were clergymen and other prominent citizens. One of the men with connections to the school was Colonel Benjamin Gold, who had entertained many of its students in his home and whose family had corresponded with people in the Cherokee Nation. Gold took it upon himself to respond to Bunce's denunciations in a letter sent to the editor. When it was not published in the *Eagle*, Gold sent a copy to the New Haven *Connecticut Journal*, where it did appear. The letter categorically denied Bunce's assertions as "base fabrications" and challenged the editor to make public the names of those local citizens who Bunce claims are outraged by the situation at the school.[7] The letter was published on August 19, 1824; a short time later, Gold's daughter Harriet asked her father for permission to marry Elias Boudinot.

Boudinot had returned to the Cherokee Nation in 1823; from there he had carried on a correspondence with the girl he loved. By summer of the next year, the couple had decided to marry. Harriet tried to reason with her shocked family, pointing out that she intended to become a missionary to the Cherokees and that this vocation would be greatly enhanced by marriage to one of the Nation's leading citizens. The Golds were adamant in their opposition, citing the family's community standing and reputation as reason enough to reject their daughter's betrothal to a relative stranger, an outlander, and an Indian to boot. Determined to put a halt to what they considered an unfortunate state of affairs, Harriet's parents sent a letter of refusal to Boudinot. At that point the young woman's health began to fail, and as time went on she became weaker and weaker. Her physician, cousin Dr. Samuel Gold, was called in, but he seemed to be powerless; after a short time he doctor feared for Harriet's life. As soon as it became apparent to the family that the patient had lost her will to live, they rescinded their prohibition of marriage and sent a second letter to Boudinot that outlined their new position.

Harriet's health improved after this, but the family kept news of the impending wedding secret until the family could be prepared for what was certain to be a vociferous reaction. Harriet's brother-in-law, General Daniel Bourbon Brinsmade, met with fellow members of the Cornwall School board to announce the news. Shortly after, one of the board members, Rev. Joseph Harvey, gave Harriet an ultimatum: If she would inform the board within three days that she had given Boudinot up, the members would keep her secret and the matter would be dropped. If she did not comply, the board would publish the banns of their marriage in any way they saw fit. A defiant Harriet Gold refused to give in to Harvey's threat, and the banns were published on June 17, 1825. In their statement, the board castigated the Gold family: anyone condoning the Gold-Boudinot connection they declared "criminal," offering "insult to the christian community" and violating the "sacred interests" of Cornwall School.[8]

Once the news was out, quiet Cornwall erupted to such an extent that it was considered unsafe for Harriet to remain at home. From a window of the home of the Clarks, a friendly neighbor with whom she had sought shelter, Harriet could see a mob forming on the village green, where they displayed paintings of a young woman and an Indian. As the sun went down the church bell began to ring, tolling as if for the soul of someone who had died. Harriet watched as the effigies of herself and Boudinot were thrown on a barrel of burning tar, the fire having been lit by her brother Stephen. After the paintings had been burned, the bell continued to ring far into the night. But Harriet Gold stood firm, enduring the scorn and animosity of former friends, fellow churchgoers, and even family members. In a letter to her brother-in-law, Harriet expressed her complete bafflement at the behavior of many of her townspeople: this was not "done merely by the wicked world," but "professed Christians attended and gave their approbation."[9]

When Elias Boudinot traveled north to join his bride in March 1826, he was careful. He had received threats while he was in the Cherokee Nation, with at least one missive decorated with a crude depiction of a gallows.[10] By the time he approached the town, the situation seemed to have calmed down; the undercurrent of bad feeling must have been almost palpable, however, since the young Cherokee thought it necessary to don a disguise before his entry into Cornwall. The couple was wed on March 28 in the Gold home. After the ceremony, Harriet's parents escorted the Boudinots as far as Washington, Connecticut, on the first leg of their journey to Boston, where Elias was due to lecture. From there they would travel to their new home in the Cherokee Nation. The Foreign Mission School at Cornwall closed for good in the autumn of 1826.[11]

Colonel Gold journeyed over a thousand miles in a one-horse wagon to New Echota in the fall of 1829 to visit Harriet and her husband. Naturally, he and the rest of the family were concerned about Harriet's welfare on the far-off frontier living with such "savages" as the Cornwall School had tried to civilize. Upon his arrival, however, he found his daughter doing quite well. With almost her first words she entreated her father to carry the message to her cousin Dr. Samuel Gold that "she does not regret" her marriage and that "she envies the situation of no one in Connecticut." And Benjamin could well believe her.[12]

Benjamin found his daughter living in a large frame two-story house, well furnished with all the comforts of life. The Boudinot children—Eleanor Susan, born on March 4, 1827, and Mary Harriet, born on October 5, 1828—both would pass for "Full-blooded Yankees," he seems happy to report. The family was well supplied with a store of staple goods from the merchants in Augusta, Georgia. Fancier goods such as tea and clothes, as well as ink and paper for the *Cherokee Phoenix*, Boudinot's newspaper, were imported from Boston suppliers. Gold says that "they have two or three barrels of flour on hand at once," the local New Echota store supplying their other wants.

Gold seems equally impressed with the rest of the New Echota settlement, noting that the town is "truly an interesting and pleasant place," a newly laid out community on level ground with 100 one-acre lots. Generously watered by a number of springs, the town had several newly built houses, all resembling those in New England. Harriet's father was especially taken with the public buildings in the center of the plat: the council house, courthouse, the *Phoenix* printing office, and four stores. All four stores were needed, he explains, only during the session of the council, when an influx of Cherokee citizens gathered in the capital from the surrounding areas. Afterward, three were removed to other parts of the Nation. The stores were as large as the best in Litchfield County, Gold goes on to say, and all are very well provisioned.[13]

Gold's letter includes high praise as well for his son-in-law, the editor of the national newspaper. The *Cherokee Phoenix*, he says, is respected throughout the United States and is well known in Europe. The *Phoenix* office regularly received around one hundred newspapers from publishers far and wide. But Elias Boudinot had other duties in addition to his editorship of the Nation's news organ. He was also clerk of the Cherokee National Council, and in 1829 he served as clerk of the Creek delegation to Congress. Gold reported that Boudinot earned from five to ten thousand dollars in a year's time.

As Benjamin Gold had pointed out, Boudinot was the editor of the national newspaper, the *Cherokee Phoenix*. In 1825, Tsalagi Tinilawigi (or Cherokee National Council) had decided to appropriate fifteen hundred dollars to establish a press. This amount was too small to buy a press, an English-type font, and a specially cast font of type in the Sequoyan syllabary. The council chose Boudinot to canvass white communities in the East to raise the needed additional funds. At the same time, they offered him the editorship of the planned tribal newspaper. Boudinot began his fund-raising tour in Charleston, later traveling to New York City, Salem, and Boston, taking a break from his lecturing to marry Harriet. The couple then traveled to Philadelphia, where his lecture was printed in the form of a sixteen-page pamphlet. The pamphlet continued to bring in funds long after the Boudinots had left for the Cherokee Nation. The gist of his message to the whites was simple: civilizing the Indians is a wise and practical course proved possible by the Cherokee experience. "It needs only that the world should know what we have done in the past few years," Boudinot said, "to foresee what yet we may do with the assistance of our white brethren, and that of the common Parent of us all." The very existence of a Native newspaper would demonstrate the Cherokees' civilized state even as it publicized the Nation's progress in other endeavors and helped to educate Native readers.[14]

After the Boudinots returned to the Cherokee Nation, Elias began teaching in the mission school at Hightower and at the same time established an important collaboration with missionary Samuel A. Worcester. Worcester had come to the Cherokee Nation to learn the language and to translate religious works

8

into Cherokee. He quickly enlisted the translating talent of young Boudinot as the pair began systematizing the Native language. This collaboration was to continue until the Cherokee's death in 1839. Meanwhile, plans to establish a press were proceeding. As soon as a press and type font were purchased and the Cherokee font was cast, the Nation built a print shop to house the operation in their capital, New Echota. About the same time, Boudinot, his wife, and infant Eleanor Susan moved into the fine new house later described by Harriet's father. The premier edition of *Tsalagi Tsu-le-hi-sa-nu-hi*, or *Cherokee Phoenix*, the first newspaper published by Native Americans, came off the small union press on February 21, 1828.

By the following year, the newspaper's title was amended to *Cherokee Phoenix, and Indians' Advocate.* The change signaled what had been one of the major objectives of the publication from the beginning, advancing the cause of the southeastern tribes in general, and the Cherokees in particular, against the onslaught of white settlement. By this time, the U.S. government's Indian removal policy had solidified from its rather nebulous beginnings under President Thomas Jefferson into a hard-line plan of action under newly elected Andrew Jackson. The Cherokee leadership knew very well that Jackson's plans had to be actively opposed if there were to be any hope of preempting them. Clearly, Boudinot and other Cherokee leaders used the *Phoenix* to present arguments that would "enlist the friendly feelings and sympathies of his subscribers abroad, in favor of the aborigines." [15] In addition, of course, a well-edited Indian newspaper signified the degree of civilization that the Cherokees had reached. However impressed subscribers in the northern cities might have been, the white citizens of the region were decidedly not. In 1828 and 1829, Georgia had extended its jurisdiction over Cherokee lands, and white Georgians began to take possession of—sometimes by force—and settle upon these lands. At the same time, the federal government increased pressure on the Native Americans to remove to the West. As the conflict intensified, the *Phoenix* focused much of its attention on this issue. Boudinot documented the actions and movements of intruders as he continued to demand from the federal government the protection guaranteed by treaties. He also attempted to appeal to the conscience of white supporters and sympathizers by reprinting copies of early agreements between the Cherokees and the government. The *Phoenix* carried news of problems the other southeastern tribes were having as well. [16]

In time, however, Boudinot's solid stand against removal began to crumble, as did the resolve of a number of his fellow Cherokees, including his uncle

Major Ridge and cousin John Ridge, influential tribal leaders. This sea change came about gradually and was caused by several factors. First and foremost was the election of Andrew Jackson in 1828, an event that had profound implications for Native Americans living east of the Mississippi, and especially for those in the South. In his first message to Congress, on December 8, 1829, Jackson announced his intention to introduce bills that would remove all American Indians to the West. This adamant stand signaled the futility of the Native nations' bargaining with and appealing to the federal government for the right to remain on their lands. Jackson's position also meant that no protection against white intruders would be forthcoming from Washington. And the intruders continued to pour in. Responding to Jackson's policy and to the wishes of many of its citizens, Georgia annexed large sections of Cherokee lands, an action that encouraged a flood of white settlers. These intruders— many of them violent men—moved into the Nation and often forcibly evicted people from their homes and farms. Around the same time, gold was discovered in the southeastern section of the Cherokee Nation, greatly exacerbating the problem. Furthermore, with the extension of its legal jurisdiction over Native territory, the state of Georgia banned meetings and elections of the Cherokee National Council. One event, however, stands out in the decision of Boudinot and his allies to recognize the futility of resistance and to acquiesce to the whites' demands: the refusal of Andrew Jackson to enforce a ruling of the Supreme Court of the United States.

Early in 1831 the Georgia legislature passed a law making it a crime for any white person to remain in the Cherokee Nation without taking an oath of allegiance to the state and receiving a permit from the governor. Two longtime missionaries to the Cherokees, Boudinot's colleague Samuel Worcester and Elizur Butler, defied this law; they were subsequently arrested by the Georgia Guard, tried, convicted, and sentenced to four years' hard labor. Worcester and Butler appealed their case to the U.S. Supreme Court. As the Court deliberated, the Cherokee leadership sent Elias Boudinot and John Ridge to Washington to offer arguments against Cherokee removal and to inform officials there about the deteriorating conditions in the Nation. Upon hearing Ridge's descriptions of the atrocities committed by intruders from Georgia, Jackson's secretary of war, Lewis Cass, reportedly said that if conditions were so bad, the Cherokees should move to the West. Seeing the futility of trying to deal with the federal government, Boudinot and Ridge traveled north to seek the support of people in Philadelphia, New York, New Haven, and Boston, venues from which they had received aid in previous years. It was on this tour that the pair heard of the Court's 1832 declaration in *Worcester and Butler v. Georgia* that the state law was unconstitutional.

Boudinot and Ridge were ecstatic at learning the news from Washington, but their elation was short lived. Rumors and newspaper reports soon began to spread the word that Jackson had decided not to enforce the Court's decision. "John Marshall has made his decision," Jackson was later reported to have said. "Let him enforce it now if he can."[17] To determine whether or not these reports were true, the pair traveled to the capital to meet with the president and put the question to him directly. Jackson replied that he would not take action against the state of Georgia, whose governor continued to keep Worcester and Butler in custody. He went on to urge the young Cherokee leaders to return to their people and convince them that their best course was to remove to the West. When they consulted with members of Congress who had encouraged them previously, they received the same message. At that point, Boudinot and Ridge decided that the best course for the Cherokees was to abandon their cause, make the best bargain they could, and take their families, slaves, and livestock to new homes west of the Mississippi. The cousins left Washington with heavy hearts and returned to their homeland.

From the summer of 1832 on, Boudinot, the Ridges, Stand Watie, and others who had reached the same conclusion worked to convince the large majority of Cherokees who remained opposed to removal that resistance was futile. Other influential Cherokees, led by Principal Chief John Ross, argued against them, calling into question their patriotism. Boudinot tried to present his faction's side in the pages of the *Phoenix*, but the Ross party forced him to resign as editor by threatening to withdraw support. Ross and his followers continued to carry out a policy of stalling negotiations with the government, hoping to outlast Jackson's administration. The Ridge-Boudinot-Watie group persevered, however, and at a council held in 1834 they drew up a memorial (a written statement of facts presented to a legislative body or executive officer) to Congress in which they announced their conviction that removal was the only course left to the Cherokee people. This message made it clear to the government that one faction, at least, was ready to enter into a new treaty. As a result, John Schermerhorn was appointed in the spring of 1835 to treat with that group. He was able to reach an agreement which provided that the Cherokee people would exchange their lands in the East for 13.8 million acres as well as a payment of $4.5 million and an annuity to support a school fund in the Nation. Twenty members of what came to be known as the Treaty party met in Boudinot's house at New Echota on December 29, 1835, to sign the pact. After adding his mark to the other signatures, Major Ridge reportedly said, "I have signed my death warrant." Boudinot and the other signers had similar feelings as they braced themselves for the onslaught of rage from their fellow Cherokees.

To add to Boudinot's public problems, his family situation was becoming difficult by the end of 1835. Harriet at first seems to have thrived in New Echota, but over time the rigors of frontier life, coupled with almost constant pregnancies, wore her down. In 1832, three years after her father's visit, she wrote to her family proclaiming her happiness with life with her husband and babies. If some in the family had shed tears for her on account of her marriage, she says, "I can now pronounce them useless tears."[18] The Boudinot family continued to grow. William Penn joined his sisters Eleanor and Mary on February 4, 1830, and was followed by Sarah Parkhill on February 24, 1832. Elias Cornelius was born on August 1, 1835, after which time Harriet was ailing, the pregnancy having been a difficult one.[19] Despite her declining physical condition, Harriet became pregnant again, and Frank was born on May 15, 1836, the mother again having had a difficult time. Three months later, Harriet Gold Boudinot died, leaving six children nine years old or younger.[20]

In a long letter to Harriet's parents, Boudinot writes of his wife's last days, of her spiritual state and her remembrances of family and friends in the North. He seems particularly eager to assure them that she was surrounded by family and friends; the Northrups were in the Nation visiting their daughter and made a call, as did members of the clergy from the area. The children are given special mention in the letter, with Harriet's instructions to the elder siblings as to the religious and social behavior she expected from them. Boudinot closes his letter with a request that "his dear parents" not forget him, even though the link that bound them is now gone.[21]

After signing the treaty, members of the Ridge-Boudinot-Watie faction deemed it expedient to remove to the new land west of Arkansas at the first opportunity. Boudinot was faced with the difficulties of settling his affairs at New Echota and making arrangement for the trek, a daunting task considering the number and ages of his children. Fortunately, his friends came to his aid, notably the Ridges and the Worcesters. Of course these families, too, were getting ready to leave for the western lands, most of the missionaries having decided to continue their work among the Cherokees. Living with the Worcesters at the time was a young missionary from New England, Delight Sargent, herself involved in making preparations for the move. Born in Pawlet, Vermont, around 1801, she remained in the Northeast until 1827, when she went to first Tennessee as a missionary, then later to Georgia.[22] In 1837, when Boudinot asked her to marry him and become mother to his children, she accepted.

In anticipation of the removal, Sophia Sawyer had closed her school in New Echota and gone to New York City on personal business, planning to join the Cherokees later in the West. Sawyer had been hired by the Ridges to teach their and the Boudinot's children. Originally, she had come to work among the Cherokees as a missionary. As a result, the older Boudinot children were sent along with those of the Ridges to William Potter's school at Creek Path, Alabama, in the autumn of 1837. Cornelius (as the family called him), Sarah, and little Frank remained at home. By the end of September, all the preparations were made, the wagons loaded with goods and children, and the great journey began. The emigrant group, consisting of the Ridges, the Boudinots, the William Lassley family, and Polly Galbreath, first traveled to Creek Path to collect their young scholars. They then made their way north into Tennessee to Nashville, where the company paused as John Ridge and Elias Boudinot paid a visit to Andrew Jackson at his estate, the Hermitage, which is near that city. The government had recommended, through its superintendent of emigration, several routes. Major Ridge, his wife, Susanna, and a group of Cherokees and slaves took one of these, largely a water route on the Tennessee, Mississippi, and Arkansas rivers. Its main advantage was that the government provided the transportation. The John Ridge–Elias Boudinot group, however, elected for another of the recommended routes, a more northerly one that ran overland.

Historian Thurman Wilkins, in his *Cherokee Tragedy: The Ridge Family and the Decimation of a People*, traces the journey of the second group from Nashville north to the Ohio River, which they crossed at Berry's Ferry into Golconda, Illinois. As they crossed that state and neared the Mississippi, the land became marshy and the traveling difficult. The party was ferried across the river probably to a point near Cape Girardeau, Missouri, from where they began a climb onto the Ozark plateau. This part of the journey was difficult as well because of the rolling terrain, but it was more pleasant traveling the wooded hills and valleys than it had been slogging through the marsh country of lower Illinois. The climate was temperate and the autumn weather generally pleasant. After six weeks or so the party reached Honey Creek, near present-day Southwest City, Missouri, where Major Ridge's party had already begun to settle in. The Boudinot family remained there for a time before proceeding south to what was to be their new home at a place Samuel Worcester had named Park Hill, just outside what is now Tahlequah, Oklahoma.

While some Cherokees like the Boudinots and Ridges moved west of their own volition, the majority did not. As a result, the U.S. government began to remove forcibly those who remained, sending in troops to round up the people and confine them in detention camps, then to escort them on one of the several routes to the West. This forced removal of the Cherokee Nation became known as the Trail of Tears. After the first group left on June 6, 1838, a steady stream followed throughout the summer and fall. The first arrivals reached Indian Territory in January 1839, with other groups straggling in over the next three months. Most of the emigrants suffered greatly from hunger, cold, sickness, and weariness, and many did not survived the forced march. An estimated forty-six hundred men, women, and children perished en route, more than one-fifth of the Cherokee population. Among those who died and was buried in an unmarked grave along the trail was Quatie Ross, the principal chief's wife. Those who reached the western lands, having witnessed the suffering and death of friends, neighbors, and loved ones, harbored a deep resentment and bitterness. It is clear that these feelings were not directed at the government officials who had formulated the removal, nor at the soldiers who had evicted them and forced them to leave their homeland. Rather, the deep feelings of the survivors of the Trail of Tears were aimed at those men who had assembled at Elias Boudinot's house in 1835 and signed the Treaty of New Echota, and specifically at their leaders: Elias Boudinot, his brother Stand Watie, John Ridge, and Major Ridge. Elizur Butler, the missionary who accompanied the Cherokees on the Trail and who documented their hardships, commented that "*All* the suffering and *all* the difficulties of the Cherokee people [were] charge[d] to the account of Messrs. Ridge and Boudinot."[23] As the exhausted bands from the eastern Nation arrived in the area where they would have to scratch out new livelihoods, the sight of the happy and prosperous families at Park Hill and Honey Creek must have greatly increased their bitterness.

One of the great ironies of the situation was that in 1829 Major Ridge had helped frame into Cherokee law a provision that anyone involved in the sale of land without the permission of the people would be put to death.[24] Many from the Ross party now clamored for the heads of Boudinot, the Ridges, and Stand Watie. Added to the Cherokees' problems was the fact that when the Treaty party had arrived they allied with the Old Settlers, accepting the government already in place in the West. The Old Settlers, or "western Cherokees," were those who had removed voluntarily from the eastern lands over a long period beginning in 1794 to settle in Arkansas and in northeastern present-day Oklahoma. When the main body of Cherokees arrived under the leadership of John Ross, they attempted to impose upon the Old Settlers and the Treaty faction the government and system of laws they had brought from the East. Neither side was inclined to give in, and by April 1839 the already-tense situation had become critical. At that point, Ross suggested that the parties meet to resolve the issue; the council was held in June, but the principals failed to reach an agreement.

Many in the Ross faction blamed the Treaty party for the council's failure, further inciting them against the signers of what they called "the false treaty." At a secret meeting, a group of Cherokees decided that under the terms of 1829 law banning the sale of tribal land, the leaders of the Treaty party were to be assassinated. They targeted Elias Boudinot, Stand Watie, John and Major Ridge, and a few others for immediate execution. Early on June 22, 1839, three execution squads were sent out. The first went to John Ridge's house, and they burst in and dragged Ridge from his bed in front of his wife and children. Out in the front yard, they proceeded to stab him to death. The second waylaid Major Ridge, who was traveling on the road near the boundary with Arkansas, and shot him to death. A third squad, made up of about thirty men, went to Park Hill, where Elias Boudinot was building his family's new house, and hid in the woods. As Boudinot was talking to some of his helpers, four of the group emerged from the trees, approached him, and asked for some medicine to treat one of their friends. At that point, a knife-wielding Cherokee attacked him from behind and stabbed him. When he fell to the ground, another attacker split his skull with a hatchet. The killers fled back into the woods as the carpenters ran to Boudinot's side. By the time they arrived, he was dead. Stand Watie and the others marked for death escaped, but the violence guaranteed continued struggle between the Ross party and what was now called the Watie party.

After the assassinations, the Ridge and Boudinot families were thrown into turmoil. Terrified for their lives, the two widows felt compelled to flee the Cherokee Nation with their children to seek safety elsewhere. Sarah Bird Northrup Ridge, along with her mother-in-law, Susanna Ridge, traveled only a short distance from their home on Honey Creek, near the present-day border of Oklahoma and Missouri, to Fayetteville, Arkansas. All of the Ridge family was to stay in the general area, with the exception of John Rollin and Aeneas, who left for the California gold fields in 1850. Delight Sargent, on the other hand, opted to take her stepchildren to the Northeast, where her family and that of Harriet Gold Boudinot still resided.

General Brinsmade and his wife, a sister of Harriet Gold Boudinot, were made guardians of the young family and apparently took their responsibility toward their nieces and nephews quite seriously. Brinsmade kept in contact with relatives in the Cherokee Nation. In his correspondence with Stand Watie, the general asked that the children not be forgotten by their Cherokee relatives.[25]

In fact, the Cherokee relatives had not forgotten. In 1844, Stand Watie and other members of the Treaty party appealed to the U.S. government for funds due them under the terms of the removal treaty. Neither the assassinated Ridges nor Elias Boudinot nor their families had received any funds from the government as a result of the treaty. While the money promised in the treaty had been paid dutifully by the government and deposited with the Nation, none of these funds were disbursed to members of the Treaty party by the Ross faction in control of Cherokee affairs. No action was taken on Watie and the others' request, most likely because the government considered it an internal Cherokee matter.

The family then took another tack. Acting for the assassinated men's families, Stand and John Watie petitioned a government claims commission, describing the fallen as martyrs who did not deserve to have their wives and children left destitute by an uncaring government. The Waties proposed that the Ridge and Boudinot families, both now residing outside the Cherokee Nation in the East and in Arkansas, be paid for their material losses and also the amounts stipulated by the removal treaty. Further, they requested that the Ridges and Boudinots receive the same educational and orphan benefits granted to other Cherokees. That they resided outside the Nation, the document went on, was caused by the fact that they feared for their lives if they dared return, and hence it should not have a bearing on their standing as Cherokee citizens. Stand and John Watie pointed out the irony of a situation in which the families were denied funds provided for by a treaty "sealed with the blood of their sires."[26] The commission members, however, claimed that they did not have the authority to address the matter, but they promised to forward the petition to the secretary of war. Once again, however, the federal government failed to act, and nothing became of the request.

The matter was not ended, however. By 1845, the bitter struggle of the two factions of the Cherokee Nation led to civil war. Stand Watie took command of the Treaty party's group of armed men and took control of Fort Arbuckle, a stronghold recently abandoned by the U.S. Army. From this vantage point he directed actions against the Ross forces. Several lives were lost on both sides, including Watie's brother Thomas. At the height of the trouble, Watie traveled to Washington to meet with President James K. Polk to make a proposal for ending the conflict. Polk and Watie agreed that the violence between the two factions that had festered since 1839 was doing irreparable harm to the Cherokee Nation, yet no reconciliation seemed possible. A solution, the two men decided, would be to divide the Cherokees into two groups. Polk then sent a commission to the Nation to investigate and to make recommendations for how the division could best be accomplished.

When Principal Chief Ross and his supporters heard this news, they quickly mobilized their resistance to what they considered an assault on the Nation's sovereignty. By the time the commissioners arrived in Indian Territory, Ross was able to persuade them against recommending a split. As recompense, perhaps, to the other side, the members did report that in their estimation the families of John Ridge and Elias Boudinot should receive ten thousand dollars each to compensate for their losses. However, by the time a new treaty was signed by both Cherokee factions and the government in 1846, this amount was reduced by one-half. [27] A further attempt was made on behalf of the Boudinot family by General Brinsmade. When he traveled to Washington to collect the family's share of the payment, Brinsmade was able to enlist the aid of Thomas Smith, his representative in Congress, to present a further petition for the family. The two men had witnessed the government's reluctance to arrive at a just monetary settlement, so they decided on a different approach: convince Congress to make a land grant of one section for each child. [28] This last petition, too, was rejected. Brinsmade, on behalf of the family, was able to collect the five thousand dollars as stipulated in 1846, but some question was raised later about its distribution. In 1855, when he was clerking in a law office, Boudinot reported to his uncle Stand that he was seeking from Mrs. Brinsmade an accounting of the family money but had so far been denied. [29] No record exists of a reply to his request. It is not clear why he approached Mrs. Brinsmade unless by this time her husband had died and Boudinot was making inquiries concerning the settlement and the Brinsmade estate. In any case, the children seemed to have been well cared for; no doubt the treaty money helped to provide for them and their education.

The Boudinot children did not remain together in the North. Sarah Parkhill died, apparently of tuberculosis, in 1845. [30] Eleanor Susan went to live with her uncle and aunt Brinsmade in Washington, Connecticut, and stayed there working as a teacher until her marriage to Henry Church in 1848. [31] Mary Harriet initially lived with her mother at Manchester, Vermont, but left to attend Mount Holyoke College in 1846. She later lived briefly with the Brinsmades in 1847 before returning to college. In 1849 Mary married Lyman W. Case and remained in the Northeast, in spite of a deep desire to return to "my country," as she asserted in a letter to Stand Watie.[32] William Penn attended school in Cornwall, Connecticut, where his guardian had found him "a fine instructor." At Brinsmade's instigation, he also worked in Philadelphia as an engraver, a profession that apparently did not appeal to him in spite of some success and his guardian's opinion that he could become rich at it. He wrote to his uncle Stand Watie in 1848 that he disliked Philadelphia and intended to move west in the fall of that year.[33] By 1850 William had moved to Fort Smith, Arkansas, where he worked for his uncle John F. Wheeler, a former printer for the *Cherokee Phoenix* in New Echota and husband of Nancy Watie, his father's sister.[34] Later, William moved to Tahlequah in the Cherokee Nation, where he edited the *Cherokee Advocate*.[35]

The "little boys," Elias Cornelius and Frank Brinsmade Boudinot, lived with Delight Sargent at Manchester. Little has been recorded about Cornelius's early years, except that he and his younger brother attended Brown Academy in Manchester and apparently did well there, as he did at Burr Seminary in Manchester and, later, at The Gunnery, a preparatory school in Washington, Connecticut. On his summer vacations from school, he worked on nearby farms.[36] In 1848, when Cornelius was not yet thirteen, William P. Boudinot in a letter to Stand Watie made this terse statement: "Frank and Cornelius are in Vt. as usual. Ma [Delight Sargent] has issued a proclamation declaring herself unwilling to take farther charge of the boys. It lies upon my Connecticut relations how to dispose of them."[37] General Brinsmade presumably took charge and provided for the boys, although Cornelius continued to live with his mother at least until 1849 as he attended school. Cornelius's education at the Burr Seminary seems to have been a thorough one, consisting of mathematics, history, science, grammar, and the classics.[38] The latter subjects were to be of critical importance to Boudinot in later life in his career as writer, editor, and lecturer. His familiarity with classical texts and rhetorical techniques especially were to serve him well as he engaged in extensive debates on issues of importance to his people and their future.

Around 1850, Cornelius left his stepmother's house and Burr and entered The Gunnery, run by Frederick W. Gunn, a son-in-law of the Brinsmades.[39] He stayed there for about a year before taking a teaching position at Danby, Vermont. In a letter to an aunt in the Cherokee Nation, Boudinot offers several details about the experience. He tells her that he is once again living with his stepmother and finds Danby to be a very "immoral place," though graced with some of a better class of people, namely Quakers. He did not feel prepared to teach, relating that he does not find the work pleasant or easy. "I hardly think I should be willing to follow it as a business."[40]

According to some sketchy accounts, Cornelius later worked as a civil engineer for a railroad in Ohio. It may be that the young Boudinot was pushed in this direction by his guardian, whose son William Brinsmade worked for a railroad from at least 1847.[41] Apparently, the physical rigors of this occupation were too much for Cornelius, as he reportedly left the railroad because of a physical inability to carry out his duties. Considerable speculation has been offered about the cause of Cornelius's limp, an affliction that followed him all his life. One commentator blames an injury to his knee that was incurred on the railroad job.[42] However, John Hallum, who claimed Cornelius as "an intimate acquaintance," reports that Boudinot had "physical injuries to the ankle, existing from early infancy," identifying that condition as the reason for quitting the railroad.[43] Hallum's statement is borne out in a letter from Elias Boudinot to Cornelius's grandfather Benjamin Gold: "Cornelius is a Pet in the family—but the poor boy is afflicted with lameness in one of his limbs, and I am afraid will be a cripple as long as he lives." Boudinot goes on to say that he has sent the boy to an "eminent physician" in Huntsville, Alabama, and hopes that eventually some relief might be obtained.[44]

Cornelius's stepmother moved to Troy, New York, and, in what might be viewed as an ironic twist, took charge of the Home for Children there in 1857. She died in that city on February 12, 1893.[45] Cornelius set out from Ohio to seek his fortune in the West.

CHAPTER 2

The Young Man in Arkansas

When he left Ohio in 1853, Boudinot did not return to the Cherokee Nation but settled close to it in Fayetteville, Arkansas, where many of his relatives and other members of the Treaty party lived. The John Ridge family had settled here after the assassination, with most of its members remaining in the district except John Rollin Ridge and Aeneas Ridge, both of whom joined the gold rush in California. Aeneas eventually returned home to northwestern Arkansas, but Rollin remained in California for the rest of his life, writing for and editing a number of newspapers and other publications.[1] Fayetteville was also home to Josiah Woodward Washbourne, son of early Arkansas pioneer Cephas Washburn (the younger Washbourne initiated the spelling change), a man who would become an important colleague of Boudinot's due largely to his family ties through his wife, Susan C. Ridge, daughter of the assassinated John Ridge. The choice of Fayetteville was also a good one for Boudinot because of its proximity to clan leader Stand Watie, who lived at Honey Creek in the Cherokee Nation, north and west of Fayetteville and very near the Arkansas border. Another member of the community, W. D. Polson, was closely connected to the Watie faction and was to become a close colleague of Boudinot's in his tobacco venture after the Civil War. Another man who became close to Cornelius in these years was William Quesenbury, publisher and editor of the *Southwest Independent*, a newspaper published in Fayetteville whose readership extended to Indian Territory and Missouri. In Fayetteville he also began a longtime relationship with Thomas M. Gunter, later an important political ally and member of the U.S. House of Representatives from Arkansas.

In the small but bustling town he met James R. Pettigrew, who was to become Boudinot's business partner and copublisher of his first newspaper.

These early years in Fayetteville were important ones for Boudinot. He was able to reestablish ties with his Cherokee family to the point where he was accepted eventually as a respected and influential member. He was also able to cultivate relationships with many people who were to become colleagues in his many ventures later in his life. Further, the social and intellectual climate of Fayetteville provided an atmosphere for personal growth. Educational opportunities were rife for whites and Cherokees alike as the area boasted many fine schools. Several competent preparatory schools and institutions of higher education had been established in the area. The highly respected Cephas Washburn led the effort in higher education, while Sophia Sawyer was instrumental in providing education for girls and women. Washburn built the Far West Seminary, the first institution of higher learning in Arkansas, the establishment of which laid the groundwork for the University of Arkansas, founded in Fayetteville under the federal Land Grant Act after the Civil War. Although it was destroyed by fire, its successor institutions ensured a firm footing for education in the area. Sawyer, a Massachusetts native, had come west after moving from Philadelphia to oversee the education of the Ridge and Watie children in the former Cherokee Nation, and she rejoined the Ridges after removal. Following John Ridge's assassination she fled with them to Fayetteville, where she established a school that numbered both boys and girls among her pupils. Later she opened a school for young women that grew in time into a highly respected academy.[2]

When Cornelius arrived in 1853 he began the study of law in the office of A. M. Wilson, where his cousin John Rollin Ridge had worked in the 1840s.[3] Wilson served as U.S. district attorney for the Western District of Arkansas, a post important to the tribes in Indian Territory as they fell under this federal jurisdiction, the seat of which was south of Fayetteville at Fort Smith, Arkansas. Under Wilson's tutelage, Boudinot passed the Arkansas bar in 1856 and was admitted to practice before the federal court in Fort Smith the following year.[4] In time his skills as a lawyer and orator were noticed by others, but inexplicably some apocryphal anecdotes concerning his prowess along these lines have been published. One such story is that Cornelius defended his uncle Stand Watie in a murder trial in which he was accused of murdering James Foreman. According to this account, the young lawyer's elocutionary efforts were so masterful that they struck all in the courtroom with shock and awe. His reputation as an attorney was supposedly fixed after this early

THE YOUNG MAN IN ARKANSAS

episode in his career. The story is a good one, but since the altercation between Watie and Foreman took place in 1842, it would have been difficult for the young Boudinot to have participated. Another story relating to his early career involves his being named clerk of the Cherokee National Council under Watie. No evidence for this claim exists, although the story may have originated in the fact that Cornelius quite blatantly tried to ride his uncle's coattails and may have acted as his secretary at one of the numerous meetings of Cherokees over which Watie presided.[5]

His prodigious legal reputation notwithstanding, Boudinot chose in 1859 to enter the newspaper business. While the professions of journalism and law might seem almost antithetical today, the combination was not at all unusual in mid-nineteenth-century America, especially in small towns where legal services were not deemed essential by most people. Although Cornelius commented in 1855 about the sleepiness of Fayetteville and environs to Watie, this was probably just a complaint of a young man who has not yet established a satisfying social life.[6] He obviously found the area as one that offered opportunities to someone with his ambitions, and after a tentative start into journalism with Quesenbury's paper, Cornelius and James Pettigrew decided to fill the void that opened up with the demise of the *Southwest Independent* in 1856. In operation since 1854 under the able editorship of newspaperman, humorist, and poet William Quesenbury, the *Independent* had previously published some of Boudinot's writing. Boudinot and Pettigrew began publication of the *Arkansian*, which quickly became one of the most influential newspapers in the state and soon had a circulation of around two thousand. In addition to the writing of Cornelius and his partner, the paper also featured contributions by Quesenbury and J. W. Washbourne.[7] Boudinot's partner in this venture was a lawyer who was born in Hempstead County, Arkansas, in 1829. Pettigrew was active politically, and he served in several public capacities: he was appointed a member of the Utah Commission and was journal clerk of the U.S. Senate. He returned to the newspaper business in Fayetteville in 1875, when he established the *Fayetteville Sentinel*. Pettigrew died in Waco, Texas, in 1886.[8]

An examination of the *Arkansian*'s content reveals Cornelius's positions on important political matters of the day, positions that may have been altered and adjusted later but which never changed fundamentally. The first issue was states' rights and the southern cause. "The Constitutional Rights of the South," proclaimed the banner of the first number, issued on March 5, 1859, setting the political tone of the publication. Of course slavery was at the forefront of the national consciousness at the time, and at no other place in the country was the issue more prominent than in the border country of Fayetteville, Arkansas. Missouri lay a few miles north and "bleeding Kansas" just a bit further on. While attending to national issues, Boudinot did not ignore the local political situation. He kept a close eye on Indian Territory and reported news from the tribes, especially of those removed from the Southeast. The *Arkansian* was also in favor of a railroad that would run from Little Rock to the Pacific along the thirty-fifth parallel and of territorializing Indian lands west of Arkansas, an issue related to the railroad. The weekly newspaper did not neglect local news, covering social and political events from Fayetteville and the surrounding area. Attention to state political issues was given as well, often in the editorial columns. From time to time the *Arkansian* printed literary efforts by persons well known to the readership, including Boudinot, his brother William P. Boudinot, and relatives J. W. Washbourne and John Rollin Ridge.[9] Publication of these works offered proof that the young editor was from a cultured background and possessed literary abilities beyond his journalistic skills.

In the first number, after issuing the usual encomiums to the sacredness of a free and independent press, Pettigrew and Boudinot set out in their "Salutatory" to establish their paper's position on national politics: "Whatever may be their merits or demerits, it should be sufficient for every true son of the South to know, that the Democratic party is the only National and Conservative political organization in the country, which can measure swords with the Hydra of Abolitionism, and stay the onrushing tide which threatens to overwhelm the South." [10] Arkansas itself, although it seceded from the Union and joined the Confederacy, was deeply split, with many abolitionists and Union sympathizers residing in the northwestern quadrant of the state. Boudinot's family, like many of the economically fortunate Cherokees, held slaves, and people of African descent were to play prominent roles in the history of the Nation and in that of other Indian nations in Indian Territory. This economic factor doubtless influenced Cornelius's thinking on the subject, but his self-image was just as important. In the young man we can see a pattern emerging that was to remain an important part of his life: the idea that he held and an image that he worked hard to project of himself as a key member of an aristocratic family. Although he was not a plantation-owning, slaveholding "Son of the South," as he might have wished, he certainly aspired to the position of cavalier, to the nineteenth-century ideal of the man who rises in his political, economic, or artistic milieu like cream to the top of the milk can. Throughout the *Arkansian*'s short history, its pages are filled with defense of the southern "way of life" and of corresponding vilification of the abolitionist point of view. In a particularly vitriolic example, Boudinot writes of the abolitionist asp in the Cherokee bosom, Evan Jones.

Jones was a Baptist missionary to the Cherokees who had much influence with the Ross party and with the tribe's full-bloods, most of whom did not hold slaves. The Watie party had opposed Jones from the beginning, an opposition that had crystallized in the sale of the "Neutral Lands" in present-day Kansas, a transaction that Jones had favored and had counseled Ross on. The Watie party had seen the land cession as favoring the Free-Soilers, as another erosion of southern influence. Jones's influence among the Cherokees was aided appreciably by his knowledge of the language and his ability to publish his opinions in the Sequoyan syllabary. In an editorial entitled "Abolitionism That Rubs," Boudinot attacks Jones and his son John,[11] as he does in subsequent issues. The paper published letters from the Nation opposing Jones and Cherokee abolitionism as well.[12]

The *Arkansian* covered other news from Indian Territory, especially that of Indian nations removed from the Southeast. From time to time, too, information appeared about other tribes brought into the area, including the Comanches, who had been cleared out of Texas. Boudinot spent much of his time in the Cherokee Nation covering elections and other political events, sending news back to Pettigrew to be published in the newspaper as letters. This was to become a staple of Cornelius's writing, and a "Letter from Boudinot" can be found in many and varied newspapers from the 1850s through the 1880s. While many of these were issued from Washington DC, he wrote from far-flung cities and hamlets as he traveled promoting his many enterprises. His missives to the *Arkansian* had one recurring theme: opposition to the Ross faction of the Cherokee Nation. Boudinot clearly took it upon himself to become the chief spokesman for the Watie faction, which would become known as the "Southern party" of Cherokees when the Civil War began. His anti-Ross prose is vehement and colorful, even by the journalistic standards of the time. John Ross's "blood-stained hand" is seen behind various aspects of Cherokee politics,[13] and the chief is accused of "hiring assassins,"[14] raiding the treasury, and other dastardly acts. Occasionally the paper would print pro-Ross letters, but these served mostly as straw men to be destroyed by Boudinot's vitriolic rebuttals. The editor was quick to point out Ross's abolitionist leanings and cheered on the "good pro-slavery fervor" he found among opposition Cherokees.[15]

The Cherokee Nation was split on the question of slavery, which was to become one of the rallying points along the Ross-Watie fracture line. The Cherokee National Council passed a resolution in 1855 that condemned abolitionist activities among the Cherokees and declared the rights of slaveholding citizens. Principal Chief Ross vetoed the measure, however, and was upheld narrowly by a later vote of the tribe. This was a defeat for the Watie faction, which had supported the proslavery stand. [16] From this time forward, many of the mixed-blood Cherokees gravitated toward Stand Watie, while many full-bloods looked to John Ross for leadership. The full-blood position was brought about, ironically perhaps, because of their reluctance to desert the federal government once the national North-South rift developed more clearly. Another factor in their position was the influence of Evan and John Jones, whose ability to speak Cherokee to spread their abolitionist ideas was doubtless a great advantage. Thus the Cherokee Nation's political situation mirrored that of the nation as the country moved toward the Civil War.

While his positions were supported by many Cherokees, others opposed Boudinot vehemently. In reactions to the *Arkansian*'s anti-Ross invectives we can see the seeds of the disdain and outright hatred of E. C. Boudinot that was to develop among a major segment of the Cherokee population. A case in point is a letter sent to Boudinot and published in the July 30, 1859, issue of the paper. "Your father was assassinated in 1839 for proving himself to be a d——d traitor to his country and others with him, a fate that he and others most richly deserved," the writer stated. "We are ready to fight you if that is what you want with knives, six shooters or anything that will cut or burn, as we are not competent to answer you with words and acknowledge that you are our superior—if we were capable of answering you with the pen, we would not waste time and words with no such d——d scoundrel as you are." Along with this diatribe, Boudinot furnished his own reply: "Mr. Sofkey may be reasonably considered a very mangy dog of Mr. Ross' who has been hissed on by his master, until he opens upon us the foregoing sickly bark." The letter, signed with the pseudonym "Sofkey," was useful to Boudinot, thus offering a rationale for its publication that goes beyond the editor's relatively mild reply. The letter, with its threat of physical violence which recall that against his father and the hostilities between the rival factions in the 1840s, firmly establishes Cornelius's credentials among the enemy's camp. Within the Watie branch of Cherokees, the letter allowed him to take his place among the leadership along with his dead father, his uncle Stand, the martyred Ridges, and other notables, thus providing a needed boost to his fortunes.

Another issue that was to remain close to Boudinot's heart was the extension of railroads into Indian Territory. In time, Cornelius would achieve some attention as being the man who drove the first railway spike in the Cherokee Nation and thus in the soil set aside for the sole use of the Indians. The *Arkansian* at this time advocated building a railroad along the thirty-fifth parallel to the Pacific, a longtime desideratum of many Arkansas businessmen hoping to extend their influence and opportunities from Little Rock west. Complicating this issue, of course, was the physical fact of the Indian Territory, a large landmass set aside for the use of the removed tribes and, in theory at least, controlled by the Indian nation's sovereign governments. The pressure for an east-west railway along the thirty-fifth parallel was increased as time went on and was quieted temporarily only by the outbreak of war. The position taken by the paper helped to cement bonds between Boudinot and the railroad interests, a group with which he was to forge a strong relationship in the coming years. It also helped him to ally himself with powerful business and political interests in Little Rock.

The railroad issue was tightly tied to another major position taken by the *Arkansian*'s editors, that being the establishment of a territory similar to others in the western United States and opening the "surplus" lands not being "used" by the Indians to settlers and ranchers, thus "opening up" Indian Territory to "economic development." Boudinot's paper threw its support to a bill proposed by Arkansas's own Senator Robert W. Johnson, who had a bill pending in Congress to this effect. Robert Ward Johnson, born in Kentucky, moved to Little Rock in 1835 to begin the practice of law. He was elected to Congress in 1846 as a Democrat and twice reelected. In 1853, Governor Elias Nelson Conway appointed Johnson to the U.S. Senate when Solon Borland vacated the seat, and Johnson was elected subsequently to a term of his own. As a member of the House and Senate he turned his attention to public lands, homesteading, land grants for railroads. When the Civil War broke out he became a delegate from Arkansas to the Confederate Congress, later becoming a member of the Confederate Senate. After the war, Johnson took up residence in Washington DC, where he became a law partner of Albert Pike. Later he returned to Arkansas, where his brother Richard H. Johnson was involved in politics. "The Family," as the Johnsons were called, dominated politics for a time in Arkansas.[17]

This was the first in a long series of territorial initiatives that Cornelius was to support in his career. Johnson's bill, introduced in 1854, came after several years of debate in Congress over the extension of the railroads westward and the subsequent settlement of western lands. Southern members were opposed to the lands being opened to both slaveholding and non-slave settlers, and Johnson's bill accommodated his colleagues. [18] Boudinot proclaimed that the pending legislation would be good for the Indian nations as well. "Upon acceptance of his Bill," the *Arkansian* thundered, "the transition from their present state of dependence to one of absolute political equality, would be easy and certain." [19] The bill called for three territories initially, to be called "Chalohkee," "Muscogee," and "Chakta" (Cherokee, Muskogee or Creek, and Choctaw), which would be later organized into one territorial entity to be called "Neosho." Chalohkee was to comprise all Cherokee lands, including the Outlet and the Seneca-Shawnee, Seneca, and Quapaw lands, provided those Indians consented as well as the Cherokees. The Cherokees, Muscogees, and Choctaws, along with members of the subsumed tribes, would elect their own governor and legislature as well as establish the qualifications for citizenship within their territories. While tribal courts would continue, federal courts with both civil and criminal jurisdiction would be established within each of the three political entities. Land survey and all it entails, including the allotment of land in severalty, was not to be carried out until the Indians made application to the federal government. Historian Morris Wardell, in his *Political History of the Cherokee Nation*, surmises that had the Cherokees accepted the provisions of Johnson's bill, factional problems would have lessened and the financial situation of the tribe would have improved, since the costs of government would have been undertaken by the federal government. [20] In the end, the bill did not come up for consideration by the full Senate; in any event, considerable opposition to its provisions had arisen in the Cherokee Nation as well as in other Indian groups.

Reasons for Boudinot's support for the Johnson bill were historical and long range as well as pragmatic and immediate. First of all, Boudinot saw the kind of government action proposed by Johnson (although his assumption was perhaps unfounded) as a way of limiting Ross and his followers' power in the future. In any case, Ross's opposition was enough to bring out Boudinot's favor for the proposal. A more immediate reason for Cornelius's support, though, was his increasing alignment with the Johnson organization within the Arkansas Democratic Party. The party was undergoing its own factionalism during the run-up to the 1860 election, with its membership split between the wing led by Senator Johnson and Governor Conway and an opposition led by Congressman Thomas C. Hindman.

Boudinot's first formal foray into politics was local. Fayetteville had been incorporated as a township in 1841, but in 1859 the leaders of the fast-growing municipality decided it was time to apply for status as a city. After the state legislature approved this change, an election was held in April 1859 in which J. W. Washbourne and Elias C. Boudinot were elected along with five others to the Fayetteville's first city council. J. W. Walker was elected mayor.[21] This election did little more than whet Boudinot's appetite for politics, and his ambition was to serve in higher echelons of the state and national political hierarchies. Accordingly, he sided with the Johnson family faction in Arkansas, a political power within the dominant Democratic Party that exerted control over much of the state at this time. This group was called "the Family" not only because two of its main figures—Robert and Richard Johnson—were brothers but also because of the close relationships among many of its leading lights. This powerful group of men had dominated Arkansas politics for some time, turning back challenges from Whigs and Know-Nothings through the years. Demographics were to play a major part in state politics as the crucial election of 1860 neared, however. As new immigrants entered the state in ever-increasing numbers, fewer people owed allegiance to "the Family"; the increasing population, too, placed great demands on the ruling faction for infrastructure, more schools, better roads and bridges, levees, and transportation facilities.[22] In addition, many of the faction's leaders were beginning to age, retire, and die, leaving empty spaces like unreplaced parts in an aging apparatus. These stresses soon opened cracks in the group's solidarity.

Thomas C. Hindman was the first major player to take advantage of these rifts. Hindman had come to Arkansas from Tennessee via Mississippi after a foray south of the border in the Mexican War, during which he served as a lieutenant in the U.S. Army. He involved himself in politics in Mississippi and traveled across the northern part of that state in 1851, stumping for Jefferson Davis against Henry S. Foote in the campaign for governor.[23] Hindman began a law practice in his adopted state, but soon he gravitated toward politics, joining "the Family" in their fight against the Know-Nothings in the 1856 election. The "colonel," as he called himself, proved to be a vicious infighter and fiery orator, attracting the attention of his party's leadership to such an extent that he was offered the nomination for U.S. representative from the Northern District in 1858. He won the election, representing a broad belt of Arkansas stretching from Helena on the Mississippi to Fayetteville on the border with Indian Territory. Once in office, however, Hindman turned on his fellows and worked to establish a group within the Democratic Party in opposition to the Johnson machine.

Many of Boudinot's associates, including his mentor A. M. Wilson, were part of the Johnson faction. It was through his contacts as well as through his own budding talents as a political writer and speaker that Cornelius began to rise within the machine hierarchy, becoming a particularly integral cog in 1860 with his appointment as chairman of the Arkansas State Democratic Central Committee. [24] A series of events during the previous year had led to this rather rapid rise, events that also caused a deep animosity to arise between Boudinot and Hindman. What political success Hindman had found in Arkansas was based largely on his abilities as a speaker; noted as a fiery orator, he drew large crowds to his speeches in small towns within and outside of his congressional district. Coverage in local newspapers was often very positive, helping Hindman to drive home the points he had made on the speaker's platform. This arrangement appeared to have been working, adding to his fame and to his faction's political base, when Boudinot announced that he had in his possession a letter purportedly written by an admirer calling himself "Viator." This particular letter had been published in the *State Rights Democrat* of Helena, a paper controlled by the Hindman faction, and was only one in a series of letters by "Viator" published in praise of the politician's speeches. Hindman was accused of writing the letters that carried fulsome praise for his own oratory and ideas; the resulting turmoil electrified the state. At first, W. L. Martin of Helena, a Hindman supporter, came forward to claim authorship, declaring that the congressman had nothing to do with the letters' writing or publication, but under increasing pressure Hindman eventually admitted that he was "Viator" and that he had written the letters praising himself. As proof, Boudinot brought forth the original letter and envelope written in Hindman's hand. The exposé had struck a serious blow against the opposition, and of course it was welcomed by "the Family." [25]

Despite the severe damage to Hindman's reputation, the political struggle between the two Democratic factions continued. The Johnson group put forth Richard H. Johnson as candidate for governor to succeed Elias Conway. Richard was editor of the *True Democrat* in Little Rock, but he planned to give up the post temporarily as he made the run for governor. As the Johnsons looked around for Richard's successor, their eyes fell on Cornelius Boudinot, who was appointed to the position, a post he accepted with relish. With his new responsibilities, Cornelius was in a position to continue to damage the Hindman forces. With most of the major newspapers within the state in the hands of or on the side of the Johnson faction, Hindman quickly saw the need for a paper in the capital city to spread his message. While he controlled the Helena *State Rights Democrat*, Hindman subsequently established the *Old Line*

Democrat at Little Rock, putting "editor-for-hire" Thomas C. Peek in charge.[26] The newly appointed editor had been most recently editor of a pro-Douglas paper in Illinois, and he was a veteran of several political wars. A native of Virginia, Peek attended law school in that state and served as a prosecuting attorney there before entering the newspaper business.[27] The first issue of his paper was published on September 15, 1859, containing praise for Hindman and declarations for his political positions. With Peek in place at the *Old Line Democrat* and Boudinot soon to be ensconced at the *True Democrat*, the battle between fire-eating editors was shaping up during the turbulent days leading up to the 1860 election.

Boudinot's political rise in Arkansas was perhaps predictable, because from early on in his career he demonstrated an enthusiastic, if not rabid, partisanship. Just as he was fiercely loyal to and vociferously defensive about the Watie faction in Cherokee politics, so too did he adhere to the Johnson machine in state affairs. Cornelius began his rise with election to the Fayetteville City Council in 1858, but it was in state politics that he made his mark. In the Washington County Democratic convention, Boudinot helped the Johnson family keep control, but he was instrumental in the passage of two resolutions dear to his heart. The first was in opposition to the sale of the so-called Cherokee Neutral Lands in Kansas, as advocated by Ross and his party and opposed by the Watie-affiliated Cherokees. The second resolution favored any efforts the Cherokees might take to oppose abolitionism in the Nation. These issues were important to many in northwestern Arkansas because of Washington County's proximity to both the Cherokee Nation and to the disputed territory in Kansas. Boudinot also was involved with the county convention's main business, the nomination of A. M. Wilson, his old mentor, for Congress to oppose Hindman.

A month later, in early April 1860, the triumphant young man traveled to Little Rock for the state Democratic convention. Before the business of the gathering could begin, however, a committee was appointed to review the delegates' credentials. The major problem the committee faced was the situation presented by the Democrats from Benton County, Washington County's neighbor to the north. Their convention had ended in a stalemate, with neither the Johnson nor the Hindman forces able to gain the upper hand. As a result, both groups met in rump session to elect delegates, with the Johnson faction family choosing two and their opponents picking three. The Hindman group, however, added a stipulation that if their candidates did not attend the gathering in Little Rock, Thomas C. Peek would act as their proxy. At the convention, according to newspaper accounts, a movement involving Boudinot and his allies was successful in arguing against the Benton County Hindman supporters. Not satisfied with this success, the Johnson supporters offered a further resolution to strip Peek of his delegate status and were upheld in this as well. The young Boudinot gleefully took his place among the delegates amid hearty greetings and slaps on the back from his colleagues. But he was not finished.

After Richard Johnson was nominated for governor, Boudinot introduced party business that would appoint an executive committee which was to have substantial powers, including picking substitute candidates should any of those on the regular ticket not be able to run. When this Democratic Central Committee was endorsed and seated by the convention, Boudinot was named its chair. Thus, in a few short months, Cornelius had risen to a post near the top of the Democratic politics—at least the dominant Johnson wing of it—in his adopted state of Arkansas. Here was clearly a young Cherokee man on the rise, positioning himself for power and influence not only within the dominant society but, as we shall see, among a prominent branch of his own people. His attention now turned to the continuing clash with the Hindman forces, among whom he had made some serious enemies.

Political maneuvering between the two factions began at the local level. In the Arkansas system, meetings were first held at the township level and then at the county stage, at which issues were debated and delegates elected to the state convention. The Johnson machine had functioned very well through the years by controlling these smaller meetings, so by the time the state conventions were held a majority of delegates were loyal to "the Family." With the machinery aging, the party apparatus was able to creak along, but certainly without the thundering engine that had once powered it. Richard Johnson was nominated as the Democratic candidate, but louder and louder rumblings were heard as the Hindman faction arose in opposition; the Democratic Party was not the monolith it once had been.[28]

A good example of the deep split within the party is found at the two congressional conventions on May 14, 1860, held in Arkadelphia, in south-central Arkansas, and at Dover, in the northwest. After considerable political bloodshed, the Arkadelphia convention ended in a tie, with neither side able to take control. Subsequently, delegates went to the state convention with no instructions on how to vote. In northwestern Arkansas, county meetings had been marked by vicious fights between Johnson and Hindman forces, mostly over the seating of delegates. In Benton County, a petition against the inclusion of the Hindman delegation to the state convention claimed to have the signatures of over a thousand voters. When the Dover convention met, the Hindman forces were able to exclude all delegates except their own, leaving them fully in control. Cornelius was singled out for especially rough treatment from his foes because of his earlier maneuverings in Washington Country and Little Rock. At Dover his credentials were rejected on the grounds that as a Cherokee citizen, he was no more white than Dred Scott, and therefore not a voter— or, for that matter, an American citizen. In addition, the Hindman-controlled convention went on to deny the *True Democrat*'s position as spokesman for Democratic policies, endorsing the *Old Line Democrat* in its place. Boudinot had resigned as editor of the *Arkansian* just prior to the May 11 Dover meeting, and although he did not take the reins at the *True Democrat* until June 9, it was well known that he would replace Johnson as editor. Here was another slap in the face for Cornelius, although it must have been a glancing blow since the Hindman partisans were certain to oppose Johnson's newspaper whoever was editor.

While Johnson was still the favored candidate, the Hindman forces searched for an effective opposition candidate. They found him within the Johnson machine's own bosom in the person of Henry M. Rector, a member of the Arkansas Supreme Court and a longtime figure in "the Family." Rector had had a varied career as a surveyor, planter, banker, and lawyer, and for his service to his political faction he had been awarded a seat on the state supreme court. The judge announced his candidacy for the governorship in late May 1860, and the obvious battle lines were drawn. The *Old Line Democrat* and the *True Democrat* followed predictable editorial paths. Peek describes Rector as a reluctant warrior, one who seeks to serve only because he sees his state in need of wise leadership: "A poor honest farmer of Saline county" who, "possessing the impress of manhood from nature, and from nature's God, at his country's greatest need, he arose like Cincinnatus of old and did his duty."[29] Boudinot, of course, scoffed at such a characterization, pointing out that Rector's farm was in Pulaski, not adjoining Saline Country, and was situated close to the state house and supreme court chambers, and moreover that the judge was a wealthy man who "is entirely innocent of plowing."

The campaign then got into full swing, with both candidates issuing printed circulars outlining their positions on issues. Following custom, a series of debates was scheduled at various venues around the state where the two men could meet face-to-face with the voters. As the Rector-Johnson debates took place, another fight was shaping up between the two factions in the congressional race, where Hindman was defending his seat against Colonel Jesse Cypert, a Whig. The campaign was confusing because in order for either Democratic gubernatorial candidate to triumph, he would need the backing of substantial numbers of Whig and American Party (Know-Nothing) voters. The Hindman-Rector faction was in the position of running against Cypert while at the same time wooing Whig and other non-Democratic voters. In the end there was little enthusiasm for Cypert even from his fellow Whigs, and Hindman was able to win handily, although as it turned out he never took his seat. The Rector-Johnson bout was turning out to be the one to watch.

In addition to the main event, the battle between the competing newspapers provided a spectacle as well. Peek was an experienced political hack with a ready cache of dirty tricks, but Boudinot, although a relative novice at mudslinging, was proving a worthy opponent. Predictably, the debate became highly personal, following the journalistic practice of the day. At the height of the campaign, Peek came out in the editorial columns of the *Old Line Democrat* with a reference to Cornelius as the "colored editor" of the opposition newspaper. In a campaign in which both Rector and Johnson were trying to promote themselves as more anti-abolitionist and pro-slavery than the other, this was a particularly serious smear. In response to Peek's resurrection of the Dover convention attack, Boudinot replied that this line has been used by "other ignorant skulking poltroons [who] have essayed to strike me down, and are well worthy of a man, who was purchased in Illinois, shipped to Arkansas, and bid by his owner to heap slander and abuse upon strangers and gentlemen." Eventually, both editors were commenting on their opponent's drinking habits, a pretty good indication that political writing had descended nearly to the level of today's.[30]

Although the Johnson forces soon imported J. H. Black, former editor of the *South Arkansas Democrat*, to relieve Boudinot of the day-to-day duties of running the newspaper, Cornelius continued as editorial writer, an occupation more in line with his political pursuits. With Black, formerly of Washington, Arkansas, an old settlement southwest of Little Rock, ensconced as senior editor, the verbal battle between Peek and Boudinot continued in the pages of their respective publications. Although Peek shied away from attacking Black, he lavished his vituperation upon the younger editor, calling him "an bitter and unscrupulous agent" who had been hired away from "a low, dirty and scurrilous sheet" to act as a political hit man for the Johnsons. Peek delighted, apparently, in playing the race card, calling Boudinot a "mongrel Cherokee," a slur upon both his father and his mother, and a "poor, lame Indian," a

THE YOUNG MAN IN ARKANSAS

reference to Cornelius's slight limp. Apparently, the readership loved it, and soon rumors circulated about an impending duel between the two. Boudinot floated such an idea, but it was rebuffed by Peek, who said that he did not consider his rival his social equal, a condition that negated the possibility of such a gentlemanly exercise as shooting at one another in a formalized setting complete with attendants. The bullets that continued to fly were made, not of lead, but of ink.[31]

In terms of national politics, Arkansas in 1860 was distinguished by its remoteness. Not a single Arkansan had been involved in the great debate going on nationally; even the war of words between Daniel Webster and John C. Calhoun had elicited no more than a passing interest. This is not to say that questions of slavery and its abolition were not argued. Outside of C. C. Danley's editorials in the *Arkansas Gazette* advocating reopening of the slave trade, most attention seemed to be turn on the state's relationships with its neighbors. Many who embraced the southern cause, such as followers of the Johnsons, came to call their opponents "submissionists" if they seemed to bend to the will of the federal government. On the other hand, Rector and others during the gubernatorial campaign referred to those allied with the Johnson faction as "disunionists" and declared secession a distant and drastic possibility. Many of those tainted with the "submissionist" label called themselves "cooperationists," referring to their preference for following the lead of the state's larger neighbors such as Tennessee. Looking to Tennessee after Lincoln's close election victory and passage of South Carolina's secession ordinance in late 1860, Arkansans saw voters there turning down calls for secessionist conventions, and for secession itself, by large majorities.[32]

The debates in Arkansas as well as in the rest of the nation began to heat up in 1861, with unionists—those opposed to secession—arrayed more and more against secessionists. Charges flew left and right as each side tried to improve its stature among the voters. Secessionists' patriotism was challenged, on the one hand, and rumors circulated to the effect that only those who owned slaves would have the vote in a post-secession South. The secessionists countered by asserting that a vote for the unionists was a vote for abolitionism and spread rumors that monarchists were growing in power in the North. The politics of the times made for some strange bedfellows: both Senator Robert W. Johnson and Representative Hindman telegraphed their views to the state assembly, calling for an immediate secession convention and for Arkansas to "join in the common councils of the South."[33] Secessionist politicians such as James Yell spoke before enthusiastic crowds, and some sections of Arkansas, such as Helena and areas controlled by planters, called for the state to follow South Carolina's lead. The question put by Johnson and Hindman to the state legislature was taken up, and in January 1861 a bill became law that provided for a statewide referendum in which citizens were asked, first, to vote on the advisability of holding a state convention on the secession question, and second, to vote for delegates to such a meeting should one be called.

At the same time, an issue arose that played into the secessionists' hands. The federal arsenal in Little Rock has been reinforced in November 1860 by sixty troops transferred from Kansas. For two or three months no alarm was expressed by public officials or the newspapers, but in January 1861 Governor Rector suddenly began to question the federal government's motives in such an action. On cue, secessionists in Helena and from cotton-producing areas offered to send five hundred volunteer troops to take over the arsenal. This would not only serve as a patriotic focus for states' rights activists but would acquire arms, equipment, and ammunition for state troops. Rector realized that the people of the capital city were more conservative on the issue than those in some of the outlying districts, so he rejected the offer of volunteers and embarked on a more moderate course. Addressing the arsenal's commander, Captain James Totten, he declared that the state would allow the facility to remain in federal hands until the state convention had decided upon the larger matter of secession. Any attempt to further reinforce the arsenal or to remove or destroy equipment or ammunition, Rector went on, would force the state to take control. The governor asked the commander to agree to these terms. Captain Totten replied that he must take his orders from the secretary of war, a higher authority in his estimation than the governor of Arkansas.

At that point a rumor spread from Pine Bluff, a city on the Arkansas River below Little Rock, that federal reinforcements were on their way to the arsenal. Rector reacted accordingly, ordering guns to be mounted on the river levees to repel this advance on the capital city by water. Reacting to Rector's action, secessionists in Helena and four other southern and eastern counties sent contingents of volunteers to liberate the facility from federal control; this in turn brought about outcries from the citizens of Little Rock, many of them unionists, who felt threatened by this invasion and were inclined to less radical action. The city council passed a resolution declaring their opposition to the arsenal's seizure by any troops not under direct control of the governor, thus placing Rector in a difficult position: he would be damned by the unionists if he took control of the arsenal, and damned by the secessionists if he didn't. In addition, there was a pressing need for action if hostilities were to be avoided between the U.S. Army and the volunteers. Rector sent a formal communication to Captain Totten requesting evacuation of the arsenal and removal from the state of the troops based there. Totten telegraphed Washington for orders, saying that five thousand men were headed to Little Rock to attack the arsenal. When he received no reply from the capital, Totten evacuated the premises on February 8, 1861, leaving its control to the state militia.[34]

With open warfare averted, the state's citizens turned to the matter of the impending convention, which the legislation had set for February 18. Blood was still running hot after the arsenal affair, and aspiring delegates worked the hustings and the newspaper offices with gusto. It was soon clear that the state was divided on secession along geographic lines: the northern and western sections were largely unionists, and the southern and eastern areas were secessionist. Northwestern Arkansas, especially the cities of Fayetteville, Fort Smith, and Van Buren, was supportive of the Union cause. The citizens of that area were greatly incensed by the removal of the federal garrison at Fort Smith shortly after the evacuation of the Little Rock arsenal. With a major source of revenue abruptly curtailed, the cities of Van Buren and Fort Smith looked with resentment on the hothead secessionists in the lowlands of the Mississippi Delta. In the pivotal area of central Arkansas, many leaders leaned toward the Union side as well, arguing that a cotton-producing state which remained in the Union would do quite well economically once the other fiber-growing regions were gone. At the polls, the people spoke, voting for a convention by the ratio of roughly two to one. Surprisingly, however, they elected a majority of pro-Union delegates to the March 4 meeting.

On the day the seventy-five delegates met in Little Rock, the rest of America was waiting to hear what Abraham Lincoln would say at his inauguration in Washington DC. At the convention, unionists outnumbered secessionists 40–35. Thomas H. Bradley, one of the few unionists from southern Arkansas, nominated David Walker, who as convention chair was assisted by the permanent secretary, Elias Cornelius Boudinot. Notwithstanding his earlier position as an editorialist for the southern cause at the *Arkansian* and his affiliation with the secessionist Johnson family, Boudinot stood with the unionists. Nominated by Hugh F. Thomason, he was elected by the same 40–35 majority that was to remain nearly constant during the convention's first session.[35] His main opponent for the secretary's post was him old nemesis, Thomas Peek. A substantial majority of the delegates were either farmers (including planters) or lawyers, and many held slaves.[36] The debates that followed at first sought to interpret Lincoln's inaugural speech, the secessionists seeing a threat in every word, the unionists finding hope for a peaceful settlement among the states. When the delegates were joined by two representatives from South Carolina on March 6, however, the arguments took up the subject of secession directly. Was it legal? Was it justified? What would be the consequences? Both sides maneuvered through oratory, but neither was able to sway members from the opposite side. Newspapers reported that the gallery was daily stuffed with men and women who cheered and threw bouquets of flowers at their favorites on the floor. Finally, on March 16, the question in everyone's mind came up for a vote and after more speeches and more "boketts," as one delegate put it,[37] the motion for secession failed, 39–35.

The convention continued to meet. After the vote on Saturday, the secessionist delegates began to look for extralegal measures to help them succeed, since their attempts at a legal victory had failed. On Tuesday the convention proper adjourned, but delegates continued to confer. A compromise of sorts was reached with four main points. First, delegates agreed to put the question to a vote of the people, deciding that the electorate would be offered the choice of "secession" or "cooperation." If the former choice was made, the convention would reconvene and fashion the appropriate articles of secession; if the latter course was decided, Arkansas would join other border states in seeking a satisfactory settlement. Second, the delegates agreed to resist any coercion by the federal government. Third, the five delegates sent to any meeting with the other border states were to be well-known unionists. The fourth point was the adoption of a series of resolutions, each of which aimed at reaching a peaceful solution. With both sides claiming victory, the convention adjourned to await the results of the August referendum.

Boudinot returned to Washington County when the convention adjourned. In addition to pursuing his law practice, the young man polished his oratorical skills, making a series of speeches in small towns in northwestern Arkansas in which he spelled out issues and arguments being debated nationally and in Little Rock. Thomas Colbert reports that in Bentonville, near the Missouri line, Cornelius was especially eloquent, offering his comments through word and gesture on the national symbol. A farmer from Elk Horn, moved by the patriotic images thus engendered, gave Boudinot a live eagle that he had captured. The orator had no choice but to keep the bird upon his return to Fayetteville, where it attracted many curious onlookers.[38] Later, the unionist friend with whom Boudinot had left the bird released it when word came that Arkansas had seceded.

But then everything changed. On April 12, 1861, Confederates attacked the

Union garrison at Fort Sumter in Charleston Harbor in response to an attempt by the federal government to reinforce the position. The pressure now was on Judge Walker in Fayetteville to reconvene the convention, and two events helped him in his difficult decision. The first was a call from Secretary of War Simon Cameron to Governor Rector to furnish 780 men to serve in suppressing rebellion. Rector indignantly refused—a popular move in the eyes of most Arkansans. In addition, Rector responded to a rumor, which later proved to be false, that federal troops were moving to take control of Fort Smith by dispatching four companies of volunteers and some cannons to prevent this from happening. As the steamboats full of volunteers paddled up the Arkansas River toward the unbeleaguered fort, Walker and other unionists got together and decided two things: first, to call the convention and pass the inevitable secession proclamation, and second, to take control of the state government before their more radical secessionist colleagues could. On May 6 the convention passed the ordinance with only one dissenting vote, the unionists throwing up their hands in surrender as the ladies threw down their bouquets from the gallery. The business of the convention was not yet over, however. It continued to sit in order to rewrite the state constitution in the face of the drastically changed situation. Most of the changes had to do with African Americans, no doubt at the behest of the agricultural interests represented at the proceedings. One very interesting alteration should be noted, one that demonstrates the young Boudinot's presence and influence: the old constitution used the phrase "all free men"; the new document read "all free white men and Indians."

CHAPTER 3

Confederate Soldier and Congressional Delegate

As the turmoil of war began in Arkansas, the situation to the west was scarcely less chaotic. In the Cherokee Nation, the early arguments between unionists and secessionists had been no less strident than in the state to the east, with many of the same arguments being offered. The result was also similar: a population with a rift down the middle; for the Cherokees, however, the split fell along old fault lines. For their part, those in the new provisional Confederate government quickly recognized the importance of the Indians' potential role in the West, and accordingly they planned to enlist the larger tribes in Indian Territory to their cause from early on. On February 21, 1861, the day the law to form a War Department was passed, the Congress of the Confederate States adopted a resolution to open negotiations with the Indians of the West. Four days later it instructed the Indian Committee to appoint agents to each of the major tribes. Among the four members of that committee was the recently arrived senator from Arkansas, Robert W. Johnson.[1] Among the first actions of the committee was to appoint Albert Pike as commissioner of the Indian tribes west of Arkansas, his duties being to negotiate with the Five Civilized Tribes and others to ensure their support. Joining with Pike in this endeavor was Brigadier General Ben McCulloch, the Confederate commander at Fort Smith.

To some extent, the way had been paved for Pike. For example, the superintendent of Indian Affairs for the Five Tribes at Fort Smith was Arkansan and secessionist Elias Rector. Several other southern sympathizers were serving under Rector, including Mississippian Douglas H. Cooper, Choctaw and Chickasaw agent; John Crawford, Cherokee agent; Boudinot colleague William Quesenbery, Creek agent; and Samuel M. Rutherford, Seminole agent. In charge of the Wichita agency was another southern sympathizer, Matthew Leeper.[2] Pike was a New Englander who had resided in Arkansas for some time, making a name there as a lawyer and poet. He had served in the Mexican War (attaining the rank of captain) and was a writer of some renown and a public figure. Pike was also a prominent Mason and as such had many important contacts in both the North and the South. Once hostilities broke out, Pike was commissioned a brigadier general, and he and McCulloch traveled to Park Hill to begin their negotiations with the principal chief of the Cherokees, John Ross. Upon hearing of their intentions, however, Ross issued a proclamation of neutrality before they arrived, asking the Cherokees to remain aloof from the controversy. The old chief had been both friend and adversary of the federal government and knew its power; he was reluctant to bring its wrath down on his people, even though Washington seemed a long way off at this time. Also, Ross probably shared many Cherokees' view that the coming conflict was a white man's war.

But many of the Cherokees, including many of the slaveholders and most of the mixed-bloods, did not agree with the principal chief's position. The old fracture lines began to form again, with the Ross party on the one side and the Watie group arrayed against them. Most of the full-bloods, greatly influenced by Baptist missionary Evan Jones, were firmly in the Ross camp. Stand Watie and his nephew had begun their own negotiations with the Confederate States early on, albeit in a more informal way. While still in Arkansas, Boudinot had befriended the older Pike, and once it was clear that Arkansas would join the other southern states, he began to discuss the Cherokee situation with both Johnson and Pike. He was, after all, in a perfect position to act as an intermediary between the Confederate leadership and the southern-leaning branch of the Cherokees. Boudinot kept his uncle Stand up on the latest news. "The State authorities at Little Rock have taken possession of the Arsenal there," he wrote on February 12, 1861. "The Southern Confederacy in Convention assembled at Montgomery Alabama unanimously elected Jeff Davis of Miss. and Alexander Stevens of Georgia President and Vice P. of the seceded states." A week before this, representatives of seven states had formed the Confederate States of America by adopting the ordinances of secession in Montgomery; this was news that Boudinot was not sure Watie had heard yet. "Active preparations are being made to commence an attack of Ft. Sumpter [sic] and the attack and capture are considered a foregone conclusion." The actual attack was still some months off, however, and did not occur until April 12. Boudinot included one more bit of news that Watie may or may not have known about: "John Ross has published a letter in the Van Buren [newspaper] in which he says the Cherokees will go with Arkansas and Missouri."[3] Ross continued to maintain his ambiguous position as long as he could, playing both sides, always looking for the advantage for the Cherokees. In the end this strategy did not bear fruit, although few alternative moves were open to the old chief.

A meeting, most likely arranged by Cornelius, was held at Fort Smith in May 1861 with Pike, McCulloch, Boudinot, and Watie attending. Later, Pike remembered the Cherokees as complaining about the rift in the tribe and asking for his help against threatened violence from the Ross party if they should "raise a Secession flag."[4] Watie, according to Pike, was apprehensive of violence from the "Pin Organization" of full-blood Cherokees. "Pin Indians" was a term applied to members of an old secret society in the Cherokee Nation, the Keetoowahs, or Nighthawks, so called because adherents wore two crossed pins to identify themselves. During the middle of the nineteenth century, the Keetoowahs sided with the Ross faction against the Watie party. Around the time of the Civil War, the organization was under the virtual leadership of Evan Jones and his son John, both of whom had decidedly abolitionist tendencies. Since most of the full-bloods did not own slaves, they were amenable to the Joneses' views; significantly, the missionaries learned and used the Cherokee language, which cemented their bonds with many traditional Indians. The Pin organization is only half the story, however. The Watie faction took part in a secret society of their own, the Knights of the Golden Circle. The Knights, begun by George Washington Lamb Binkey in Cincinnati, was originally a "filibuster" organization; that is, it was founded to extend U.S. hegemony over Central and South America. Binkey's plan was to impose "the superior Anglo-American civilization" on Latin America; an ancillary object was to make Binkey and other Knights rich.[5] When the Civil War broke out, many Copperheads, as politically active, anti-abolitionist, conservative Democrats came to be called, turned to the Knights organization as a means of opposing Lincoln's Republican administration. In the Cherokee Nation, the Knights were formed partly to resist the acts of the Cherokee Light Horse police, under the control of Cah-skeh-new Mankiller, a noted Keetoowah.[6] Watie's Knights probably had a very local flavor, as the immediate abolitionist threat was the influence of Jones on Ross and his followers. Another family member, however, embraced the organization vigorously. John Rollin Ridge, exiled to California for killing one of the Ross party, campaigned for the Knights in his newspapers and for a while traveled his adopted state to recruit members.[7] The rise of these organizations had ominous undertones, however. All the tinder for the Civil War bonfire that was to engulf the Cherokee Nation, it seemed, awaited the spark.

Watie had been assured of official Confederate support by Pike and Mc-Culloch, but he had other allies as well. In Arkansas, those organizing for the southern cause saw early on the importance of securing the western border through an alliance with the Cherokee Nation. Although Boudinot had conferred with Pike, Johnson, and others on this issue soon after the state's secession, nowhere was the need for defense greater than on the western border, where the old Ridge-Boudinot-Watie network was alive and well. In May 1861, A. M. Wilson and J. W. Washbourne wrote to Watie "as a private and public citizen" of the Cherokee Nation, urging him to unite with anti-abolitionist forces in the region. Promising the support of troops, guns, and ammunition from Arkansas, they asked Watie to train his men as a force for the Confederate side. If he would come in on the Confederate side, Wilson and Washbourne assured Watie, "we would afford you all the aid we could." They added that "a certain number of guns, good guns, have been granted to the State of Arkansas, for the use of the Cherokees in the defence of their and our frontier." Wilson and Washbourne also mention that action by Watie would constitute "service for the Cherokee soil" and also would "serve Arkansas effectively." The need to organize was urgent, the Arkansans pointed out, since close by in Kansas the ardent abolitionist James H. Lane had been elected to the U.S. Senate. Lane's intention, they assured Watie, was "subjugation of the Cherokees" and the "overwhelming of the race by the hordes of greedy Republicans." Wilson and Washbourne urged Watie to act, but to act in secret because of federal forces in the area as well as the many Union sympathizers in this border area.[8]

After Watie and Boudinot had assured Pike and McCulloch of their loyalty to the South, Pike's delegation continued on to Ross's residence at Park Hill outside Tahlequah, the Cherokee capital. In order to sweeten the offer, Pike offered to purchase the eight hundred thousand acres of Cherokee territory in Kansas and Missouri, but this was not enough to win the old chief over. When Ross refused to throw in the Cherokees' lot with the Confederates, the pair left, Pike to negotiate with other tribes in Indian Territory and McCulloch to return to his command at Fort Smith. While Ross resisted the South's overtures in May 1861, forces were at work to make him change that stance. The first of these was Pike's success with the other tribes. On July 10 the Creeks allied themselves with the Confederacy, followed on the twelfth by the Choctaws and Chickasaws. When the Seminoles signed their treaty in August, the Cherokees alone among the Five Civilized Tribes were neutral. While all of the tribes were divided in their sympathies, it is clear that Pike's work for the southern cause was notable. By the time he secured a treaty with the Plains tribes at the Wichita Agency on August 12, it was evident to all that he had gained a significant advantage for the Confederacy. Even the federal government seemed to agree, because by this time most of their troops had withdrawn from the area. At this juncture, the Cherokee Nation seemed left out in the cold. Even the genial Pike had turned his back on Ross, withdrawing his offer to purchase the Kansas and Missouri lands and refusing to negotiate further with him.[9]

With assurances of support from Arkansas and from Pike and McCulloch, Watie raised a troop of three hundred cavalrymen, among them his twenty-six-year-old nephew Cornelius. Watie was commissioned a colonel in the Confederate army on July 12, 1861, and his supporters attempted to raise the Stars and Bars over the capitol square in Tahlequah.[10] As pressure rose in his own neighborhood, Ross was informed of the Confederacy's decisive victory at Bull Run in July and the defeat of the Union army at Wilson's Creek in southwest Missouri in August. Some of Watie's men were pressed into service in those confused days of the summer of 1861. According to one eyewitness, J. M. Keys, Boudinot took part in this battle and cut a powerful figure, "his long black hair floating on the breeze" as the Confederates fought to victory.[11] To make matters worse for Ross, the southern newspapers made Colonel Watie the hero of this battle, although Watie himself wasn't even there. Nonetheless, the leader of a small band of irregular cavalry became an instant hero in Indian Territory, Arkansas, and southern Missouri.[12] This fame doubtless made Watie's recruiting job easier, as the new colonel was still organizing his forces at this point.

The convergence of the forces of Confederate battle success and Watie's actions close to home gave Ross no choice but to capitulate his neutral position. To do otherwise would have unleashed a Cherokee civil war that the chief hoped desperately to avoid, given what seemed to be the inevitable outcome. Accordingly, he invited Pike back to Park Hill to negotiate a treaty and, not incidentally, to reestablish himself as the Cherokee leader. After some days of negotiation, the treaty was drafted. Called the "Treaty of Friendship and Alliance between the Confederate States of America and the Cherokee Nation," the document was signed on October 7, 1861. Its major stipulations are as follows: protection from hostile invasion, guarantee of the institution of slavery, representation in the Confederate Congress, immunity from debts incurred by the Confederate States of America, and in general, replacement of the authority of the United States with that of the Confederacy. The Cherokees were to allow the construction of forts and roads in their territory and to furnish a regiment consisting of ten companies of cavalry plus two reserve companies. However, the treaty stipulated that the Cherokees serving in such a regiment would not be forced to serve beyond the limits of Indian Territory and that the troops would receive the same pay and allowances as other Confederate soldiers. Interestingly, the treaty also called for the payment of $10,300 each to the claimants of the Ridge-Boudinot-Watie party, an unsettled claim going back to the Cherokee Treaty of 1846. Stand Watie was authorized to dole the money out to legitimate claimants. [13] Once the treaty was signed, Ross and Watie shook hands warily as Cornelius looked on.

Preparations for war now began in earnest. Instead of one Cherokee regiment, two were organized. This was largely due to the fact that both Ross and Watie had begun to raise troops before the treaty was negotiated, Watie's cavalry to prepare a force to fight either for the South or against the Pins, Ross's Home Guard for any eventuality. Now the two groups remained separated. Colonel John Drew commanded the First Regiment of Cherokee Mounted Rifles, while Watie led the Cherokee Mounted Volunteers. McCulloch appraised the regiments in a letter to L. P. Walker, the Confederate secretary of war, dated September 2, 1861. Drew's regiment was mostly full-bloods, he reports. Watie's forces, which he has already employed in the Neutral Lands and in Kansas, he describes as "half-breeds, who are educated men, and good soldiers anywhere, in or out of the Nation." He goes on to state his intention to keep the two regiments distinct and separate. [14] At first McCulloch directed both regiments, but when, on November 22, 1861, the Department of Indian Territory was created, the command was given to the Confederate army's newest brigadier, General Albert Pike.

As later events made clear, Watie had considerable talent as a military tactician and leader of men, but he had little or no interest in the administrative details of command. In the electric atmosphere in the months before the war reached its full, roaring horror he was beset with advice, applications, and entreaties, some of it well meaning, some of it self-serving, most of it a little of both. Among the applicants and advisers was Cornelius Boudinot, who hoped to secure for himself a post in Watie's regiment with responsibility and authority. Although he had no military experience outside the Wilson's Creek skirmish, hardly anyone else did either, since the Mexican War had been more than twenty years before and the serious Indian Wars had yet to begin. Boudinot found himself clamoring for Watie's favor among a group of Cherokees eager to don a uniform on the southern side, as indicated in his letter of October 5, 1861, by which time he was in the Cherokee Nation at Honey Creek, an early Treaty party settlement. The catalyst for the letter was a conversation he had had with Tom Taylor in Tahlequah, in which Taylor related that he would be appointed "Lt. Col."—that is, second in command to Watie. "I hope there is some mistake about this for of all men I think him least deserving and least fitted for that post; he is as you know a timid flexible wavering unstable speculating politician always ready to profit by the labors of others and selfish to the last degree," Boudinot writes, seeming hurt and bewildered, thinking that he has been overlooked by his uncle. "I deserve something from your hands," he goes on to say. "I venture to ask from you either the Lt. Col. or the Major's place." He goes on to point out that John Ross had appointed *his* nephew, William Potter Ross, to lieutenant colonel in Drew's regiment, this being a good way for the chief to keep himself apprised of developments there. If Ross can engage in nepotism, Cornelius seems to say, perhaps Watie should follow his example.[15]

In another comment, Cornelius speculated that his appointment "would give dissatisfaction to some," acknowledging the fact that he already had enemies, or at least detractors, within the ranks of the Confederate Cherokees. This was no doubt due to three major factors: first, that he was a relative newcomer to the ongoing Ross-Watie conflict; second, that he seemed to exploit the blood link with his uncle; and third, that he was developing a reputation as an "operator," a man with high ambition and the Machiavellian tendencies to further his career. Tom Taylor may or may not have had a conversation with Watie concerning the lieutenant colonel's post, but two thing are certain: Taylor knew that Cornelius wanted that position badly and that the excitable Boudinot would be upset by being told that another might possibly get the appointment instead. In this case, Cornelius's temper did not get him into trouble, as it would later. Boudinot was clamoring for a position in the regiment and had his eye on being second in command. His letter to Watie on the matter gives us an interesting perspective on the situation as Cornelius saw it: "If any accident, which God forbid, should happen to you so that another would have to take your place, you will see the importance of having some one in responsible position to keep the power you now have from passing into unreliable hands."[16] Boudinot, even at age twenty-six, saw himself as Watie's successor not only in the family but as leader of the anti-Ross faction. Perhaps wisely, Watie talked his nephew into taking on the rank of major and gave the higher ratings to men in the Cherokee Nation. Once the fighting began, Boudinot found that he had all the military responsibility he wanted. His official service record, dated December 4, 1861, has him listed as a major in Watie's regiment of Cherokee Mounted Volunteers.[17]

Cornelius was no doubt happy that Watie had indeed been judicious in his choice of officers, especially in his appointment of two senior aides, Lieutenant Colonel William Penn Adair and Captain James M. Bell. The latter was Watie's brother-in-law, as Sarah (Sallie) Watie was Bell's sister. Bell became very close to Sallie after the death of his wife, Caroline, and of Stand, and he became a close associate of Boudinot's in many ventures after the war. Cornelius's association with Adair was not as cordial; in fact, after the war they became bitter enemies as Boudinot pushed for the opening up of Indian Territory while Adair fought to retain the status quo for the Cherokee Nation. Within the regiment, however, Watie had established a cadre of like-minded men who would serve him well. In this, his first major administrative duty, he had performed brilliantly.

The Confederate War Department had specific plans for the Indian troops in the Territory. They were to serve on the western flank, preventing Union troops from taking control south of Kansas and Missouri, and engaging in guerrilla-style fighting to keep the enemy off balance. Watie's particular orders, dated September 20, 1861, involved taking up an "advanced position" in either the Neutral Lands or Kansas, "acting with great prudence." On October 22, General McCulloch reports, "I have instructed Col. Stand Watie, with one regiment of Cherokees, to move into the neutral land and Kansas, and destroy everything that might be of service to the enemy." He adds that he plans "to lay waste to Kansas."[18] General Pike was put in charge of the military district of the Indian Territory established in November 1861, with his first objective made clear: to neutralize the Indians who had not entered into treaties with the South. The most important contingents of these were a group of Muscogees, or Creeks, under Opothleyahola, and one of Seminoles under Halleck Tustenuggee. The groups were estimated at between eight hundred and twelve hundred men, two hundred to three hundred African American slaves, and an undisclosed number of women and children, all encamped at the juncture of the Canadian River's North and Deep Forks in the Creek Nation.[19] Opothleyahola and Halleck Tustenuggee prepared to leave Indian Territory with their followers for federally controlled Kansas, thus avoiding confrontation with relatives and neighbors. When Pike was called to Richmond to report on the status of the war in Indian Territory, Colonel Douglas

SOLDIER AND DELEGATE

H. Cooper took command of the southern troops, including the Cherokees; Cooper decided to move on the river encampment and to capture the Creeks and Seminoles before they could move. However, when his forces reached the camp on November 15, 1861, he found it deserted. Cooper and his fourteen hundred troops followed the refugees and overtook them four days later at Round Mountain in the northern part of the Creek Nation. The Creeks and Seminoles defended themselves but were soundly defeated. Before Cooper could consolidate his forces and carry out his capture plans, he was called away to defend against a Union force moving from Missouri.

Cooper's intelligence told him that Opothleyahola's forces were about to attack his position on the Arkansas River, perhaps in conjunction with the Missouri contingent. He decided to take the offensive and surprised the Creeks at their camp on Bird Creek in the Cherokee Nation, forcing them to withdraw. Cooper's forces were at this time made up of Choctaws, Chickasaws, southern Creeks and Seminoles, Texas cavalry, and the Cherokees of Drew's regiment. The Cherokees had lately joined Cooper, and after their first taste of killing other Indians they were reluctant to continue. Faced with this problem and with the need to resupply, Cooper chose not to follow Opothleyahola's forces when they withdrew. He soon found out that a southern force under Colonel James McIntosh had moved from Van Buren, Arkansas, and was chasing the retreating forces. Watie's regiment was ordered to join McIntosh and cut off the Creeks. The Confederates engaged Opothleyahola's forces at Shoal Creek in the Cherokee Outlet. In the battle, known as Chustenahlah, McIntosh's men soundly defeated the Creeks, who fled in disarray.[20] Watie's men pursued a large group of between five hundred and six hundred fighting men over difficult terrain until the enemy stopped to fortify a position in the hills. Watie, with three hundred men under his command, split his forces into two groups, one on the left and commanded by Boudinot, the other moving to the right. Once in position, the Cherokees attacked the superior forces and, after a fierce battle of two hours or so, forced the enemy from its position. In his official battle report, Watie stated that twenty or twenty-one of the enemy had been killed and many others wounded, while his command had no casualties. Boudinot's report says that he moved into a ravine and engaged a group of the enemy, resulting in at least eleven dead. McIntosh put the number at fifteen and said that in addition, Boudinot had captured seventy-five prisoners and twenty-five or thirty packhorses.[21]

Basic supplies had become a problem for the Confederate troops in the West from the beginning of the war. Watie's forces were perhaps better off at first because they knew where the region's resources were located and because they had friends and relatives among the civilian population. Writing to Stand Watie in March 1862, William Quesenbery marks his letter from Fort Gibson as "very private" and then goes on to say that he is sending supplies to Watie that are expected by other regiments. Do not "make any noise about it," he cautions, as they have been "obtained by a high handed move." As always, Quesenbery delighted in telling a good story. In closing his letter, he sends his respects to "Boudinot and other good friends."[22] Watie's confidential advantage was not to last, however, as the war ground on. As early as June, Albert Pike complains to Major General Thomas C. Hindman, commander of the Trans-Mississippi District, that all the treaties and deals he has made with the Indians prior to the war have now been broken. Orders from Hindman for Pike's white troops to help at the siege of Little Rock "finishes the ruin of my command," he writes. Little support has been forthcoming for the Indian troops, the Cherokee officers have not been paid, and all his cannon powder has been ordered to Little Rock. Pike reports that he has sent Boudinot to Corinth, Mississippi, in search of replacement ammunition. In July he sends a similar complaint.[23]

In May 1862, Boudinot fought with Watie's regiment at Pea Ridge, in northwestern Arkansas, a battle marked by confusion and lack of communication in the Confederate ranks. The fighting resulted in the retreat of the southerners down the Boston Mountains to the area around the Arkansas River near Van Buren and Fort Smith. General Pike describes the battle, including the conduct of Watie's troops, in some detail in his official report.[24] The picture he paints is not a pretty one: communication among units was almost nonexistent, and rumors superseded official orders in many cases. Some troops—and Pike singles out the Cherokees under Drew especially in this regard—were almost totally undisciplined, to the point of ignoring direct orders from superiors. Watie's forces, on the other hand, were more trustworthy; Pike used them judiciously, he reports, for crucial situations such as securing artillery positions. Boudinot is mentioned only once in the report and appears to have been used to communicate with the elusive General Earl Van Dorn and his constantly moving command post. Evidently, Pike felt that he could trust Boudinot to keep his head in the midst of this especially chaotic situation and to give an accurate reading of Pike's predicament. In addition, Boudinot knew the terrain better than many and carried some additional authority as Watie's nephew. In any case, despite the efforts of Pike, Watie, and Boudinot, the Union forces scored a decisive victory at Pea Ridge.

Boudinot saw action again when a Union force—described as an "Indian expedition"—from Fort Scott, Kansas, proceeded into the Cherokee Nation in May 1862. Drew's and Watie's regiments were sent to repulse them, with reinforcements from Missouri under Colonel James J. Clarkson. In short order, Drew's men deserted—chagrined, perhaps, at having to fight other Indians. Clarkson's troops were dispersed as the fight went on, but Watie's men resisted, "with a courage never surpassed," as General Hindman reported to Adjutant and Inspector General Samuel Cooper. "On one occasion," Hindman wrote, "a portion of his regiment, under Major Elias C. Boudinot, repulsed the federal advance of fivefold greater strength." [25] Later that year, on July 27, Boudinot took part in a skirmish at Bayou Bernard, Indian Territory.

Boudinot was elevated to the rank of lieutenant colonel after one of the skirmishes in which Watie's regiment was involved that summer.[26] Tom Taylor, the man whom Boudinot had warned his uncle about as the command was being formed, was killed, leaving a vacancy among Watie's staff. Boudinot filled this post, acquiring the title of "colonel," an honorific that he would attach to himself for the rest of his life. Boudinot's service record, however, carries the designation "Major/Major," indicating that he entered the service as a major and left with the same rank. His promotion was most likely made on the battlefield and did not make it into any official record. Boudinot's role in the war was to change in a very short time anyway, as he moved from the military to the Confederate Congress.

In the summer of 1862 in the Cherokee Nation, the fighting was furious. Union forces under General William Weer decisively defeated Colonel Clarkson, commander of all the troops within the Cherokee Nation, at Locust Grove, north of Tahlequah, on July 3. Watie's forces were engaged elsewhere and did not take part in the battle. Weer marched triumphantly into the Cherokee capital and placed Ross under arrest, later releasing him on parole. Weer urged Ross to deliver the Cherokee Nation to the Union side, since many of Drew's men had deserted to the Union forces soon after the fight. However, the Union army had exceeded its supply lines and was forced to retreat in spite of its successes. As it withdrew from Tahlequah in July, Ross went along, giving the reason that he needed to confer with President Lincoln concerning the status of the Cherokee Nation. After meeting with government officials in Washington, the chief retired to Philadelphia to wait out the conclusion to the war.[27]

With Ross gone and many of his supporters scattered, there was a power vacuum in the Cherokee Nation. With the Union troops withdrawn, there was a temporary lull in the fighting as well. Taking advantage of the situation, the Confederate Cherokees, now in control politically as well as militarily, convened in Tahlequah on August 21. There they elected Stand Watie principal chief and chose his nephew Elias Cornelius Boudinot as Cherokee delegate to the Confederate Congress under the terms of the treaty signed earlier by Ross and Pike.[28] The convention continued to function as a legislative body, meeting from time to time during the war to enact ordinances for various issues as they arose. When the southern Cherokees, as they came to be known, were forced from the Nation and into the Red River area and Texas later in the war, the convention ceased to function as a political body. One session worthy of note was held in May 1863 at Coody's Creek across the Arkansas River from Fort Gibson. At this point, three pressing issues needed discussion: recruitment of men for the Indian regiments, establishing camps for the numerous refugees forced to flee from the Union advances into the Cherokee Nation, and organizing a school system for the refugee children.

Boudinot offered a plan to help recruit soldiers into the Indian regiments. Wardell has described this plan as "sinister" because it provided for white settlement of Cherokee lands in the West, perhaps for the first time by a Cherokee citizen. While the Confederate government promised a brigadier general and colonel's positions should the measure be accepted by the council, no direct benefit to Boudinot has been identified in spite of some intensive research efforts. [29] Boudinot's plan, as it appeared in the form of a series of resolutions proposed by a subcommittee comprising J. A. Scales, James M. Bell, Hooley Bell, Dr. Adair, D. R. Nave, and M. C. Frye, proposed that 160-acre plots be assigned to white men loyal to the Confederacy who would enlist in the Indian brigade that would be formed under the agreement. The brigade was to combine the Indian regiments from the various tribes under the command of a brigadier general, presumably Watie. The offer was open to both Indian and white soldiers who served in that command, but the total number of "bounties" was not to exceed one thousand. Excluded from settlement was land in the eastern half of the Nation as far north as the Spavinaw River. Generally included was the Cherokee Outlet and the Texas panhandle region. Morris Wardell reports that the resolutions were never put to a vote; however, the discussion is notable because of its potentially far-reaching consequences.

In September 1862, Union forces had once again occupied northwest Arkansas and were threatening the Cherokee Nation. This time, however, instead of answering the call to arms, Major Boudinot left for Richmond, convinced that he could do more for his people there than on the front lines. Other tribes in

Indian Territory that had signed treaties with the Confederacy sent delegates as well. S. B. Callahan represented the Seminoles and Creeks, Robert M. Jones the Choctaws, and Peter Pitchlynn the Chickasaws.[30]

On October 7, 1862, Representative Felix I. Batson of Arkansas introduced Boudinot to the Confederate House of Representatives. Although Cornelius was not officially accepted as a delegate at this point, he was invited to take a seat and view the activities on the House floor. Meanwhile, his credentials were forwarded to the Committee on Indian Affairs for that body's recommendation.[31] Two days after this cordial reception by the membership, Cornelius met with the committee. The members inspected his credentials and declared him duly elected and entitled to his seat. However, his position as delegate from the Cherokee Nation was defined as being for the following purposes: to propose and introduce measures for the benefit of the Cherokees and to be recognized to speak in regard to such matters in both the committee and on the House floor. While this stipulation seemed to limit Boudinot's responsibilities in the Confederate Congress considerably, he was also given the right to speak on other topics in which the Cherokee Nation might be particularly interested, a privilege that allowed him some latitude. Boudinot's reaction to these restrictions is unclear. The treaty with the Confederate States of America stipulated only that the Cherokee Nation would be allowed a delegate in Congress, a position for which the Cherokees and other nations had petitioned the U.S. government for years. While the Confederates granted this request, they did not spell out exactly what the delegate's rights and responsibilities were until it was time to seat the member. If Boudinot and his fellows in the Cherokee Nation were expecting full membership in the House of Representatives, with voice and vote in all matters considered by that body, they were disappointed. It is very likely that Cornelius, as the political animal he had become, held his tongue publicly and lobbied friendly congressmen whenever he needed to.[32] His subsequent actions in the Confederate Congress made it clear that he was trying to consolidate as much authority in his position as he could.

But Boudinot was not merely a lobbyist for the Cherokee Nation in Richmond. During the war he split his time between the Confederate capital and the West, traveling to Arkansas, the Cherokee Nation, and later, when Cherokee refugees had fled there, to Texas. In a letter to Watie sent from Little Rock in January 1863 he says, "I delayed proceeding to Richmond until I could know something definite concerning the fate of our army here, upon which rested the only hope of *our* country. I wished to carry such intelligence of the State of Affairs as would enable me to do more at Richmond than I could otherwise."

He gives Watie a synopsis of the war news from Arkansas and Missouri and then mentions the money due the southern Cherokees as stipulated in the treaty with the Confederate States. "A good deal of money is due us and I suggest that the convention assemble and adopt the accompanying resolution authorizing me to receive such moneys, if they will pass this ordinance I am satisfied I can get the money, and with a full treasury you know what new life will be infused into our infant government."[33] Boudinot eventually became the conduit for money and commodities to the Cherokees, meager as they were. More importantly, he saw control of the Cherokee government as continuing in the hands of southern Cherokees after the war. The implications for his personal ambitions is obvious.

Back at Richmond, Cornelius decided to test his limits for the first time on April 1, 1863. By this time he had reestablished contacts with politicians from his region and made some alliances that both sides considered mutually beneficial. This became evident because when he rose to speak on the floor of the House, he did so after a motion to suspend the rules was made and passed, an indication of both his "special" status as a delegate and his personal stature among the members. His business before the House was to introduce two bills. The first was to establish regulations for delegates from "certain Indian nations," with which he meant to clarify not only his own position but also that of delegates from other nations from Indian Territory. The Muscogees, Choctaws, Chickasaws, and Seminoles had all ratified treaties similar to the one between the Cherokees and the Confederate States, with stipulations for representation in the Confederate Congress. His second bill was a supplement to an act passed on February 15, 1862, to establish "judicial courts" in Indian Territory. Both measures were referred to the Judiciary Committee for further action.[34] By this time, the leadership had recognized his status by issuing him a regular seat on the House floor.[35]

Cornelius continued to travel back to Arkansas in support of Watie's efforts. In a letter from Fort Smith dated June 27, 1863, he says that he was en route to Watie's headquarters until he learned that the regiment was "on the scout," referring to the Indian troops' guerrilla activities. On this trip he engaged in securing ammunition boxes and other supplies and having them sent to regimental headquarters. Apparently, he found doing this sort of business impossible by long distance and felt he needed to deal with suppliers face-to-face because of shortages of goods and the unreliability of dealers and traders. Boudinot also uses this letter to comment on actions of the convention, the governmental body established by Watie's wartime Cherokee government. Cornelius's brother William Penn Boudinot was in Tahlequah and sending news of the convention's various ordinances, including a conscript law. Boudinot was well aware of his powers as congressional delegate and attempted to influence the body through William and Stand Watie.[36]

On December 10, 1863, Boudinot introduced a bill called "An Act for Filling Vacancies of Delegates to Congress in Certain Indian Nations," an attempt to beef up the strength of Indian representation in the Congress. On the same day, Boudinot ally Thomas B. Hanly, a congressman from Arkansas, introduced a motion that "one of the Indian delegates" would attend meetings of the Committee on Indian Affairs. Four days later, the Speaker announced that he had appointed Boudinot "corresponding member" of that committee, effectively giving him voice but no vote in all matters affecting Native Americans that came before the Confederate Congress.[37] On December 18, acting on pleas from Watie and others back home, Cornelius introduced legislation that called for the appointment of a commissioner of accounts for the states and territories west of the Mississippi and another for payment of all accounts due to commissaries and ordnance officers west of the river. The situation was becoming desperate in the Cherokee Nation. Union troops had occupied its lands since April 1863, Stand Watie complained in a letter to Colonel Sutton S. Scott, the Confederate commissioner of Indian Affairs, yet the South had done nothing to dislodge them or to support Watie's troops, let alone the Cherokee civilians. He also charged that funds and goods promised to the Cherokees had been diverted to others in the Confederacy.[38] Boudinot was able to borrow $10,000 on his own credit and sent the money to Watie in hopes of alleviated some of his people's suffering. He also promised a further $40,000 within two months. Apparently, he was having trouble with Colonel Scott, who seemed reluctant to disburse any funds to the Indian troops or refugees.[39] At Richmond in December 1863, Cornelius put up an appropriations bill for the payment of $100,000 "for the use and benefit of the Cherokee Nation," a reflection not only of the impecunious state of the Indian troops fighting for the Confederacy but of the dire predicaments of southern Cherokee civilians, many of whose crops and dwellings had been destroyed in the fierce, often internecine fighting in Indian Territory.[40] President Jefferson Davis signed the bill on January 22, 1864, but the payment's effect was diminished, partly by runaway wartime inflation and partly because of reluctance on the part of many people to accept Confederate currency, especially at face value.[41]

One of the difficulties facing Watie in the field was what he saw as incompetence in military leaders sent from Richmond for command in Indian

Territory. A particularly sore spot in this regard was the conduct of Brigadier General William Steele. Watie complained that he had tried to apprise Steele of the situation in the Territory and how different tactics were necessary in the West than in the East, but his advice had been disregarded. The Cherokee leader could not understand how Steele could continue a strategy that "allows a vastly inferior force of enemy to ravage the land with impunity." Even after Steele received reinforcements to help him dislodge Union forces from the area, Watie reported in August 1863 that "the same lethargy and procrastination prevail, and our prospects look more gloomy than ever." [42] Adding insult to injury, Steele had Colonel Adair, one of Watie's trusted lieutenants, arrested for "disrespect." Adair's trial was to be held in Little Rock, but in the turmoil of war it was soon forgotten. [43] Boudinot complained to Confederate officials in Richmond, including Secretary of War James A. Seddon, with whom he was developing a political relationship. By November, Watie was exasperated, and his nephew knew it. It was at this point that Cornelius demanded General Steele's removal, suggesting to President Davis a major realignment of the Confederate leadership in Missouri as well as in Indian Territory. [44] While Boudinot's wide-ranging plan was not put into place, Watie was put in charge of two Creek regiments and the Choctaw battalion over the objections of Steele. Even Brigadier General Douglas H. Cooper got into the act, complaining to General Edmund Kirby-Smith that Steele was "at the hazard of losing our Indian allies, and with them the Indian Territory." [45] Soon, Steele was replaced by General Samuel B. Maxey, who later was replaced by Watie's ally, General Cooper. Steele blamed Boudinot for his machinations against him in Richmond. His dismissal was "the result of a scheme originating, I believe, with the Hon. E. C. Boudinot, delegate from the Cherokees for raising several Indian brigades for permanent service in the Indian country, the whole to be commanded by a major-general, and it was feared that if it should appear that my administration were successful, that I might be selected for the command. Hence the necessity for traducing me." [46] Without mentioning Boudinot by name, Steele in another letter makes reference to "a class of men whose whole aim is to sway the councils of the Nations for their own selfish ends." The context makes clear that he is referring to Boudinot and others whose influence seems to be powerful in Indian Territory. [47] In any case, the thorn in Watie's side had been removed.

As the war continued and casualties mounted, the Confederacy was particularly hard pressed to provide for the care and relief of wounded soldiers and incapacitated citizens. With tremendous strain on the South's dwindling treasury, people in the West were often forgotten or ignored. Boudinot introduced legislation to pay the claims of the officers and men of the Indian Territory in early 1864, their petitions not having been included in the regular claims for the Confederate army; he also rose to amend a bill that provided for wounded and disabled soldiers, adding the words "Indian Territory" to the list of states and territories covered in the original act.[48] This may have caused some tension between the Cherokee champion and other delegates trying to provide for the relief of their own constituents, because when Boudinot introduced a memorial relative to Indian Affairs on the House floor on February 20, 1864, it was remanded to the Committee on Indian Affairs "without being read."[49] In May a bill for "the relief of the Cherokee Nation" was sent to the committee as well.[50] Cornelius's personal fortunes were not doing so well at this point, either. In a postcript to a letter to Watie of April 20, 1864, he comments, "I pay $350 per month for board and received $230. per month salary—So see I am making money."[51]

The situation for the southern Cherokee troops in February 1864 was desperate. Union troops launched a campaign to rid the Indian Territory of southern forces at this time and pressed toward Texas with a furious, scorched-earth attack. Low on basic supplies like food, clothing, and ammunition, Watie's men were forced ever southward as morale sagged. The troops were aware that their families were suffering similar hardships and in some ways were worse off than the combatants; they longed to return to their farms and loved ones. At this dark hour, aware of the resistance to Boudinot's pleas in the Congress, Jefferson Davis attempted to rally his Indian troops. In a letter to Watie and other southern Indian leaders, he admitted that some Confederate officials had neglected them. Promising to reprimand those responsible, he promised to give his "earnest consideration" to the soldiers' problems. He closed by saying that all "treaty stipulations between us shall be sacredly observed and carried into effect to the full extent of my power as President of the Confederate States."[52]

But by the end of 1864, Boudinot was still struggling to call attention to the plight of Confederate Indians and the Cherokees in particular, but it appeared he was fighting an uphill battle. It is telling that bills he was introducing were reminiscent of the myriad memorials and proposals sent to the U.S. Congress and to federal officials throughout the nineteenth century calling for recognition of various aspects of treaties. Boudinot had taken Davis at his word considering the sanctity of the Confederate-Cherokee treaty. When no changes in action seemed to be forthcoming, however, he felt compelled to act. In December he proposed legislation that would "carry into effect the treaty with the Cherokee Nation." Another proposal, made on December 30, 1864, called for "the relief of the Indian nations with which treaties have been made by the Confederate States."[53] The wording of these proposals indicates that he was still having trouble getting recognition from the Confederate government, let alone aid for his people.

Boudinot was able to score a major coup in 1864, in terms of recognition if not in relief for the Cherokee troops and people, when he was instrumental in securing Watie's promotion to brigadier general. Since the fall of the Ross government and the dissolution of Drew's forces, Watie had been in command of all the Cherokees fighting for the South. Cornelius worked behind the scenes to get Watie's appointment, enlisting Secretary of War Seddon as an ally. Seddon suggested to Davis early in 1864 that Watie be promoted to general and Maxie elevated to major general as a concurrent effort was made to raise additional troops for their forces.[54] The secretary's recommendation was approved by Davis, and on May 10 the action was approved by the Confederate Senate. With his brigadiership, Watie took over the First Indian Brigade, a command that included troops of other Indian Territory nations. Thus, with Boudinot's sponsorship, Stand Watie became the only Indian to reach the rank of general during the Civil War, a tribute to his military skills and to his nephew's diplomatic ones. For their part, the Confederate authorities were aware that the promotion could only help recruiting for and morale of the Indian soldiery.

Boudinot's letter to Watie announcing the promotion demonstrates Cornelius's pride in having secured the brigadiership and also throws some light on the circumstances. He writes that Arkansas senators Robert W. Johnson and Charles B. Mitchell, "our steadfast and warmest friends," sent a joint letter to President Davis urging the promotion. "Their high appreciation of you and your services were there," he continues, and "the interest they have ever shown for our people and country should be noted and remembered by every Cherokee." He comments on the great impact in the capital of the news of Watie's success near Boggy Depot, intimating that perhaps the new general himself might take a bit of credit. Boudinot goes on, making suggestions for the staff needed for the increased responsibilities. He knew that Watie disliked paperwork and administrative tasks, being much more at home in the field with his men, and so Cornelius stressed the importance of choosing the right staff, especially an adjutant who would be loyal and able to take the administrative load off his shoulders. Seizing the opportunity, he also included plugs for their common relatives, J. W. Washbourne and Andrew Ridge, the latter a son of the slain John Ridge. Boudinot ends this lengthy missive by assuring his uncle that he is actively raising money for troops and civilians alike, but he closes with some ominous words: "The great battle so long pending between Lee and Grant was fought yesterday and today; full official reports have not yet been recd. Enough is known however to convince us that we are again victorious."[55] He was referring to the Battle of the Wilderness, the bloody and violent beginning of Grant's campaign into northern Virginia, defended by Lee's army, which numbered just half of the Union strength.

We can get a glimpse of what life was like in Richmond as the Union troops closed in through Boudinot's words to his brother William Penn a month later.[56] The capital, of course, was rife with rumors, punctuated by the sounds of cannon and small-arms fire as the fighting drew near. At one point, Cornelius reports, "the city fairly shook with the thunder of artillery. I was awakened by it—the firing was terrific and very rapid. I counted looking at my watch 30 guns a minute." As General Philip Sheridan menaced the city, "alarm bells were rung and intense excitement prevailed, the govt. packed up." The townspeople found out that all the railroads into the city were cut, and Cornelius jocularly comments that those "who would escape the halter were admonished that they must take their feet in their hands and be ready for locomotion." As for himself, he reports that "I was called up at 1 o'clock by the Arks senators [Johnson and Mitchell] but after going down town and seeing no Yankees, went to bed again." This is not to say that Cornelius intended to surrender if the city was captured. "I had determined in the hubbub which would naturally take place when the Yankees entered the city," he writes, "to retire to our army, south of James river—a walk of 12 to 15 miles." But the present danger subsided even as the enemy was at the city's edge. Confidence in Lee's abilities soared as reports put Union losses at more than 55,000 men, nearly the total of the whole southern force in that area. Everyone in Richmond believed that "Lee will whip the enemy as he always does—You wouldn't dream if you should walk through town and see the self satisfied air of everybody that a hostile army of 150,000 men were almost in sight of town, on bloody thoughts intent." Nonetheless, the attacks went on for some time. "This morning at day light the heavy firing was reopened," he writes in a postscript. "I hear it now as I write."

Boudinot includes some personal news as well in his letter to William. "Laflore was incorrect in his speculation about my approaching *nuptials*," he writes, apparently in response to a comment in one of William's letters. "I went to Lynchburg to see your old friend Ciss Chisolm, now the wife of Col Owen."

Ciss was Narcissa Chisholm Owen, a Cherokee woman who had married the president of the Virginia and Tennessee Railroad. Later she was the mother of Robert L. Owen, who returned to Indian Territory, entered politics, and served for many years as U.S. senator from Oklahoma. Probably of more interest to William, however, was news of his youngest brother, Frank. "I got a letter from Frank by flag of truce the other day—he wrote from Winchester Va—in the yankee lines—," Cornelius reports. "He wanted me to meet him at City Point, but of course we couldn't do so, he gave no news of himself." Boudinot then comments on his brother's penmanship, probably sharing a family joke with William. Frank, unlike his brothers, remained in the East when he finished school and became an actor. He was married and had one son, Frank, who also was an actor. The youngest Boudinot enlisted in the Union army and, as Cornelius indicates, was involved in the fighting for Richmond. In one of the battles for the city Frank was wounded, and later he died as a result. In another piece of news, Cornelius writes about his personal finances; in so doing, he reveals the rising rate of inflation. "I pay $450. for board per month," he writes, saying that laundry and "other contingencies" bring the total over $500, "without indulgence in whiskey." He continued to practice law, representing clients in claims cases, taking 10 percent of the awards as his fee. This, he writes, "enables me to squeeze through without selling my watch." Boudinot also mentions that he has written a long article "on Indian matters" for the *London Herald*, an indication that he was using all his talents in an attempt to scrape by. [57] This was a habit he would be forced to continue for many years.

After the siege was lifted from the Confederate capital in early July 1864, Boudinot again traveled west. In July he wrote Watie twice from Washington, Arkansas, in the southern part of the state where the Confederates were in control, indicating that he was trying to reach Watie's headquarters. He was carrying orders for the general's command but, reflecting the conditions at the time, was prevented from traveling further because he did not have a good enough horse at his disposal. In September he wrote from Paris, Texas, twenty miles south of the Red River, this time carrying a duplicate copy of Watie's commission as general, demonstrating the uncertainty of lines of communication between Richmond and the West. Boudinot's plans were to proceed first to the Indian brigade's headquarters, then to Rusk Country, Texas, where Stand's wife, Sallie, was living as a refugee with her sister Nancy. [58] Among other things, Boudinot was checking on the status of the southern Cherokee families who had fled the Nation and who were trying to eke out a scant living south of the Red River. In a letter in October from northern Texas, he introduces his plan to procure cotton cards for the refugees as a way of earning cash or at least gaining the ability to barter. Cotton cards were implements used to make raw cotton fiber ready for spinning into threads, which in turn could be used to weave cloth. The plan, Cornelius's brainchild, was to put these tools in the hands of the refugees, most of whom were women. There was no shortage of cotton in the South, since the Union blockade of the ports had shut down exports to the textile mills of England. Several profiteers began shipping cotton to Mexico, from where it could be exported, but this required resources beyond the Cherokees' means. With cotton cards, however, the refugees would be able to transform raw cotton that they could purchase for almost nothing in Texas into cloth and even clothing that they could use and sell. In the end, the plan was only partially successful due to a shortage of cards and even some profiteering within the Cherokee ranks.[59]

The fighting that took place within the Cherokee Nation caused vast destruction of houses, farms, and businesses. Control of the area changed hands often, and as a consequence, when Union forces were in control, "southern" farms and ranches were raided, buildings were destroyed, and crops, livestock, and horses were appropriated. The reverse was true, of course, when the Confederates were winning. Stand Watie, for example, burned Rose Cottage, John Ross's house at Park Hill near Tahlequah, to the ground. In addition, bushwhackers from Kansas raided with regularity, and groups like William Quantrell's were indiscriminate in choosing their victims.[60] Naturally, "those who must stay at home" were terrified and did not stay at home; "northern" Cherokee women and their families fled to Kansas and other areas, while the "southerners" packed a few belongs and went to the Choctaw Nation, to refugee camps along the Red River, or to Texas. A major factor in this exodus for the southern Cherokees was the Act of Confiscation of July 1862, passed by the U.S. Congress. It called for the seizure and sale of all property held by those who fought for the Confederacy and added more fuel on the fire of hatred burning out of control between the Cherokee factions. For the Waties, the confiscation was compounded by the fact that the new home they had built just before the war was burned to the ground by Union troops. The hardships suffered by the refugees went beyond displacement and disarray in their lives. Simple needs often went unmet, and the correspondence of the refugees is full of comments about the shortage of food and potable water.[61] Boudinot was especially concerned with the plight of the refugees, traveling to the camps along the Red River and to areas in Texas where some Cherokee families had landed. He met frequently with Sallie Watie on his journeys, and at one point he offered to take the younger Watie children back with him to Richmond where they could attend school. Sallie was reluctant to send her children away, especially in such desperate times, so the two girls remained with her.[62]

In October 1864, Boudinot wrote to Watie from Washington, Arkansas, to report the death of an ally, Senator Mitchell, and to say that Robert W. Johnson had been hurt and was in bad health. It is clear that Cornelius was not eager to return to Richmond, but he knew he must do so. He closes his letter with another reference to the cotton cards: "For God's sake and the sake of the naked refugees let some person go across the river and buy cotton cards—and let them do it quick, it will soon be too late."[63] The river, of course, was the Mississippi, and the urgency was due to the increasing presence of Union gunboat patrols.

Boudinot returned to Richmond, and as one of his last acts in the Confederate Congress he got a bill passed that transferred a quantity of baled cotton which General Kirby-Smith controlled to the Cherokees in partial payment of the debt owed them by the Confederate government. In a letter to Watie, Boudinot proposes acquiring transportation for the bales so that they could be conveyed to Mexico for sale. He is not clear, however, on how the transportation problem is to be solved. At the same time, William Musgrove was involved in selling cotton for the southern Cherokees in Matamoras, Mexico, their sole market for that commodity. Cornelius's letter, sent from Shreveport, Louisiana, also reports to the general the state of affairs east of the Mississippi, where, according to Boudinot, the war was virtually over with Lee's surrender at Appomattox, and the people were in a state of "absolute submission."[64]

Even though Watie had not yet surrendered his command, Boudinot knew the war was over. With Augustus Hill Garland, his colleague from the Confederate Congress, he made the melancholy trip from Shreveport through southern Arkansas to Little Rock. Both men surrendered to the Union commander there, Major General J. J. Reynolds, on May 26, 1865.[65] Reynolds gave them permission to enter Little Rock as private citizens, but it is clear that both men were attempting to enter into negotiations with the U.S. government. Reynolds flatly refused their overtures, and while he seemed sympathetic to the plight of the private soldiers who had fought for the South, he had little patience with their leaders. Garland and Boudinot were not confined or punished, but it was clear that their service in the Confederate government had forfeited any authority they might have had in the postwar period in Arkansas.

Garland had been elected representative from the Southern District of Arkansas, and when Charles Mitchell died in office, Garland succeeded him as Confederate senator. Born in Tennessee in 1832, Garland had moved to Arkansas early in life. He was admitted to the bar in Arkansas in 1850 and to practice before the U.S. Supreme Court in 1860. Pardoned after the war by President Andrew Johnson, he returned to his law practice, taking part in two important decisions that had an impact on Reconstruction in the South.[66] Garland was elected governor of Arkansas in 1873 and U.S. senator in 1876, and he was appointed attorney general of the United States under President Grover Cleveland in 1885. He was a staunch ally of Boudinot's during the latter's attempts to pass legislation for white settlement of Indian Territory.[67]

When Watie surrendered at Doakesville on June 25, 1865, he was the last Confederate general to do so. Although hostilities with the United States ceased with this act, there were still the northern Cherokees to be reckoned with. A measure of reconciliation was offered by the Northern Cherokee National Council on July 13, when it passed an act of amnesty and pardon for members of the southern branch. The pardon and restoration of citizenship, however, was predicated on the swearing of a loyalty oath to the Cherokee Nation and its constitution. Resentful of the implication that they had been disloyal to their people and Nation, Watie and other southern Cherokee leaders refused the oath and were not granted pardons.[68] It appeared that peace had not yet come to the Cherokee Nation. Watie and his men decided to bide their time until September, when a peace conference would be held with federal representatives. They returned to what was left of their homes, were reunited with loved ones, and attempted to start over with their lives. In this they were joined by Elias Cornelius Boudinot, who had left Arkansas and returned to Indian Territory. Always the optimist and schemer, he hoped he could still salvage a place for himself among the wreckage of the war.

CHAPTER 4

Peace Negotiator

Cornelius Boudinot's purpose in traveling to Little Rock with A. H. Garland at the end of the war was to offer his services as a negotiator in the peace deliberations between the U.S. government and the Indian nations in Indian Territory. In a letter to General J. J. Reynolds, commander of the U.S. Army in Arkansas, and to Arkansas governor Isaac Murphy dated May 26, 1865, he states, "I believe I can be of service in restoring peace and quiet upon the frontier, and it is for this object and no other that I have come."[1] He chose Arkansas as his starting point because, as he puts it, "The interests of these nations are so blended with those of Arkansas that they will and must follow her fortunes." He is referring to the Indian nations in the plural, and it is clear that he is thinking of himself as taking on a wider role in the coming discussions than that of a representative of the Cherokees. This is made clear later at Fort Smith, where he speaks for other delegations from time to time. It is easy to picture Cornelius as an eager speaker, willing to substitute when the main delegate has temporary business elsewhere, trying to establish a wide constituency for himself among the Indians, but more importantly to establish himself as an influential figure to the men in power in the dominant society. In his letter, Cornelius goes on to write that he was invited to Little Rock to make his offer of assistance at the invitation of "prominent citizens of the State at Washington." However, Reynolds and Murphy seemed not to be impressed by Boudinot's offer and refused it flatly. His project thus stillborn in Arkansas, Cornelius headed west.

After he surrendered at Doakesville on June 25, 1865, Watie attempted to negotiate with the northern Cherokees for an equitable peace settlement with them. The terms of his surrender were temporary, he understood, and could be changed by the upcoming negotiations with the U.S. government to be held at Armstrong Academy on September 1. In the meantime, Watie tried to effect an understanding with the northern Cherokees so that the Nation could present a united front to the government treaty makers. The Northern Cherokee National Council was conciliatory, at least to some extent, and passed an act of amnesty and pardon to their southern brethren. However, old antagonisms ran deep; the National Council added a stipulation that in order for the southern Cherokees to have their citizenship "restored," each would have to swear an oath of allegiance.[2] The majority of the southerners found this to be an insult, as they did not consider their citizenship to have been lost, taken away, or renounced. The whole oath-of-allegiance business seemed to be a major mistake: it was almost certainly going to fail and to exacerbate (if that were possible, given the extent of animosity that existed) the split between the two groups. The split, of course, played right into the government's hands. Further, the northern Cherokees had even more to lose than the southern side by emphasizing the bipolar condition of the Nation at this critical time: their chief, the venerable John Ross, was under attack from the government, his position and very authority threatened. A united front may not have held back the attacks by the determined federal negotiators, but the dueling delegations that presented themselves at the conference table certainly played right into the white men's hands.

Troops loyal to Ross had been fighting under Union command for the second half of the war and were mustered out as the end approached in May 1865. As they returned home, they seemed to have little to fear; they had ended up on the winning side and so expected that any repercussions from the conflict delivered by the government would fall on the heads of their southern kinsmen. Furthermore, during much of the war their principal chief had been in the East, directing delegates from the Cherokee Nation to Washington and communicating with government officials. While Watie had been declared chief by the Southern Cherokee Council, Ross's party had reelected him to his long-standing position in August 1863, and it was from this post that he carried out his intercourse with the federal officials. While he had not been sworn into office in the Cherokee Nation following his reelection, Ross took his oath in Washington before a justice of the peace in April 1865 before returning to the Cherokee Nation.

It was pretty clear that Ross felt vulnerable on the oath-of-office issue, as he took pains to file an affidavit attesting to his act with the Office of Indian

Affairs. Perhaps he was crossing his legal T's because he had caught wind of government intentions for the upcoming peace negotiations. An astute politician like Ross could read the winds issuing forth from the Office of Indian Affairs as well as the Department of the Interior under which the office functioned. In the debate over the Harlan territorial bill before the Senate in March 1865, Ross made known his opposition to the proposed legislation, angering Senator James Harlan from Iowa and Senator James H. Lane from Kansas. Harlan's bill called for the reorganization of Indian Territory, dissolution of tribal jurisdictions, and settlement by whites. During the debate, Lane made claims before both the Committee on Indian Affairs and the Committee on Territories that Ross had no legal status as Cherokee principal chief because he had not been properly sworn in. Now, at the end of the war, Harlan was secretary of the Department of the Interior and thus director of the government strategy in the treaty negotiations. Ross expected trouble, and of course he got it. [3] At the same time, Boudinot and the southern Cherokees watched Ross's position vis-à-vis the government crumble and vowed to make the most of it.

The peace conference of 1865 began, ironically enough, with a breakdown in communication. While many of the Indians were expecting the venue to be Armstrong Academy near Fort Washita in the Choctaw Nation, near present-day Durant, Oklahoma, others got the word from the federal negotiators en route that the site would be Fort Smith, Arkansas, just across the line from Indian Territory. Thus the government took the psychological advantage of meeting on its own turf, as it were, giving better accommodations in Fort Smith as the reason for the last-minute switch. Watie decided to meet with delegations from other Indian nations at Armstrong Academy on September 1, 1865, no doubt hoping to gain some advantage through formulating a multilateral strategy that could be carried out against a common adversary. This meeting had its roots in the second of two grand councils held by the Indian nations of the Territory near the end of the war in order to develop a common policy toward the U.S. government. That meeting had been held at the Armstrong Academy, established by the Choctaws as their capital in 1862, and was attended by delegations from most of the tribes that had signed treaties with the Confederacy. The September 1 meeting was held with the Fort Smith negotiations in mind, the result being a series of resolutions signed by Watie and other Indian leaders addressing what they believed the government's position to be. By this time, Boudinot had joined his uncle as a member of the southern Cherokee delegation; the group decided that the best plan was to split their forces, with the main body of delegates remaining at Armstrong

Academy while a reconnaissance contingent consisting of Boudinot and Josiah W. Washbourne traveled east to cover the proceedings at Fort Smith. Boudinot and Washbourne were to protect the interests of the southern Cherokees until the main force arrived. Watie's plan was to bring his delegation to Fort Smith on September 15 along with the other negotiators from Armstrong Academy, swooping down on the proceedings with a large body united with a common purpose.

The strategy was to have little effect on the negotiations, however, since once they arrived, the delegates found the members of the government commission thoroughly dug in, adamant in their demands and showing little taste for compromise. Talks had begun a week earlier, on September 8, with the following Indian nations present: northern Creeks, Osages, Quapaws, Senecas, Senecas and Shawnees, northern Cherokees, Seminoles, Shawnees, Wyandotts, Chickasaws, and Choctaws. The party of government officials appointed originally included Elijah Sells, superintendent of Indian Affairs, Southern Superintendency; James M. Edmunds, commissioner of the General Land Office; Major General Francis J. Herron; Brigadier General William S. Harney; and Colonel Ely S. Parker. This group was led by Dennis N. Cooley, the commissioner of Indian Affairs. Edmunds, an ally of Secretary of the Interior Harlan, had to decline the appointment at the last minute due to the press of business in Washington, as did General Herron. In their place, Thomas Wistar, a Quaker from Pennsylvania, was appointed by Harlan under orders from President Johnson; Harlan also authorized Cooley to use other clergymen if he saw fit.[4] Seneca Ely S. Parker, an aide to General Ulysses S. Grant during the war, was the lone Indian member of the commission.[5]

After the first day's perfunctory meeting, at which mainly housekeeping matters were discussed, the meeting on September 9 took on an entirely different tone. And well it should, since the events of this day, according to Morris Wardell, mark the beginning of a new Indian policy.[6] On the second day, the commission introduced its "Stipulations," at once demonstrating its reluctance to bargain or even to hear what the Indian delegates had to say. The seven stipulations were as follows:

> **1.** Each tribe is to enter into a "treaty for permanent peace and amity with themselves, each nation and tribe, and the United States." The "themselves" obviously refers to situations such as the Cherokees', in which the nation was split.
>
> **2.** Tribes of Indian Territory must aid the government in compelling the Plains

Indians to maintain peaceful relations with each other, with the Indians of the Territory, and with the United States. The government was enlisting the aid of the tribes already settled in Indian Territory against, if need be, new arrivals from Kansas and elsewhere; it also seemed to be anticipating the Indian wars of the plains that were in the offing.

3. Slavery was abolished, emancipation effected, and the former slaves "incorporated into the tribes on equal footing with the original members, or suitably provided for." The third part of this stipulation was nearly universally reviled by the Indian nations, who saw it for the attack on sovereignty that it was. In the Indians' eyes, with this unprecedented pronouncement one nation attempted to dictate and define citizenship in another.

4. Slavery or involuntary servitude shall never exist, except as punishment for crime.

5. Land was to be set aside for the Kansas Indians and others, the terms of the land cessions to be agreed upon at the time they took place.

6. The Indian Territory would be consolidated along the lines of other territories in the United States. Ramifications and consequences of this stipulation were not lost on the Indians, who saw it as a clear threat to sovereignty and as the start of a process that would end in tribal dissolution.

7. White people were prohibited from Indian Territory except for those there on official business and those formally adopted into the tribes. This stipulation almost seems at odds with number 6, but perhaps it was meant as a sop to those fearful of its consequences.[7]

On the third day, delegations from various tribes made their somewhat shell-shocked replies to the stipulations; then the next day, September 12, the government delivered another salvo. The sins of John Ross were recounted before the gathering, with the commission's statement culminating in a declaration that it did not recognize Ross as the principal chief of the Cherokee Nation. His transgressions, according to the statement, included signing the treaty with the Confederacy, encouraging Opothleyahoya to sign a similar treaty for the Creeks, raising troops to fight the United States, and encouraging his people to unite under the southern banner. By the sixth day, September 14, the "loyal" Cherokee delegation protested, saying that Ross was their duly elected chief and that he had signed the Confederate treaty "under coercion of the rebel army." The commission's response on the next day was unrelenting. Ross, referred to as the "pretended 1st chief of the Cherokees," is "still at heart an enemy of the United States" who is "disposed to create discord," responded Cooley in his opening remarks on the afternoon of September 15. He added that the commission still refused to recognize him, in effect deposing Ross as chief. It is important to note that these pronouncements were in no way those of the commission alone; Cooley and his colleagues were operating under orders from Harlan and, in fact, were in daily contact with the secretary via the military telegraph. In one important missive sent along the wires, Harlan says that in relation to the treatment of John Ross, President Johnson is not only in agreement but "authorizes and directs you to say that on your understandings of the facts as stated your action is approved. Should he [Ross] persist you are authorized to recognize such other party or parties as representative of the Cherokee Nation, as may appear to you to be the true representatives of their sentiments and wishes."[8] Johnson and Harlan thus rendered their complete backing to Cooley and his commission.

The commission's secretary, Charles Mix of the Office of Indian Affairs, reported that a "brief colloquy between" E. C. Boudinot, John Ross, and Cooley occurred at this point in the proceedings, with adjournment shortly afterward. However, some vital details about that afternoon's proceedings are left out of the official reports of both Mix and Superintendent Sells. Annie H. Abel reports that an account written by a newspaperman named Wilson for the *New York Herald* completes the story.[9] According to Wilson, on the afternoon of September 15, Ross defended himself against the government's charges, rising to reply to the commissioners' statement. He denied the charges and challenged anyone to prove them. He gave a history of his actions during the war, including communications with the president, and denied disloyalty, saying that he resisted until the last, signing the treaty with the Confederacy only under duress and against the counsel that he had been giving his own people and the other Indian leaders. Once Ross had finished his statement, Cooley asked other delegates to speak on the issue if they wanted to. Cooley's action seems odd in many ways and may have been a setup for what happened next. As if on cue, Boudinot rose to his feet and delivered a stunning renunciation of Ross. After a few perfunctory remarks informing the commissioners that the Watie delegation had arrived, he went on to refer to the charges against Ross that the chief had just sought to refute: "The Gentleman (Jno. Ross) who has addressed the Commissioners respecting a paper read by the Prest. [Cooley], desires to know who the person or persons are who have charged him with duplicity & bad faith. So far as those particular charges are concerned, I do not suppose that any member of the delegation from the South has had anything to do with it." At this time, it must be noted, Boudinot and Washbourne were the only members who would have had a chance to make such charges, since the others had just arrived. Boudinot continues:

> But, Sir, there are serious charges which I will make against him, & I here announce my willingness and intention to make such charges, to state such facts & to prove them too, as will prove his duplicity. The fact is the Cherokee Nation has been long rent in twain by dissensions & I here charge these upon this same John Ross. I charge him with it here today & I will do it tomorrow. I will show that the treaty made with the Confederate States was made at his instigation. I will show the deep duplicity & falsity that have followed him from his childhood to the present day, when the winters of 65 or 70 years have silvered his head with sin; and what can you expect of him now.

At this point, Cooley broke in with a totally disingenuous statement, denying the very tactic that he was employing: "The object of this Council is not to stir up old feelings. The paper you have heard read was drawn up out of a sense of duty, by the Commissioners, to the interests of the U.S. & as an act which was due to the loyal portion of the Cherokee Nation." Cooley was referring to the commission's statement deposing Ross as principal chief. He goes on,

> I trust that no one may come into this Council and attempt to stir up bad feelings which ought to have been buried years ago . . . I wish it to be understood that the document read here today will not give any license to different portions of your nation to bring up matters that long ago ought to have been buried in oblivion. We trust that Jno. Ross will be able to exculpate himself from the very serious charges which have been made against him. We hope he will be able to fully explain his actions so that we can shake hands too with him in peace & amity.

Cooley's timing was masterful. His statement was also incredibly hypocritical. The situation was now changed from one in which the government was attacking Ross to one in which Boudinot had taken on that responsibility. The government's role had gone from attacker of a venerable figure to mediator between the two squabbling factions. Cooley's goal was now "peace and amity," while the Cherokee brethren continued their hostile maneuverings against one another. Boudinot had seemingly fallen into Cooley and Harlan's trap, becoming their chessman to be moved with impunity.

But was Boudinot an unwitting pawn, or had he been part of the plan from the beginning? Cornelius was very much a participant in the proceedings even before the delegation of which he was a part had arrived at the conference and was still deliberating at Armstrong Academy. He and Cooley had met behind the scenes as Cornelius jockeyed for position, and he had been given a copy of Secretary Harlan's territorial bill, which had passed the Senate in the previous congressional session. Senate Bill 459 had been opposed vehemently by John Ross when it was being debated in Washington in March 1865, this being one reason why Harlan's underling Cooley attacked the Cherokee chief. Although the Harlan bill passed the Senate, it had not become the law of the land, and the interior secretary and his allies were trying to use the Fort Smith conference as a way to get it enacted via the back door. [10] Cooley's strategy in carrying out this assignment included soliciting the cooperation of some of the former secessionists, making, perhaps, offers of compensation that never made it into the official record. One of the first persons Cooley approached was Boudinot.

The provisions of the Harlan bill as originally drafted may be briefly summarized. The first provision calls for the formation of a regular territory within the boundaries of the existing Indian Territory. It also provides for the introduction of government machinery similar to those found in other organized territories of the United States. Under this plan, a governor and a secretary would be appointed by the president for terms of four years. The governor was to be, in effect, superintendent of the Office of Indian Affairs, and he was to have an absolute veto over the proceedings of the legislative assembly, or council. The council was to be made up of delegates selected by the various nations in a number based on their populations. If the tribe preferred, or should an election fail to take place, the delegation was to be composed of tribal chiefs. The legislative power vested in the governor and legislative council was to be extensive, covering all domestic matters. However, fiscal affairs were to be controlled by the U.S. Congress. Finally, the territory was to be represented in Congress by a delegate, to be chosen by an unnamed process. [11] No doubt it was this latter position that Boudinot had his eye on; no doubt Cooley knew this and made his moves accordingly.

On the fourth, fifth, and sixth days of the conference—September 13, 14, and 15—the delegations lined up one-by-one to sign a Treaty of Peace and Friendship, a general pact of amity with few details. The finer points were to be made later after negotiations with each of the Indian nations. Watie's main body and the other delegates from the Armstrong Academy arrived on the afternoon of September 15, but they did not make their official appearance before the government officials until the next day, Saturday. At that time,

Boudinot presented the southern Cherokee credentials, then went on to make a statement concerning the government stipulations. The delegation acceded to all except the third, the incorporation of freedmen into the Cherokee Nation, and the sixth, the organization of a territorial government. The statement, drafted by Boudinot, went on to give a brief history of the conflict between the Ridge-Boudinot-Watie Cherokees and those under John Ross from 1835, when the New Echota removal treaty was signed. Recounting the history of violence between the two factions, Boudinot says, "We should not be expected to live in an undivided country" because of the blood that has been shed and the bitterness "in the bosoms of our brethren." He also cites President James K. Polk's suggestion in 1846 that the Cherokees be divided into two separate nations.[12] At this point, the record states, a "short controversy" ensued between Boudinot, John Ross, and William Potter Ross. The meeting adjourned shortly afterward until Monday. On the intervening Sabbath, the Ross Cherokees prepared their answer to Boudinot's charges and the proposal to split the Nation, while no doubt Cornelius and Stand Watie conferred with Cooley.

When the conference reconvened on Monday, September 18, the northern Cherokees offered their rejoinder to Boudinot and the southern Cherokee delegation, but by this time it was clear that the officials were not listening very hard. On Monday, William P. Adair rose on behalf of his delegation to question the officials on the status of what came to be called the Matthews Truce, the agreement reached by Stand Watie and the Union officer to whom he surrendered in June. Cooley answered, saying that treaties can only be made by the Department of the Interior, not by representatives of the War Department, so the truce had no standing. When asked about the forfeiture law in the Cherokee Nation, Cooley replied that while the government has authority, it needs to look at the matter more closely.[13] On the next day, Richard Fields rose to state the southern position on another matter: the forfeiture laws passed by the Cherokee National Council. The council, Fields charges, had made those who had fought on the Confederate side as well as their families "homeless paupers" by confiscating their property—that is, their buildings, tools, and livestock—and removing their means of making a living. The citizenship issued had also removed their right to farm or ranch on the Nation's land, so they were left destitute. Further, Fields states, an appeal to the council to rescind the forfeiture law had failed.[14]

After Fields finished, Boudinot rose to offer a plea for the Cherokee families who were forced to flee south when Union troops arrived in the Nation. Of course, a similar fate had befallen other Cherokees who had been forced to become refugees in Kansas when southern forces controlled the area, but Boudinot felt responsible only for the refugees on whose behalf he had been working for the past two years. He gave their number as six thousand, saying that they were residing in the Choctaw and Chickasaw Nations in the vicinity of the Red River. Most of them "are in destitute condition, having been since the termination of the late war dependent on the bounty of said nations and the adjoining country of Texas for subsistence; they are without money, and, with a few exceptions, without property of any description." What he says here is without exaggeration, because in other correspondence on the matter he is concerned that some did not have clothes to wear. Cornelius goes on to make a plea for "some definite plan" to be devised for the relief of these people. The government's answer was delivered by Superintendent Sells, who doubtless saw the refugees as pawns in his game of control with the Cherokees, to be held in reserve for use at some future time. Sells declared that the subject of Cherokee citizens displaced by the war was not on the conference agenda. On the following day, Boudinot rose to speak on the issue again, this time presenting the case for Seminole war victims as prepared by Seminole leader John Jumper. The Seminoles received much the same reply as the Cherokees had.

As one of his last acts at the conference, Boudinot made a statement that can perhaps be seen as a clue to the prize he has fixed for himself, namely, the office of delegate to Congress from an Indian Territory reorganized along the lines of the Harlan bill. In this statement, on September 21, Boudinot says that he was the author of the southern Cherokee reply to the commissioners' stipulations, in which the territorial reorganization was rejected. Since that time, he goes on to say, he has read the bill, and the scales have dropped from his eyes. He now sees Harlan's scheme as "one of the grandest and noblest schemes ever devised for the red man, and entitles the author to (as I believe he will soon receive) the lasting gratitude of every Indian."[15] Cooley and Sells made sure Boudinot's remarks were duly entered into the record of the conference's proceedings. With these words, Boudinot had attached himself to the "Territorial Ring" and all the alliances this entailed. On the same day, the conference was adjourned sine die; the next step was for the Indian nations to negotiate detailed treaties with the federal government in Washington DC.

The U.S. government had set things up entirely to their advantage when the Cherokees came to the capital to draw up the treaty in early 1866. On the surface it appeared that the southern Cherokee delegation was in the ascendancy, while the northern Cherokees were struggling. When the maneuvering began in January it seemed a foregone conclusion that the Nation would be split, with the Ridge-Boudinot-Watie party fulfilling a longtime dream to preside over an autonomous land base within the present boundaries of the Cherokee Nation in Indian Territory. Their preferred locale was the southwestern section known as the Canadian District, bounded by the Canadian and Arkansas rivers on the south and Sallisaw Creek on the east, comprising Muskogee County, the northeastern area of McIntosh County, and the western part of Sequoyah County in present-day Oklahoma. The Creek Nation was to the immediate west, and Tahlequah District in the Cherokee Nation was directly north. As Boudinot and William Adair began advance operations in Washington, this goal seemed not only feasible but probable. The other side was no less anxious to begin the deliberations on a sound footing.

The delegations had been formed in Indian Territory, each led by its prospective chief, John Ross and Stand Watie. In addition, the northern Cherokee group had retained General Thomas Ewing as legal counsel, while Watie's group took on Daniel W. Voorhees. Voorhees, a congressman and later senator from Indiana, shared many of Boudinot's ideas and was to become an important ally later on. Voorhees was born in 1827 in Ohio but grew up in Indiana. He was admitted to the bar in 1851, shortly thereafter moving to Terre Haute, which became his permanent home. He was defeated in his run to Congress from there in 1856, but President James Buchanan appointed him federal district attorney for Indiana. In 1861 he was elected to Congress, where he opposed the war and abolitionist policies. In and out of Congress, Voorhees was appointed to the Senate in 1877 and served there for the next twenty years. He was a staunch supporter and friend of Boudinot's in several endeavors. Called the "Tall Sycamore of the Wabash," he was instrumental in establishing the Library of Congress.

In April 1866 the southern Cherokee delegation signed a contract with Perry Fuller, a former Indian agent. Fuller's main task, according to the agreement, was to make sure the southern faction received their just share of the Cherokee treasury as well as any funds they might receive from the sale of the Neutral lands or other areas and payments from railroads that might accrue from a treaty.[16] It is clear from the Fuller agreement what the southern delegation was expecting.

Watie did not take part in the deliberations, leaving that to the official southern delegation, which included Boudinot, Adair, Watie's son Saladin, and Richard Fields, a merchant and former partner of Colonel John Drew. J. A.

Scales and Stand Watie also acted with the delegation, especially during the April and May, their main duties being the formulation of a new government for the Canadian District. A surprise delegate was John Rollin Ridge, the eldest son of John Ridge and a nephew of Stand Watie. Ridge had been in California since the gold rush, leaving his farm near Honey Creek in the Cherokee Nation when he killed a member of the Ross party in an altercation over a horse. Ridge had made a career as a writer and editor of several California newspapers, including the *Sacramento Bee*, was a poet of some renown, and was the author of *The Life and Adventures of Joaquin Murieta, the Celebrated California Bandit*, generally acknowledged to be the first novel written by an Indian.[17] The idea to include Ridge came from Josiah Washbourne. Washbourne was jubilant that Ridge was "recognized by the Government as the *loyal* chief of the Ridge party," feeling that the delegation was thus strengthened.[18] The "loyal" tag is ironic because although Ridge never took up arms against the Union, he propagandized heavily against Lincoln and his government before and during the war.

At first the delegation seemed poised for victory. Washbourne had written his wife in mid-January that Boudinot was in daily contact with the Department of the Interior, and "they agree in the main, and he is consulted in the affairs of it daily, and his counsels obtain." Ross, on the other hand, "is dead for ever, with all of his kith, as to public influence . . . Boudinot is to-day far stronger with the Government than he is, or ever was, and is, practically, the Cherokee Nation."[19] While Washbourne cannot be seen as the most reliable source, it is clear that Boudinot and his fellow delegates had been made to feel that they had clout with those in power.

Acting in the fall of 1865, the Cherokee National Council met to formulate a strategy to have Ross once again recognized by the U.S. government as their chief and to appoint the delegation to Washington to hammer out a treaty. Members of the delegation were Smith Christie, White Catcher, Daniel H. Ross, Houston Benge, John B. Jones, James McDaniel, and Thomas Pegg. John Jones was the son of Evan Jones, the influential abolitionist and Baptist missionary to the Cherokees, who had been admitted to Cherokee citizenship on November 7, 1865, four days after the official delegation has been appointed.[20] As Morris Wardell points out, as the delegations traveled to Washington, "Chief Ross and Boudinot, with their able assistants, waged a battle . . . that is unique in the story of Reconstruction."[21]

Boudinot and Adair struck first, their tactic to keep up pressure on Ross. In a letter to Cooley on January 12, 1866, the pair inquired about funds paid to

Ross by the Confederacy in 1861 or 1862, in the amount of $250,000.[22] None of Watie's group had received any of this money, the letter goes on, and it was received into the national treasury controlled by Ross, whom they refer to as the "constituted authority" of the Cherokee Nation. The purpose of the letter was twofold: first, to distance themselves and their comrades from an official link with the Confederacy, and second, and more important to Cooley and Harlan, to cast Ross in a negative light. That Cooley saw this second purpose is clear from the annotation he affixed to the letter's envelope, according to Abel: "File for use in our negotiations with 'Cherokees.'" On the face of it, having Boudinot and Adair—one a delegate to the Confederate Congress and the other a staff officer in a Confederate army unit—attack Ross for his links to the Confederate government is ludicrous; the fact that their argument was taken seriously by Cooley and Harlan, however, shows the extreme lengths to which the government was willing to go to bring about their desired ends. As he had in Fort Smith, Boudinot was blatantly supporting Cooley and Harlan's position that the "constituted authorities" of the Cherokee Nation had been disloyal and thus were liable to any penalties deigned proper by the government, including cancellation of earlier U.S.-Cherokee treaties and loss of their land and sovereignty.

The northern Cherokee delegation knew it was being attacked on two fronts and did all it could to defend itself. And the defense came quickly. On January 24 they addressed a memorial to the president and Congress that presented their side of the history of the past four years, outlining their relationship with both the Confederate and U.S. governments. The emphasis was on their ultimate loyalty to Washington, maintaining their position that the Confederate treaty was signed under duress and was abandoned at the first opportunity. Most of all, they stressed Ross's deep-seated loyalty to the federal government.[23] Moreover, Ross was not entirely friendless in the national capital. He had made many lasting relationships in his years of service to his people, and as came to be increasingly clear, much of his power and influence remained. A week after the first memorial, another was issued, but this one was sent to the president alone. It recalled President Lincoln's pledge, during the war, that the Confederate treaty "should never rise up in judgment against the Cherokees, nor stand in the way of perfect justice being done them under their treaties with the United States."[24]

Boudinot and Adair received a copy of the first memorial from Cooley and responded on January 30, trying to finesse the issue of Ross's chieftaincy. They referred to the Fort Smith proceedings, saying that since the government had deposed Ross at that time, there was no need to regard the words of the Cherokee delegation under his direction. They were careful to point out that "a due regard to these Treaties [the Treaties of Amity and Peace separately signed by both sides] and *your acts* [emphasis in original] as Commr of Indian Affairs, seem to require of us no notice of him or his Dellegation [*sic*]."[25] Both delegations were forced to deal with Cooley, although both made appeals to other officials in Washington. For his part, Cooley seemed more favorably disposed toward the southern camp, both because of his relationship with Boudinot and also because he expected to be able to promote his own agenda and Secretary Harlan's by treating with them rather than with Ross. Probably at Boudinot's suggestion, he contacted Albert Pike, who had landed on his feet and was practicing law in Washington. Cooley's choice was an illustration of this southern bias, as there is no record that he attempted to contact other witnesses who may have had conflicting opinions on the matter. Pike replied to Cooley in a characteristically careful but long-winded letter. He said what the commissioner wanted him to say, in effect that Ross had been disloyal to the United States and that the signing of the treaty justified his deposal. If he mentioned it, Pike was careful not to dwell upon Ross's recalcitrance when initially approached by the Confederate emissary during the war.[26]

Through the spring, the delegations worked and sent drafts of treaties to Cooley. In May the northern delegation delivered a reply to a list of twelve stipulations that the commissioner insisted be part of the treaty. Three of these were not challenged, and the delegation said in their reply that they agreed with five more: restoration of confiscated property; general amnesty; civil rights and political privileges to the southern faction; sale of the Neutral Lands; and acceptance of the North Carolina Cherokees as citizens. However, the remaining four stipulations were still opposed, and these the northern delegation took up one by one. First, Cooley had demanded land for railroads through the Nation—not only right-of-way for the tracks, but alternating sections of land along the route. This land, the Cherokees knew, would be sold to pay the costs of constructing the railway and the infrastructure needed to support it. Cooley's proposal was rejected on the ground that it opened the Cherokee Nation to white settlement. The second issue was a territorial government consistent with the Harlan bill. The Cherokees saw this as an attack on tribal sovereignty, but they did agree to discuss the matter after consultation with the National Council. The third stipulation they opposed was the sale of Cherokee land in addition to that in the Cherokee Outlet for the use of removed tribes from other parts of the country. Again, the

Cherokees rejected the stipulation but agreed to discuss it further. Finally, Cooley demanded a division of the Nation along the lines proposed by the southern faction. The delegation replied that the principle in question was exactly the one proposed by the southern states to the Union before the Civil War; further, they said, their people, like the people of the United States, would never submit to "national dismemberment."[27]

For their part, the southern Cherokees saw the northern delegation's refusal to submit to Cooley's demands as a sign that they were winning. In an address "To the Southern Cherokees," which Stand Watie had printed and distributed to his supporters in the Nation and to the southern refugees still in the Choctaw Nation and Texas, four issues were identified as government demands: the sale of lands for the removal of Indians from other parts of the country; acceptance of a territorial organization; provisions for railroad construction through the Nation; and acceptance of the abolition of slavery with incorporation of the freed people as citizens. The address went on to say that the land sale could be accepted, granted further concessions by the government. The territorial issue was dismissed, as it was a foregone conclusion that the Harlan bill would pass in the next session of Congress. The southern delegation accepted the cession of alternating sections of lands to the north-south and east-west railroads as demanded by Cooley, going so far as to name the railroads the Leavenworth, Lawrence and Galveston, and the Atlantic and Pacific. As to the abolition question, this was seen as a non-issue, since it had been settled nationally. The address goes on to state that these provisions have been accepted by the government, including the division of the Nation, and that a treaty embracing them was very close to ratification. So confident was the delegation that Stand Watie and J. A. Scales left Washington for the West. Washbourne kept them informed, writing to Scales on June 1 that "Ridge, Adair, Fields and Boudinot, with Fuller and Voorhees had an interview with the President. They are in high spirits. *The President has ordered that a treaty be made with us for our own pro rata share of the Nation. This is positive.* On the 22nd of May they were drawing up the treaty. It is duly signed before this."[28]

On June 14, Cooley announced that articles of agreement had been signed between the United States and the southern delegation. Through Secretary Harlan, Cooley sent the treaty to the president, but Johnson did not act on it. Meanwhile, sensing that their efforts to maintain the Nation as one entity were about to fail, the northern delegation made one last effort at compromise. Under their ailing leader, another round of discussions was carried out. When it became clear to the southern delegation—the Ridge delegation, as it was now being called—that Johnson was not going to accept their treaty and looked to one offered by the Ross faction, they entered into the talks. A stipulation, later to become Article 29 of the treaty, was introduced by Ridge and Boudinot that called for payment for "expenses of the delegates and representatives of the Cherokees invited by the Government to visit Washington for the purpose of making this treaty." This stipulation was carefully worded so as to include the southern delegates as well as the official signers of the treaty for the Cherokee Nation, namely, Ross's delegation. The clause was a signal of the southern delegation's collapse; Johnson returned their treaty and sent the Ross treaty on to the Senate, where it was signed on July 19.

Several factors had gone into these fast-moving events. First, Harlan's star was waning in the administration firmament; soon after the treaty was settled he resigned as secretary of the interior. Second, Ross still had much influence, apparently, in Congress and among other government officials. Third, Ross had gone to the public for support, writing letters to newspapers in New York City and other eastern cities, calling for pressure to be placed on the government to prevent the dismemberment of the Cherokee Nation. Newspaperman John Rollin Ridge tried to neutralize this effort, but as it turned out, what influence he might have had in California did not extend to the eastern seaboard. Fourth, the government had manipulated the situation, bringing pressure on the Ross delegation by seeming to favor the southerners. They were helped, of course, by the fact that Cooley and Harlan probably did favor Boudinot and company for the simple fact that they were more in harmony with Harlan's ultimate aims. The major determining factor was, perhaps, that Johnson saw the force of Ross's argument that a Nation which had sacrificed so much in order to protect its own Union would be morally amiss in effecting a successful secession in another. At any rate, the treaty was ratified by the Senate and signed by the president; on December 7, 1866, it was adopted by the Cherokee Nation and its articles were accepted into its constitution.

In the end, both the government and Ross's faction had compromised. The treaty terms included some issues that were already settled, such as the abolition of slavery and the voiding of the treaty with the Confederacy. Other matters were settled for the first time, such as amnesty for all who had fought against the Union. Confiscation laws were nullified and property restored to former owners. Southern Cherokees were allowed to settle in the Canadian District, and if this land was insufficient they would be given land further north as well; as a matter of fact, many of the southern families had by now returned to their former homes. Former slaves were allowed to settle in the Canadian

District as well. Initially, some autonomy was granted to the southerners, but in no way was the Nation divided. The treaty approved a general Indian council, which came to be known as an international congress, but this was a far cry from the territorial organization called for by the Harlan bill. Two railroads were allowed, one north-south and one east-west, and federal courts were to be established within Indian Territory. These later two issues were dear to Boudinot's heart, as subsequent events will show. Indians from mainly Plains tribes would be placed on Cherokee lands, west of ninety-six degrees, the purchase price to be worked out among the tribes and the government. The Cherokee Outlet and the Neutral Lands were ceded to the United States in trust, later to be sold. The government agreed to survey Cherokee land and allot lands to individual citizens of the Nation whenever such action was requested by the National Council. Finally, the United States was to maintain military posts within the Cherokee Nation and to keep the peace. In addition, of course, the government agreed to pay the expenses of delegates who had contributed to the treaty-making process.

This last issue was not quite as clear-cut as it might appear for Boudinot and the southern delegation. When Ridge agreed to travel to Washington to join his kinsmen, there was general jubilation at the reunion. Washbourne went so far as to rhapsodize to his wife that he, Ridge, and Boudinot were planning the purchase of a newspaper in Little Rock, Arkansas, after the treaty was signed. Using the paper as a springboard for their ambitions as well as a showcase for their talents, they planned to restore the family to its former political and economic power. Their plans were doomed—not so much, it turns out by their failure at treaty making as by their own penury and greed, especially on the parts of Ridge and Boudinot.

After the treaty was ratified and the participants had submitted bills for what were loosely termed "expenses," an appropriation was made for $28,825. Apparently, no disbursement method was set up by Cooley's office, and this lack led to the argument about who should receive what amount. Cooley made an initial payment on October 31, based on bills that had been submitted to him, in the amount of $10,000, to Ridge, Adair, Fields, and Saladin Watie. The remaining $18,825, Cooley explained, would be forthcoming when the government sold the Cherokee land in Kansas. Scales and Stand Watie were to receive shares, but they were back in the Territory, so they did not collect. Boudinot, who was in Arkansas when Cooley made the payment, was cut out of his share as well. When Boudinot returned, he protested, saying that he had not received any expense money from the government; Ridge objected to his cousin's statement in a "certificate" he circulated to the members of the delegation and to Cooley's office. In that document, Ridge charged that Boudinot had "sold himself" and "made $1500 off the other delegates and no telling how much more." [29] Ridge went on to say that Cooley told him Boudinot had gotten $1,500 of the $6,000 paid to Perry Fuller, the attorney hired to make sure all payments were in order.

Boudinot responded explosively, denying Ridge's accusations. He wrote to the new secretary of the interior, O. H. Browning, charging that he had been "grossly swindled by my brother delegates under a misrepresentation of Mr. Ridge." He charged that the $10,000 from Cooley had been given to Fields, acting as attorney for Ridge, Saladin Watie, and Adair, and that the four had split the money equally. He demanded his $2,000 share, forgetting for the moment the money due Scales and Stand Watie. Furthermore, Boudinot demanded that the remainder of the $28,825 not be disbursed until he got his share. The delegation itself became involved, with Saladin and Adair jumping on Boudinot's side and Fields backing Ridge.[30] Boudinot also wrote to Cooley and Fuller asking them to sign statements denying Ridge's charges.[31] Cooley and Fuller complied, but unfortunately for Boudinot, Ridge had returned to California with his expense money. Furious, Boudinot wrote his cousin a letter, saying that Saladin and Fields had informed him of "the malicious and dishonest part you played in my absence to injure my reputation and steal my money." Apparently lacking any legal recourse, he promises to exact revenge in another way. "I have written to your wife, brother and sisters, that all friendly relations between you and me have ceased forever, and that you have proved yourself a faithless and ungrateful friend, a slanderer and a liar, a thief and a coward." He goes on, saying, "I had so much at heart and for which I had labored so long and unselfishly," and then asks a final question of his cousin and erstwhile friend: "What motive under Heaven could have moved you to this insane and futile attempt to malign and injure me? I would have laid my energies and my means at your feet to have advanced your personal and political fortunes." At this point, Boudinot seems to be mourning the stillborn future he and Washbourne had laid out for themselves. "It has been said that 'all men have their price,'" he continues. "this *may* be true; but my price, must be more than $500." The amount is Ridge's share of the money due Boudinot. Then, after maligning Ridge's blood and pretensions, he finishes with one more irony: "In conclusion, let me remind you that you owe me $30, which you borrowed a few days before I left Washington; if it is convenient, please forward it by mail to me here. Care of Commr. Ind. Aff."[32]

Boudinot spend the winter of 1866–67 doing what was to become a familiar task: trying to collect from the government, claiming a total of $4,569.56. On April 10 he received one-fifth of the $18,824 owed the delegation. The remainder was disbursed to Fields for distribution to the other delegates. Apparently Stand Watie never received his share, partly because of John Ross's objection. Before his death on August 1, 1866, the old chief was able to deliver one last blow against his old enemy.[33]

CHAPTER 5

The Tobacco Tycoon

The Cherokee Tobacco Case embodies significant irony. To begin with, here we witness white Americans restricting Native Americans' use of tobacco, a commodity that had been presented to whites initially by American Indian giftgivers. But the irony does not stop there. When the English first established settlements on the western shores of the Atlantic in the early seventeenth century, the Native people introduced them to several new agricultural products. One of the most important of these was tobacco, a plant that achieved almost instantaneous popularity back in England, and from there on the Continent. The acceptance of tobacco use among Europeans gave the North American settlers a cash crop that could be exported in exchange for cash and manufactured goods. Thus the Native Americans' gift to the white settlers greatly aided the colonists' chances for survival in the "new" world and helped to establish firmly their beachhead for the all-out invasion that was to follow.

Two and a half centuries later, tobacco was the centerpiece in a dispute that ended up severely curtailing the independence of Native Americans and fundamentally altering the status of the American Indian nations. The Boudinot case did away with the concept that a "nation" could exist within the borders of the United States, independent of the federal government but coexistent and interactive with American society. The U.S. Supreme Court decision that ended the dispute asserted the supremacy of laws passed by Congress and ratified by the American political system and decreed that these laws take precedence over treaties in place since before the beginning of the republic.

The case had other implications as well. It marks the first time that the U.S. government levied a tax on Native Americans, even though at the time they were not U.S. citizens. At the same time, it highlighted the growing importance of excise taxes to the federal government. Because it invalidated a key provision of the 1866 Cherokee treaty with the United States, it demonstrated the impact of rules imposed on "conquered" peoples who had been allied with the Confederacy during the Civil War, rules that formed the basis for Reconstruction in other parts of the country. Finally, the tobacco decision encouraged the would-be settlers and corporate interests that cast envious eyes over Indian Territory. Insofar as the action eroded the Indian nations' sovereignty, it encouraged boomer groups and corporations to disregard the Native Americans' laws and to look to political means to achieve their ends. One result in subsequent years was a steady flow of intruders into Indian Territory, culminating in the Oklahoma Run in 1889 and the dissolution of tribal land titles a few years later. Another result was a flood of bills presented to Congress endorsing allotment in severalty for Native American lands, territorial status or statehood for the region, the extension of U.S. sovereignty over Indian Territory, and a host of schemes for exploiting the natural resources of the area. Ironically, as we shall see, many of these bills were written and defended by Boudinot after the Supreme Court had made its decision on his case.

These far-reaching and drastic consequences had their seeds in one of Cornelius Boudinot's schemes for fortune and fame. After ratification of the U.S.-Cherokee treaty of 1866, the always-opportunistic Boudinot looked around for a way to make his fortune. It is not surprising that his attention was attracted to tobacco. One of the last sights Cornelius had had of Richmond was the burning tobacco warehouses, set afire by the Confederates to deny the Yankees a fortune in the one commodity most akin to legal tender.[1] And he knew that tobacco, in the form of sweetened plug, played an important role in postwar Indian Territory, Kansas, Missouri, and Arkansas. Like other regions, this area was cash poor, and the people had to rely on or invent other systems to conduct business. One way was to barter, but this ancient practice was inefficient to say the least, and much of the time it was downright impossible. The warrant system came into widespread use, but it, too, had its limitations. This was basically a way of trading IOUs; if a farmer sold a mule to another person who lacked cash but whose credit and assets were otherwise sufficient, the buyer could issue a warrant for the amount of the debt. This certificate, in turn, could be used by the mule's seller to buy fodder to feed his remaining livestock, provided he could find someone to accept it. Obviously, the system had its drawbacks. Plug tobacco, however, was in universal demand by chewers and smokers, and the raw material was grown throughout the region. It soon became a medium of exchange with an established value. For example, Stand Watie's offer to settle a debt with James M. Bell for twenty-five pounds of tobacco and some cows reflected common practice in the years immediately after the war.[2]

Boudinot knew that even before the war, northwestern Arkansas and southwestern Missouri were tobacco-growing areas, producing mostly red burley, a good variety for making sweetened plug.[3] That same area was an excellent potential market for the product. The catch was that the factories which processed the raw tobacco leaf into plug were in St. Louis, which with Louisville, Kentucky, was a major tobacco-manufacturing center in the Midwest. The leaf had to be shipped to St. Louis, where it was made into plug and then shipped back over the Ozark Mountains to southern Missouri and Arkansas to be sold. An additional complication arose in 1862 when the federal government, looking for a revenue source to finance the war, hit upon the excise tax on tobacco as well as on other goods such as alcohol. The tax was imposed on the plug makers, so when the red burley made its return trip it had transportation and manufacturing costs plus a hefty tax added to its price. At the time Boudinot opened his factory in 1868, the federal levy on a pound of tobacco was thirty-two cents. The financial advantage was obvious: Boudinot could manufacture plug in the Cherokee Nation from tobacco grown in the area and sweetened with native grape juice, avoiding both the cost of transportation and federal excise stamps. He could sell his plug for less and still make a substantial profit.

Boudinot made plans for his tobacco venture in the spring of 1867, shortly after his return from Washington and service with the ill-fated delegation of southern Cherokees. He persuaded Stand Watie to enter the business with him as a partner who would provide much of the financial support needed for the operation's startup and for day-to-day administration of the business. This latter role was a necessary one because Cornelius expected to be away from the business much of the time, engaged in other affairs. Watie was the key to success of the tobacco business. In addition to backing the venture with his money and his supervisory experience, he backed it with his name. The product Boudinot sold was called "Boudinot & Watie," taking advantage of the general's Civil War reputation as well as his name as leader of the minority faction of Cherokees.[4]

By January 1868 Watie had agreed to enter the tobacco business, and his nephew was delighted. In a letter from Washington dated the ninth of that month, Cornelius predicts that "we will be able to make a handsome thing of it this year. And do better and better every year." He is equally sanguine about retirement of the initial investment, calculating that "all expenses will be paid up in the spring and then we will have clear sailing."[5] The prospect of success has him thinking about other ventures as well. "I wish to put up in conjunction with the factory a steam flour mill," he suggests, asking his uncle's opinion of it. He will finance the flour mill from the payment received as Cherokee delegate, he goes on to say, but he does not regard that sum as automatically forthcoming. Often delegates were paid amounts stipulated by the agreements they were negotiating, as Boudinot was bitterly aware from his participation in the 1866 treaty talks. Furthermore, the letter voices concern that others in the delegation are plotting to throw him "over board." As ever, though, his planning was not deterred by lack of capital; he tells Watie that if he fails to raise a sufficient amount in Washington, he will finance the flour mill from proceeds from the tobacco factory and "give you an interest."

Characteristically exuberant when his prospects seemed bright, Boudinot used the same letter to announce other plans to Watie for a venture beyond the scope of the factory and mill. While he saw these ventures as being essential to secure his financial well-being, he had a larger mission to carry out in the affairs of men: "I have drawn up and have introduced an important railroad bill; *It is my own invention* and I am entitled to a patent right therefore; The bill incorporates the central Indian R. R. Co the first directors to be apportioned to the several nations according to population; and the subsequent directors to represent the several Nations in proportion to the stock subscribed; My plan is to allow the Indians to build their own road and own it; They have got the land and money to do it. And it will be their own fault if they don't." In closing, Boudinot exhorts Watie to take personal charge to "have the necessary buildings put up as soon as possible about the factory and move up and take possession." He begs his uncle to "keep my affairs straight at home and we will make money." With money and brains, he concludes, "we can win in spite of family malice and ignorant prejudices." He is doubtless alluding to animosity toward the Watie-Boudinot family within the Cherokee Nation and to racist attitudes outside it.

By fall the tobacco operation was up and running. It was situated at Wet Prairie in the Cherokee Nation, about one hundred yards west of the Arkansas boundary, three miles south of Mayesville, Arkansas, and four miles south of the northwest boundary of Arkansas. This location, while seen as provocative by tax agents because of its proximity to Arkansas, was actually in the area of the original Ridge-Watie-Boudinot settlement after removal from Georgia. Six miles southeast from Watie's home, the factory was approximately the same distance due south from John Ridge's home on Honey Creek. The factory had been up by the end of 1867 and the other buildings by summer of the following year. The Boudinot-Watie enterprise operated in two two-story frame buildings, each twenty by forty feet, surrounded by a number of smaller log or frame structures. A longtime resident of the area recalled that they also had a deer park, although it seems superfluous in such a game-rich region.[6] A post office was established on the site, although later the Court of Claims pointed out that "there was nothing but the factory to require a post office there."[7] But doubtless Boudinot had plans that would require a post office. Perhaps he meant for his workers to move close by. He estimated that the factory employed over one hundred people at its peak.

Apparently the Boudinot & Watie brand sold well from the beginning, because when the general tried to get some for himself he was told that there was no tobacco at the factory, it "being all sold or sent off."[8] Business was doing so well soon after opening that it was necessary to purchase more hydraulic presses and other equipment to keep pace with demand. Boudinot purchased machinery from a Carthage, Missouri, plug manufacturer who may have kept a connection with Boudinot after the equipment purchase. By November 1868 the partners had found it necessary to hire managers and a foreman for the day-to-day operation. Joseph C. Henderson of Nevada was hired as business manager and remained in that capacity until the factory was shut down. There is evidence that Dr. W. D. Polson and J. W. Washbourne also worked at the factory as managers of operations. Polson was married to Flora Ridge, daughter of John Ridge, and had served as Watie's regimental surgeon during the Civil War. Washbourne was Polson's brother-in-law, having married Susan Ridge, Flora's sister. Both men were allied with Cornelius in other ventures as well. Boudinot was at the factory at this time supervising the installation of the equipment, but he planned to return to Washington as soon as this was accomplished. The machinery purchase was apparently quite extensive since shipment required fourteen wagonloads over a month's time at a total transportation cost of fifteen hundred dollars.[9] Cornelius and his uncle had agreed by this time to pay expenses and then share the profits equally, which they expected to start rolling in by February 1869. And their expectations were not unfounded.

With the new machinery, the factory had the capacity to manufacture five thousand pounds of tobacco per day. According to Henderson, the operation comprised 120 people who were involved in sweetening the cured tobacco, compressing the leaf into "flat goods," weighing and packaging the product, and transporting it to market. The Boudinot & Watie brand was distributed to and sold in stores throughout the Cherokee and Creek Nations, in addition to outlets in Kansas, Missouri, and Arkansas.[10] Obviously no cottage industry, the factory was bound to attract the attention of the large St. Louis tobacco dealers, as it must have cut into their business appreciably. Boudinot was able to sell his plug, reputedly a high-quality product, for approximately half of what the St. Louis factories were asking for theirs in Indian Territory, and in some cases even less than half.[11] It is easy to see why Boudinot had attracted the attention of the larger tobacco companies.

By the middle of August 1869, Boudinot had returned from Washington and wrote Watie about his plans.[12] He says that he has just visited the factory and "found things in a prosperous condition." However, he does not expect to get out of debt as soon as expected, and now he plans to personally supervise his affairs at the factory. "In the mean time," he adds, "I think we can agree up on some combination to make money which will suit you better than an interest in the factory in the future." This is the first recorded mention of Boudinot's intention of buying out his partner. Apparently, Watie was not doing well financially and was in need of ready cash. Boudinot's hands were tied, of course, because the factory was still in debt and he, too, was short of funds.

An undated, unsigned document that outlines a proposition concerning the tobacco venture has survived in Stand Watie's papers and seems to constitute an agreement to buy out Watie's interest. It specifically mentions Polson and Washbourne and appears to be a vehicle not only to allow Watie out of the enterprise but to allow Polson and Washbourne in, perhaps as payment for their managerial duties. The document stipulates that the undersigned, Watie, will relinquish rights and interest to the factory at Wet Prairie to Boudinot for an advance of one thousand dollars in money and four thousand dollars in tobacco goods, reckoned at twenty-five cents a pound. Watie would repay the four thousand without interest on January 1, 1871, in cash or in tobacco valued at the agreed amount. The agreement further states that "the parties in interest of the said factory" will pay "amounts due me [Watie] by Dr. Polson and Washbourne in money." Presumably, under the terms of the agreement, Watie would be able to make a profit on the tobacco advanced to him, thus raising some much-needed cash. Finally, the undersigned would agree "to participate in any new undertaking [upon] which the parties may hereafter embark." Always planning ahead in spite of present difficulties, Boudinot aimed to establish claims along the right-of-way of the putative Central Indian Railroad

THE TOBACCO TYCOON

for himself and his partners.[13] The agreement outlined in this document was never consummated, and Watie never received compensation for his interest.

At its inception, the enterprise seemed to be poised to make a lot of money for Boudinot; he was certain of fulfilling his dream of becoming a man of means and influence. Precisely at that point complications began to set in. Boudinot's work as a delegate on the 1866 treaty meant, of course, that he was well versed as to its provisions. Article 10 of that treaty, which Boudinot seems to have written himself, had particular relevance to his plans.[14] It provided that "every Cherokee and freed person, resident in the Cherokee nation, shall have the right to sell any products of his farm, including his or her live stock, or any merchandise or manufactured products, and to ship and drive the same to market without restraint, paying any tax thereon which is now or may be levied by the United States on the quantity sold outside of the Indian territory."

So by terms of the treaty, Boudinot was certainly within his rights to make and sell plug in the Cherokee Nation without giving the excise tax a thought. To sell his product in Arkansas or Missouri, however, was another matter, and the law and the treaty clearly provided for it: Boudinot, as the manufacturer, had to buy the excise stamps—thus paying the tax—and affix them to each packaged plug. One problem, however, became immediately evident: according to the tax codes, the stamps must be purchased from the U.S. Internal Revenue Office in which the manufacturer conducted business. Boudinot, working from within the borders of the Cherokee Nation, was outside any revenue district. How was he to proceed, then, if he intended to sell his wares in Missouri and Arkansas?

In characteristic fashion, Cornelius wrote directly to John E. Risley, the deputy commissioner of Internal Revenue in Washington, on May 8, 1868. His experience in that city led him to ask the right questions of the right person. His letter was short and blunt: "Sir: I have a factory for the manufacture of tobacco, situated in the Cherokee Nation in the Indian Territory. Will you please give me your official opinion as to whether I have a legal right to sell tobacco manufactured at such factory without the payment of the revenue tax thereon, at any place I shall choose to sell the same, whether in the Cherokee Nation, or elsewhere in any of the United States."[15] Commissioner Risley made prompt reply on July 14, saying that in his opinion, "under existing laws" no tax may be legally assessed or collected from such a factory, whether its products are sold in the Cherokee Nation or elsewhere in the United States. Risley is careful to add, however, that he is not offering an opinion on the effect of a bill pending before Congress.[16]

Cornelius knew he was walking on eggs with the taxation issue. He had already heard rumors that the plug manufacturers in St. Louis and elsewhere were not happy about his business success so far and that they were determined to protect the monopoly they had become accustomed to.[17] While in Washington with the Cherokee delegation negotiating various aspects of the 1866 treaty, Boudinot determined that his competitors were also in the capital, "moving in hostility to his interests."

Although other plug factories had sprung up in Indian Territory near the border with southern Missouri and northwestern Arkansas to compete with the large St. Louis mills, Boudinot's operation was most worrisome to them because of tax implications posed by his Cherokee citizenship.[18] Citing potential tax fraud, the St. Louis tobacco magnates went to the federal government for protection and found their solace there. Congress passed a measure that became law on July 20, 1868, the one to which Risley had referred in his May letter, which provided the following: "That the internal revenue laws imposing taxes on distilled spirits, fermented liquors, tobacco, snuff, and cigars, shall be held and construed to extend to such articles produced anywhere within the exterior boundaries of the United States, whether the same shall be within a collection district or not."[19] Of course, the Indian Territory was within the "exterior boundaries," so Congress with this act had extended the excise tax to cover items produced, sold, and consumed by Native Americans.

While this portion of the law, known as Section 107, seemed to settle the matter, Boudinot was not finished. He called for clarification of the issue, especially on what he says is his method for paying the tax on goods sold outside the Cherokee Nation. On November 20 he sent a letter to James Marr, supervisor of Internal Revenue at St. Louis, stating that when he sells tobacco in the states he reports those transactions to the nearest government assessor. The assessor then marks the packages, Boudinot goes on, and collects the tax. He then asks Marr for permission to continue the practice, specifically in the Southern District of Kansas and at Carthage, Missouri, and Kansas City.

Of course it is difficult to know whether or not Boudinot had been following this procedure before attention was drawn to his business. After all, the tax added greatly to the price, the potential for underselling one's competitors was high, and the profits from untaxed goods luxurious. To one who played the angles as Boudinot did, the temptation to sell untaxed tobacco in the states must have been almost irresistible, especially when the legal aspects of the situation were so gray. But, while we know that Cornelius was not above exaggeration or downright misrepresentation, it seems senseless for him not to tell the truth about his dealings with government agents when it would be so easy for the supervisor to check on the veracity of his statements, especially at a time when the St. Louis interests were complaining about potential tax fraud. Marr, sensing the delicacy of the matter, declined to provide Boudinot with an independent ruling and instead, on December 3, referred the question to his superior, the supervisor of Internal Revenue in Washington. In a cover letter, he did recommend that Boudinot be allowed to continue with the practice outlined in his query letter.[20]

The acting commissioner of Internal Revenue, Thomas Harlan, gave Marr and Boudinot a prompt reply. In a letter dated December 26, 1868, Harlan laid out the details of the procedure Boudinot was to follow if he wished to sell tobacco in the states. He would have to buy and affix revenue stamps to the packages he sold outside Indian Territory, Harlan ruled. Tax collectors nearest the place of manufacture, he went on, were obliged to furnish Boudinot with stamps. Once this procedure is carried out, Harlan states, "his tobacco will pass current in any of the States where he may desire to ship it and will be free from any liability to seizure or detention."[21] Many people would have taken Harlan's letter in stride and complied with his instructions. After all, Cornelius was still able to sell his tobacco wherever he desired, and his chances of running afoul of the law were minimal so long as he adhered to the rules as understood by all parties.

But Boudinot considered this an "onerous" ruling and was determined to contest it. As always, his reasoning was complex, and as always, money played a big part in his decision. First of all, Boudinot seems determined to insist upon the supremacy of the terms of the 1866 treaty over any laws that Congress might pass. Part of this was based on principle and part on his personal feelings. Protecting the sanctity of treaties, in spite of the fact that the treaty path is strewn with the shards of former pacts, is the sine qua non of Native American policy, then and today. These documents contain all the obligations and concessions agreed to and expected by both parties. For Indians, if the treaties fail, chaos results. In addition, this particular treaty was one in which Boudinot had a personal and emotional stake. As we have seen, he had risked his political reputation and invested a great store of his time, labor, and emotions in the negotiations. In the end, even though his side lost and he personally suffered loss of face and effort, there stood the treaty, a solemn document carrying the design for U.S.-Cherokee relations presumably far into the future. But now, in Boudinot's eyes, with the ink hardly dry, Congress had tossed aside the treaty and with it what little dignity Cornelius was able to escape with from Washington and the excruciating deliberations. Another factor was in the mix as well. As we have seen, his tobacco venture was doing very well. While the operation was not yet out of debt, significant profits were in sight in the form of a mountain of unprocessed tobacco for which there had proven to be a ready market. Boudinot's gamble was ready to pay off. His personal prestige—always an important consideration—had risen as well, now that he had created a host of jobs for people who had been living for years in desperate economic straits. The outward trappings of success were also there— the factory with its adjacent buildings and acres, Boudyville and its post office. The Cherokee Nation had even seen fit to include him in their delegation to Washington, although that appointment was not altogether popular with some of his and his family's old antagonists. Given this set of circumstances, perhaps Cornelius was tempted to try throwing his weight around a bit. There would be no better way to antagonize many people in the Nation and in the surrounding states, people like business and political rivals and federal revenue agents.

Several weeks later, after he had had a chance to digest Harlan's letter, Cornelius wrote back, stating his objections and suggesting an alternate course of action. His first sentence invokes the 1866 treaty, which guarantees, Boudinot says, "the right of any Cherokee citizen to send any article manufactured in the Cherokee Nation to market without restraint." It is on that last phrase that he centers his argument. No one engaged in the trade can afford to pay taxes on tobacco until he knows what portion of his product will be sold outside the Nation. Because there is no way to anticipate the size of this portion, he argues, his ability to do business is restrained by the requirement that he buy revenue stamps for the tobacco before the sale. He closes his letter with a different plan, one that would allow him to pay the tax like a good citizen, but only on actual sales. He asks that he be allowed to deposit his product with revenue officers in a number of places he anticipates doing business: Baxter's Springs and Fort Scott, Kansas; Fort Smith, Fayetteville, and Bentonville, Arkansas; and Kansas City, Carthage, and Neosho, Missouri. The tax would be paid and stamps affixed when he withdraws it from the revenue collectors for sale in the various communities. [22]

Cornelius did not have to wait long for a reply. In his letter, Deputy Commissioner Risley addresses the "restraint" issue at once and, quoting Article 10 of the treaty, says that Cherokees are free to ship their goods "without restraint by paying any tax thereon." Risley, however, accedes to Boudinot's plan and stipulates that the tobacco should be clearly marked and the revenue agents sufficiently notified when and how much tobacco was to be shipped. Risley also directed that copies of his letter be sent to revenue agents in Kansas, Arkansas, and Missouri.[23]

While no record exists of the reaction to Risley's letter from the agents involved, it is not too much to speculate that the new arrangement did not sit very well. While Boudinot's system was not without precedent (the bonding of whiskey is a similar practice), it is doubtful that the agents had the facilities for storing the tobacco, let alone the stomach for the additional task of keeping the necessary records. The fact that Boudinot was a Cherokee, one who presumed to contest the decisions of the revenue agency's higher officials and get concessions from them, probably didn't sit well with the district officers either. Finally, Boudinot had been a Confederate. He had served as secretary of Arkansas's secession committee, advocated secession as a Little Rock editor, fought in the Cherokee regiment, and served as a delegate to the Confederate Congress. Federal employees in Kansas, Missouri, and Arkansas at the time almost invariably held anti-Confederate sympathies, especially in Arkansas, where they were part of the Reconstruction machinery.

In late February 1869, Boudinot had the Internal Revenue system on his side, and his business future looked bright. It didn't take long, however, for things to change. In March, Ulysses S. Grant was inaugurated as president and a change of guard ensued in the nation's capital. With the change in personnel came a decided change in attitude toward tobacco manufacturing in Indian Territory. In August, R. W. Wishard, the collector for the Third District of Arkansas at Dardenelle, received a letter from J. W. Douglass, acting commissioner of Internal Revenue. Douglass's opening paragraph signals the reversal in agency policy: "I am informed that for the purpose of avoiding the tax imposed upon manufactured tobacco, parties have established factories in the Indian Territories, in some cases just across the boundary lines where tobacco is manufactured on which no tax is paid, and it is further intimated to me, that this tobacco is intended to be sold—at least, large portions of it in the States adjoining the Indian Territories."[24] This, of course, was the standard line of the St. Louis interests. Instead of acting on actual violations, Douglass decided to act on the alleged intentions of the new factories as identified by their competitors. Clearly, the tobacco lobbyists were still at work in Washington and had found sympathetic ears. Douglass's letter goes on to outline action needed to thwart the intentions of new purveyors of plug. He orders Wishard to seize "every pound" of tobacco "found outside of a factory or bonded warehouse in your district" that does not bear the revenue stamp proving that the excise tax has been paid. In addition, he orders that the sellers and manufacturers of the tobacco be arrested and charged for violation of the July 20, 1868, revenue act.

At first glance, Boudinot's operation would seem exempt from Douglass's decree, since his tobacco was not "outside of a factory," but he felt threatened, probably with good cause. In any case, Cornelius was scandalized, and, wrapped in a cloak of righteousness (since he hadn't been charged with any wrongdoing other than a vague "intention"), he promptly applied for reconsideration of the order. In response, revenue officials in Washington informed him that the new commissioner of Internal Revenue, Columbus Delano, had taken an even harder line. Delano, Boudinot was told, was determined to collect taxes on alcohol and tobacco manufactured in Indian Territory no matter where they were to be sold. Apparently, Delano was following the "exterior boundaries" stipulation of the July 20, 1868, law.

An Ohio native, Columbus Delano had served one term in the U.S. House of Representatives as a Whig (1844–46) and two terms as a Republican (1865–69). In 1867 he was a part of the radical faction in Congress that favored a military government for the South, and in 1869 President Grant appointed him commissioner of Internal Revenue. While in this post, Delano was unable or unwilling to end the whiskey revenue frauds that had been rife for some time. In 1870, Grant appointed him secretary of the interior.

By 1869, Cornelius was feeling distinct hostility emanating from the offices of Internal Revenue. He knew, too, that heretofore the good graces of the Washington-based officials had stood between his good fortunes and the tax collectors back in the Third District of Arkansas. As he was not getting anywhere personally with Delano or his subordinates, Boudinot decided to enlist the aid of his old friends Albert Pike and Robert Johnson. Both Pike and Johnson had listened to Cornelius's tales of his problems as they spent evenings together in Washington. The pair were prominent attorneys with political connections, and Boudinot felt that this show of force might be enough to stop the Delano's efforts. Pike and Johnson immediately challenged Delano, citing a violation of the 1866 treaty.[25]

Delano's response was to wheel in a big gun of his own, Judge Charles P. James, whose opinion on the matter was rendered in a memorandum of opinion. James and Delano contended that it was not Cherokee citizens who were being taxed but rather goods that happened to be manufactured in the Cherokee Nation and which "might be carried thence" into the states. Thus, in James's opinion, the revenue laws were not being extended to Indian Territory in violation of existing treaties.[26]

Boudinot accepted James's pronouncement as "the final settlement of the question" and continued to operate the business in compliance with the law, according to a statement he made later.[27] On December 20, 1869, John McDonald, supervisor of the Van Buren, Arkansas, office of Internal Revenue, and John A. Joyce, one of his agents, seized the factory at Wet Prairie and all the materials in it. With assistance from U.S. Marshal William A. Britton, they also seized tobacco from stores throughout the Cherokee and Creek Nations. The operation seemed well planned and coordinated. For example, about 5,000 pounds of plug and smoking tobacco were seized at Fort Sill, Indian Territory, in a shipment just received from Boudyville, some four hundred miles distant. Deputy Marshall J. G. Owens, acting under Britton's orders, seized 7,500 pounds of manufactured tobacco at the factory, leaving more than 100,000 pounds in leaf and "lump" tobacco impounded on the premises. According to the clerk of the U.S. marshal's office, James W. Donnelley, the manufactured tobacco was taken to a house about five miles from Mayesville, where it was stored under the charge of two deputies until it could be auctioned. There it remained for weeks because of bad roads caused by inclement weather. When Internal Revenue officers went to retrieve the tobacco to take it to nearby Bentonville, they found that much of it had been destroyed or stolen "through the negligence of the deputies left in charge of it."[28] What was left was auctioned.

Boudinot was worried about the tobacco impounded at the factory. He appealed to Britton to allow him to attend to the goods before they spoiled, but Britton replied that he lacked authority to condone the action. Boudinot kept trying to impress upon the marshal the idea that the seizure was all a mistake, the result of a breakdown in communication between the Internal Revenue authorities in Washington and their agents in Arkansas. Britton's reply was that he was only following orders. The huge stock subsequently spoiled and was deemed worthless. In addition, according to Donnelley, at least 35,000 pounds of Boudinot and Watie's tobacco were seized in stores, only 18,000 pounds of which made it to the Internal Revenue office in Van Buren. The rest was left at different points in Indian Territory on account of high water and lack of transportation, according to reports made by deputies. "The tobacco," Donnelley states, "was scattered about over a territory about as large as the State of New York."[29]

Boudinot was beside himself. His whole empire had crumbled, his bright future darkened. But this was not the last indignity he was to suffer in the matter. As he was arguing with the deputy marshals who had set upon his property, Internal Revenue supervisor John McDonald and his agent John A.

Joyce arrested him, charging violation of the revenue laws within the Indian Territory. The furious Boudinot demanded that McDonald show some proof of his authority, knowing that internal revenue law did not extend to the Cherokee Nation and its citizens, except for goods that were to be sold in the states. McDonald replied that his authority came from Columbus Delano himself, who had urged both the seizure and the arrest. But when Boudinot demanded to see a written order or letter from the commissioner, McDonald angrily replied that none was needed. Boudinot then told the supervisor that he was sure that McDonald's actions were "voluntary and wholly unauthorized," accusations that McDonald hotly denied.[30] Cornelius then threatened to sue McDonald personally for trespass, damage, and injury.

Fuming, Boudinot was taken into custody and brought before McDonald's superior in the Third District of Arkansas, R. W. Wishard. When Boudinot arrived in Dardenelle, he found that Wishard had summoned his legal adviser to the meeting. Here, Cornelius outlined his allegations against McDonald and showed them Delano's October letter to Pike and Johnson, which took the position that the internal revenue laws did not extend to Indian Territory. In the light of the letter, he insisted, McDonald could not have been following Delano's instructions.

Wishard replied calmly that he had seen a copy of Delano's letter in October when it was sent to Pike and Johnson. At that time, he said, Washington officials had told him that the letter had been sent to Boudinot's lawyers for the purpose of "quieting their complaint." At the same time, Wishard continued, Delano was urging McDonald to hurry up and make the seizure and arrest. Boudinot was devastated. He had believed initially that a terrible mistake had been made and that as soon as the proper authorities in Washington found out about it, all would be well. He had made this case repeatedly to Britton and his men when the marshals appeared at the factory door. Now it was clear that the treachery lay not only with McDonald, whom Boudinot now considered a sworn enemy, but also with the powerful commissioner of Internal Revenue himself. Defiantly, he refused to post bond, but Wishard was too timid to put him in jail. Boudinot traveled to Fayetteville, from where on the following day he wrote of his plight to Pike and Johnson. His near desperation comes through that letter when he writes, "I am completely broken up; my employees scattered to the four winds."[31]

Pike and Johnson lost no time in protesting to Delano, demanding that the arrest order be rescinded and Boudinot's property returned. Curiously, Delano's reply seems to have been a verbal one, so no record of it exists outside

Boudinot's memorial to Congress. Delano told Pike and Johnson that he had reversed his former decision and stood behind McDonald in his seizure of the tobacco and factory and in his arrest of Boudinot. Cornelius's lawyers protested that the defendant had not been given any notice of the policy reversal and had been acting in accordance with the rules set down by Delano previously.

By mid-January 1870, Cornelius had traveled to Washington to assist Pike and Johnson in the coming battles. McDonald had arrived days earlier to consult with Delano and his other Washington superiors. When Boudinot arrived, he was astonished to discover that McDonald had placed paragraphs in the local newspapers "containing misstatements of facts and law and imputations against the undersigned" designed, Cornelius charged, to damage his own reputation and to justify McDonald's actions. Although McDonald's forays into journalism were pointed out to Secretary of the Treasury George S. Boutwell as being unprofessional and damaging the department's reputation, no acknowledgment of the complaint was ever made.

It was not until January 25, 1870, that Delano issued an official order extending the internal revenue laws of the United States into Indian Territory and published regulations for the assessment and collection of taxes there.[32] Boudinot immediately appealed Delano's actions to Secretary Boutwell in a long letter in which he gave a history of the dispute and presented a legal argument to the effect that Delano had acted in defiance of the 1866 treaty. Two days later, on January 28, Boutwell replied, saying that he not only concurred with Delano's actions but had consulted with the commissioner on the matter beforehand. Facing this stone wall, Boudinot decided to try to go in another direction by requesting from Delano permission to resume business. This request was summarily rejected.[33]

Pike, Johnson, and Boudinot could see that they were getting nowhere with the executive branch, so they looked to Congress, where they knew they had friends. An attempt to bring pressure to bear on the Treasury Department designed by Senators Alexander McDonald and Daniel W. Voorhees appeared on the Senate floor in the form of a resolution. This act, passed on February 19, 1870, asked that the body be informed "if any officer of the government has, contrary to article 10 of the treaty of July 19, 1866, with the Cherokee nation, enforced or sought to enforce the payment of taxes by Cherokees on products manufactured in the Cherokee nation and sold within Indian Territory." The resolution was submitted to the executive branch, and five days later a reply was received from Delano. The commissioner says that his office has ascertained that tobacco manufacturers—chiefly white men who are not citizens of the Cherokee country—had perpetrated "extensive frauds." He states his determination to collect all taxes due, citing his authority under the June 20, 1868, statute. Both the Senate and the commissioner had neatly avoided mentioning Boudinot's case specifically, and after Delano's reply was read into the record, the issue was allowed to rest for the moment in the legislative branch.

Meanwhile, the court case against Boudinot was proceeding apace back in Van Buren, with Judge H. C. Caldwell presiding. President Johnson had appointed Caldwell to the Western District of Arkansas post in 1865, a position he would retain until 1873, when he joined the Eighth Judicial Circuit.[34] As the case opened, the defense attorneys took issue with the district attorney's contention in the original charge that the factory and equipment belonged to Boudinot and "white persons and white men" unknown to the prosecution.[35] This part of the charge, it seems, lay at the heart of the case for fraud. If the authorities believed that Boudinot had conspired with white tobacco manufacturers from Carthage, Missouri, or elsewhere to move their operation a hundred yards inside the Cherokee Nation to thwart the internal revenue laws and gain advantage over the big St. Louis interests, the seizure and arrest would make sense. However, a conspiracy of this kind was never specifically alleged; the "white persons and white men" part of the charge was the only allusion to anything of the kind. Interestingly, once Boudinot claimed that he and Watie were the sole owners and proprietors of the operation, the "white" connection was dropped.

Pike and Johnson petitioned the judge to instruct the jury that the revenue act of July 20, 1868, was not in force in Indian Territory at the time of the alleged infraction; that Article 10 of the 1866 treaty between the United States and the Cherokees was in force at the time, guaranteeing Boudinot's right to conduct his business without restraint; and that the act of July 20, 1868, required that revenue stamps be sold only to tobacco manufacturers in collection districts, so that it was illegal under the act for Boudinot to purchase the stamps. The judge refused to instruct the jury according to these terms, and Boudinot was found guilty as charged. The judge then entered a judgment of condemnation that provided for the sale of the seized property. In response, Pike and Johnson filed a writ of error with the U.S. Supreme Court.

The Court heard the case in its December 1870 term, so the principals did not have long to wait for a decision. Boudinot, Pike, Johnson, A. H. Garland, and Benjamin F. Butler represented Boudinot and Watie. Historian Robert K. Heimann writes that the Cherokee National Council retained Pike and

Johnson in December 1870 for fifteen hundred dollars,[36] but Boudinot wrote to Watie in May 1871 saying that the money ought to be paid by the Nation, indicating that if it were the council's intention to pay, they had not done so by that time.[37] The Nation does seem to have hired Butler, however, who had served as legal representative to the Nation before. Pike and Johnson submitted a brief, and Butler filed a second one. A comparison of the two briefs is interesting in that Pike and Johnson seem to focus on the particular case, while Butler addresses its broader ramifications.

The Pike-Johnson argument outlines a history of the case, then makes the case that if the July 20, 1868, internal revenue law is allowed to take precedence in this case, it effectively repeals Article 10 of the 1866 treaty and extends the revenue laws over Indian Territory. This should not be allowed, they contend, as the power of taxation does not give Congress the right to abrogate treaties. They go on to say that if precedence is given to the tax law, it will bring about a sea change in the relations between the United States and the Indian nations. The Native Americans' "treaties and titles were as worthless as waste paper" if the decision of the lower court is allowed to stand.[38]

In his argument, Butler reviews the history of treaties between the United States and the Cherokee Nation, alluding to Article I, Section 8, of the U.S. Constitution and citing its relevance to the 1866 treaty. After his review, he makes the following points:

> First. That in all these treaties the United States have dealt with the Cherokee nation as an independent power, of limited sovereignty, under the protectorate of the United States.
>
> Second. That all interference with the Cherokee nation by the United States Government in changing their legal relations have [sic] been subordinated to the provisions of such treaties and to acts of legislation carrying into effect those provisions.
>
> Third. That the United States have never claimed to exercise general jurisdiction independent of treaty provisions over the Cherokee nation, but have always legislated in subordination to those provisions. This will very clearly appear from the provisions of the treaty of 1866.[39]

With the Court assembled, Boudinot's attorneys made their case, going over the arguments made in the briefs.[40] They asserted, too, that in order for the government to tax citizens of the Native nations, it would need to secure the consent of those citizens. They added that the United States has never claimed general jurisdiction, except for what was outlined in treaties, over the Cherokee

Nation. For a law such as the revenue act of July 20, 1968, to apply in the Nation, it would have had to include a stipulation to that effect, the "plainest, and most unequivocal and distinct enunciation of the law," in order for the act to abrogate or infringe on treaty provisions. The lawyers then present their argument as to the precedence of Article 10 of the 1866 treaty over the revenue law.[41]

The prosecutors, Amos T. Akerman, attorney general of the United States, and B. H. Bristow, solicitor general, made several points generally affirming the right of Congress to legislate over "subject matter" taken up in treaties, in this case, taxation. *U.S. v. Rogers*, they argued, had decided the issue of consent before taxation.[42]

When the decision was made, it was an easy one, according to Associate Justice Noah H. Swayne, who wrote for the majority, which included Justices Clifford and Strong. In cases where the outcome is a tie, the verdict is with the status quo. In this case, then, the government had prevailed. Justices Bradley and Miller wrote dissenting opinions, Justice Davis concurred in Bradley's dissension, and Justices Chase, Nelson, and Field did not take part in the proceedings. Swayne, of Ohio, had been on the Court since 1862, when Abraham Lincoln appointed him. In his opinion, issued May 1, 1871, he pinpoints the central issue: Does Section 107 of the July 20, 1868, revenue act apply to citizens of the Cherokee Nation, given Article 10 of the 1866 treaty? "Considering the narrowness of the question to be decided, a remarkable wealth of learning and ability have been expended in their discussion. The view of counsel in this court have rarely been more elaborately presented." But the issue is an important one: either the law or the treaty has precedence over the other. "The repugnancy is clear and they cannot stand together," Swayne writes. In cases such as this one, when conflict arise, the conflict must be resolved by the "Political Department of the Government," he goes on. "They are beyond the sphere of judicial cognizance. In the case under consideration the Act of Congress must prevail as if the Treaty were not an element to be considered."

Swayne continues with a statement that sets the stage for further action. Referring to Boudinot, he says, "If a wrong has been done, the power of redress is with Congress not with the judiciary, and that body, upon being applied to, it is to be presumed, will promptly give the proper relief." The final paragraph of the decision supports this unusual statement. It makes clear that "there is no ground for any imputation upon the integrity or good faith of the claimants who prosecuted this writ of error." They acted, he says, "under a misapprehension of their legal rights." Swayne's comments on the possibility of redress led to a situation in which Boudinot did not find "proper relief," from his point of view. And whatever relief he did receive cannot be deemed "prompt" by any measure.

While Swayne wrote for a "majority" of three, the case drew two minority opinions, one by Justice Joseph P. Bradley of New Jersey, newly appointed to the Court in 1870, and the other by Justice Samuel F. Miller of Iowa, sworn in during December 1861. Bradley's opinion, in which Justice David Davis concurred, was founded on legislative intent in Section 107. There is nothing to indicate that Congress intended its provisions to extend to Indian Territory, Bradley writes, and "it would have been very easy to say so." He concludes that if Congress had so intended, it would have made that intention clear, given that the "exempt jurisdiction" depends on a "solemn treaty" between the United States and the Cherokee Nation.

Reaction to the decision was not long in coming from several sectors. From Washington, Boudinot wrote to Watie, "The Supreme Court has decided the tobacco case against me. It is the death knell of the Nations."[43] The significance of the decision was not lost on Boudinot: if laws passed by Congress took precedence over treaties, then the treaties were only "waste paper," as Pike and Johnson had predicted. The legislative and executive branches could work their wills with Native Americans, Boudinot knew, and no relief was to be found in the judicial. The Court's decision and the conclusions Boudinot drew as a result of it drove his most important actions from this time forward.

The "Nations" that Cornelius had spoken of—the Native groups of Indian Territory—were meeting in Grand Council just after the decision was announced, and in the autumn of 1870 they issued a memorial regarding it to the U.S. Senate and House of Representatives. The Supreme Court's ruling "imperils, we feel, all our rights. It commits us wholly to the 'political department' of the government, and places us entirely at its mercy. In our ignorance we have supposed that Treaties were contracts entered into under the most solemn forms, and the most sacred pledges of human faith, and that they could be abrogated only by mutual consent. We are now taught differently."[44] After printing the memorial, Cornelius's brother William, the editor of the *Cherokee Advocate*, adds his own comments on what he calls the "unexpected decision." Native Americans regard the ruling as "a confession by the Government that they have been deceived and mocked." They recognize that they have been "deluded" in thinking that they enjoyed all the rights pertaining to them "as members of the ancient Indian Nations," rights not expressly relinquished by the treaties they had made with the "new Power in whose shadow so many Tribes have withered." The editor goes on to say, "They are now rudely told that all these assurances have been worthless or deceptive. . . . And so the Indians are reduced to beg their vaunting Protector not to destroy them. What have we done that our rights and our liberties should be thus taken away. What but that we occupy a country whose merits are magnified four-fold by covetousness, and is pronounced one of the finest in the world." The rights of Native Americans are endowed by the Creator, the editor says, and "it was in their exercise that we fostered the infant Power which now in its arrogant strength would fain deny or destroy them."

Some citizens of the states bordering the Cherokee Nation saw the injustice in the government's actions. James Donnelley, chief clerk of the U.S. marshal's office for western Arkansas, says in his affidavit that Boudinot "had the deep sympathy of all, and it was supposed to be an act of favor to him to bid off his tobacco at the lowest possible price" lest the government assume a profit at the Cherokee's expense.[45] Others, however, had a different slant on it. William Boudinot reported in the *Advocate* on a speech given in Kansas, where a number of people were eager to settle in Indian Territory:

> Mr. Laughlin made what the [Baxter, Kansas] *Bulletin* considers a "remarkably eloquent speech." In the support of his position and that of the settlers generally, that all Indian lands are the property of the United States and subject to the disposition of Congress and no other power, Mr. Laughlin cited the well-known Boudinot case . . . where it has been decided by the Supreme Court of the United States that the Congress of the United States has power to abrogate any treaty with the Indians, and that the revenue laws are of higher authority than Indian treaties. The decision also says that the Cherokee Nation is a part of the territory of the United States, and subject to be dealt with as the Congress may see proper.[46]

The *Advocate* editor writes that Laughlin's is a correct interpretation of the ruling. It authorizes Congress to allow squatters to settle on vacant Indian lands and stay there. While the decision is "monstrously wrong," it nonetheless means that Congress can take away the Indian nation's lands as long as "we hold them in common" and give them to others. He then reaches a reluctant conclusion, one he was to rescind later: "The only way to save the country now is to cover it with individual titles." This was a gospel that his younger brother Cornelius would preach until his death.

THE TOBACCO TYCOON

While the matter of the tobacco seizure was now settled, the criminal charges against Boudinot still applied, even in the face of what the Supreme Court had said about "integrity and good faith." Similar charges were pending against other tobacco manufacturers who had been operating out of the Cherokee Nation. Judge J. H. Huckleberry, U.S. attorney and prosecutor in Boudinot's case, and later commissioner in probate for the Northern District of Indian Territory, recalled that after the civil cases were decided against the manufacturers, a nolle prosequi was entered "in all cases except one, that of Elias Boudinot." Huckleberry said that he wrote to the attorney general for authority to dismiss the remaining case, but his request was denied. "There had been a personal difference between Inspector MacDonald [*sic*] and Boudinot," he recalled, "and the former used his influence to have the latter prosecuted."[47]

Following the advice of the Supreme Court, Boudinot applied to Congress for redress, outlining the situation as he saw it. In his memorial to the House, he mentions Huckleberry's attempt to get criminal charges dropped and the government's refusal. He also compares his case to those of the other tobacco manufacturers who had been tried in civil court but who had had charges against them dropped. The four other manufacturers—all "white men," according to Boudinot—operated out of the Choctaw and Cherokee Nations and, "knowing they were responsible as citizens of the United States to the laws of their country, they took no appeal to the Supreme Court." In consideration of not appealing their cases, Boudinot charged, the criminal prosecutions against them were dismissed, even though in their trials it had been proved that "they had intentionally defrauded the Government by selling tobacco in the State of Arkansas without the payment of any tax."[48]

Boudinot then adds a personal note on his motives for going into business in the first place: "Your memorialist further represents that he is the only Indian on record who has ever been known to embark in the business of manufacturing; that he flattered himself he would demonstrate to the world that Indian civilization was not a failure; but that, under the benign and fostering care of this great country, he would present to his red brethren a notable example of the benefits of industry, enterprise, and energy." Boudinot's next statement is remarkably self-revelatory: he writes that he was "ambitious not alone to amass wealth, but to rank first of his race who had ever rivaled the enterprise and success of the white man." While money was obviously important to Boudinot—he spent much of his life in pursuit of it—the major driving force in his life was the restitution of his family's former station in the Cherokee Nation and, indeed, in the country. When Boudinot's father and uncle, along with the Ridges, signed the Treaty of New Echota, the family fortunes were at their highest. The elder Boudinot was an acknowledged leader among the Cherokees and a favorite of the politically important missionaries. He was well known in the eastern capitals of business, commerce, and government and a respected prototype of the civilized savage, an important symbolic cultural figure in the nineteenth century. The elder Boudinot was successful as a journalist, orator, and translator, as successful, it can be argued, as any white man. In addition, he and his relatives had amassed wealth and property to an extent enjoyed by few Native Americans. After the Trail of Tears, however, the wheel of fortune turned, and the Boudinot-Ridge-Watie clan suffered a significant loss of prestige and worldly goods. Cornelius Boudinot, along with relatives such as John Rollin Ridge, sought with their own lives to restore the family's former status and saw personal success in the white man's world as a way of achieving this goal.

The House Judiciary Committee appealed to Attorney General Akerman to drop the criminal charges against Boudinot on December 18, 1871. Akerman complied the following February. [49] Cornelius then turned his attention to recouping some of the financial losses suffered at the hands of the government's action. His efforts in this direction were stymied by a classic case of buck passing. Embedded in the Supreme Court decision was a key statement: "If a wrong has been done, the power of redress is with Congress not with the judiciary, and that body, upon being applied to, it is to be presumed, will promptly give the proper relief." [50] With this utterance, the Court deftly handed off responsibility to the legislative branch, effectively telling members of Congress that if they thought Boudinot had been treated unfairly, they ought to do something about it.

Cornelius petitioned Congress for damages due to the seizure on November 12, 1877, but he did not receive any prompt relief. His friends in Congress sought to help him, but they were unable to get their colleagues to agree to the extent they had wished. Their job was made more difficult by the fact that by the 1880s, Boudinot had made many political enemies inside and out of Congress by his vigorous support of such controversial issues of territorial status for Indian Territory and allotment of tribal lands. After years of maneuvering behind the scenes, Senator Voorhees of Indiana, Boudinot's longtime friend and colleague, introduced a bill (S. 120) in 1880 that did not award any damages but did allow the injured party to bring his grievance to the U.S. Court of Claims. Voorhees's bill passed the full Congress on June 4,

THE TOBACCO TYCOON

1880. Congress thus took the responsibility passed off from the Supreme Court and presented it to the claims court.

Boudinot filed his original claim with the court on June 17, 1880, asking judgment for $98,050, but he revised it upward in February 1883. The judges on the claims court were not amused with Congress's legerdemain. In their opinion they say, "In no instance, probably, in the history of the court has a special act authorizing a party to sue the United States here, been couched in terms so liberal to the claimant as those of this statute." The court then goes on to list the far-reaching consequences of the legislative act: "It removes any ground for questioning the right of an Indian to sue in this court," thus setting an important precedent. Further, the opinion states, Congress has given the claims court jurisdiction over a claim against the government based on "an alleged tort committed by its officers," another precedent. In addition, the judges point out, Congress has deemed that a decision of a U.S. district court, upheld by the Supreme Court, has constituted a "wrong" done to the claimant. The legal issues all having been decided by Congress, the claims court then states somewhat peevishly that there is "nothing for this court to do in the case" except "merely" assess the amount due to right the wrong.

This the court proceeded to do. Boudinot claimed that between 95,000 and 150,000 pounds of leaf tobacco had been seized by the government, but, the court noted, the marshal's statement to the district court put the amount at 4,500 pounds. Since the district court's judgment was based on this figure, the claims court used it to calculate Boudinot's loss at $675. The claims court also tabulated the cost of the manufactured tobacco seized, putting the value of it at $1,147.25. It allowed $300 for losses and damages to the factory as a result of the seizure. The court took exception to Boudinot's figures for living and traveling expenses, noting that for much of the time he claimed expenses he was employed by Congress and would have had to travel to Washington from the Cherokee Nation and pay room and board in any case. They allowed him $1,000 of the $4,109 claimed. Boudinot had also claimed $36,000 for prospective profits lost, which the court disallowed entirely. Finally, the court agreed with the claim of attorneys' fees, $150. In all, the court authorized Boudinot to recover a total of $3,272,25.

The other partner in the tobacco venture, Stand Watie, had died on September 9, 1871, leaving his widow, Sallie, and their children in dire financial condition. Ironically, his time of death coincided with the time that Boudinot had predicted they would become wealthy, but as far as is known, Watie had never received a dime from the business. But hope for some kind of proceeds from the ill-fated Watie survived even after his death. In a letter written in early 1872 to her brother James M. Bell, Sallie writes:

> Ask C. Boudinot if he intends to give me any thing for the Gens share in the factory you can tell him that I am perfectly destitute for I have let the last thing go that would pay a debt if I had just enough to send Jack to school it would help some and I want to have the Gens grave fixed up and if I can do that it will greatly releave my mind if I could only get one or two hundred at this time it would greatly releave me at present you know that I can not collect any tell him that if he can to let me have two hundred and I will return it just as soon as I come if there is nothing coming to Stand but he left on a piece of paper that he would take six thousand for his share now if he will give me one third of that it will make me even with the world and do a great many other things that I must do.[51]

In all fairness, Sallie and the children were very much in Cornelius's mind. His problem was that he wasn't very well off financially either. Boudinot involved Mrs. Watie in many of his ventures in the Cherokee Nation in the coming years, but she never made much money from any of them.

Stand's role in Boudinot & Watie lived on after his death, but instead of profits, his estate realized only debts. As late as 1873, Sallie Watie received a dun for $60 from Bentonville, Arkansas, requesting money for tobacco that "Standwaitie" had purchased. After demanding remittance of the debt at once, the writer informed the destitute lady, "The interest we will not require."[52]

1. Stand Watie, Boudinot's uncle, commander, and business partner.

2. Sarah C. (Sallie) Watie, Cornelius's business partner, wife of Stand.

3. Elias Boudinot, father of E. C. Boudinot.

4. Chief John Ross, longtime leader of the Cherokees, nemesis of the Watie-Boudinot faction.

5. Saladin Watie, son of Sallie and Stand.

6. Elias Cornelius Boudinot

CHAPTER 6

Railroad Man

H. Craig Miner calls the events of 1865 and 1866 the "hinge" on which the fortunes of the Five Civilized Tribes swung in their relationship with white corporate interests. [1] This relationship, of course, came to determine the fate of the Native nations themselves, culminating in their dissolution early in the next century. At the time, however, most people did not perceive the turning of the historical hinge, least of all many of the participants in the process. Boudinot, it may be argued, was one of the few Indians who did see the swing; his pronouncements, both public and private, and his actions make this clear. His early years working for the railroad in New Hampshire helped him to see and understand the fervor and sense of destiny that impelled those in the forefront of the expansionist movement driving American society. More important, however, was his intimacy with the white power brokers during his experiences in Washington and Richmond. As an outsider looking in and yearning to join the inner circle, Boudinot came to know the dynamics—political, economic, and emotional—that powered the white locomotive bearing down on Indian Territory.

Cornelius Boudinot was involved in one of the key issues facing the Cherokees and other tribes of Indian Territory after the Civil War: the coming of the railroads. It is generally acknowledged that the expansion of railroads across the American West hastened the demise of the lifeways of the people who lived there by rapidly transporting settlers to take their land, soldiers with the latest weapons to defeat them when they resisted, and microorganisms to infect them physically before resistance could be built up gradually. Instead of fighting the railroads or attempting to stall their movement west, Boudinot welcomed them, working closely with the people and corporations bent on laying track up and down and across the continent. His decision to cast his lot with the railroads embroiled him in one of the hottest controversies of the time. As time when on, his close dealings with railroad adherents led him into other areas of contentious debate among not only the Cherokees but the other inhabitants of Indian Territory as well. These issues were the labor permit system and town lot speculation.

Boudinot advocated railroads in the Cherokee Nation early. He had introduced a bill in Congress in 1868 to incorporate "A Central Indian Railroad Company, to be owned and operated by the Indians of Oklahoma."[2] This bill did not get very far because the railroad interests saw as anathema a competing line, the profits from which would line pockets other than their own.

With the end of the Civil War, the federal government and many business and commercial interests were able to redirect their attention to western expansion. While the transportation medium, the railroad, was ready to roll, the movement could not get up a full head of steam until the Native inhabitants of the western lands could be dealt with. For many of the tribes that found themselves in the way of the juggernaut, the result was removal, a continuation of the process that had "cleared" in turn the Southeast, the old Northwest Territories, Iowa, and Missouri. The first groups slated for removal after the war were those who still inhabited parts of Kansas, some of whom had been settled there upon their removal from Iowa, Illinois, and Wisconsin. A key provision of the postwar treaty with the Cherokees was the settlement of many of these groups within Indian Territory on lands ceded by the tribe, generally west of ninety-six degrees, in the Cherokee Outlet, or Strip. The treaty provision called for compensation for the loss of land, money that was to be kept in trust funds for the Nation. Some Indian groups, like the Delawares, treated directly with the Cherokees and worked out the terms of their land purchase and of the political status of their people.[3]

Another impediment to white western expansion that needed to be disposed of was the area known as the Cherokee Neutral Lands in southeastern Kansas. A twenty-five-mile-wide tract of eight hundred thousand acres, this prime farm- and ranch land extended fifty miles north of the Cherokee Nation along the Missouri border. Ceded to the Cherokees in the 1835 removal treaty, it was now seen as an "unnatural" extension of the Cherokee Nation, one eyed by prospective settlers, speculators, and corporate interests. While the issue of Indian removal from Kansas and the plains as well as the disposal of the Neutral

Lands had been addressed in principle by the 1866 treaty, both matters had yet to be carried out.

The clearing away of these two impediments to white expansion had enormous repercussions for the Civilized Tribes, especially the Cherokees. The most obvious result was that lands previously closed to white settlement were opened, bringing European Americans to proximity across their northern boundary. The Cherokee Nation now found itself abutted by Kansas on the north and Missouri and Arkansas on the east, with Texas not far from its southern line. All these neighbors were soon casting envious glances at the Cherokee's "unused" tracts of land, timber, and other natural resources. As energy built for the westward explosion that was to come, pressure for a corresponding southward expansion grew as well, as whites in Kansas, Missouri, and other sections of the Midwest began to think of linking their territories with those on the Gulf of Mexico.

The second result of the removal of Kansas Indians to Cherokee territory and the sale of the Neutral Lands was just as far-reaching if not so obvious. This was the disposal of the funds the Cherokee Nation and the other Civilized Tribes received in trust as a result of the agreements that settled these matters and of the funds received by the removed tribes for their land in Kansas. This money, held in trust by the federal government, was sometimes invested by the Office of Indian Affairs directly in financial instruments issued by the railroads and often in state and U.S. bonds issues that guaranteed corporate financing of ventures involved in western expansion. As Miner points out, both the Cherokee National Fund and the Orphan Fund were invested in bonds supporting the Union Pacific Railroad, which at the time was cutting timber illegally on Delaware land in Kansas. Muscogee and Chickasaw funds were likewise invested in bonds pledged to support railroad expansion.[4]

Boudinot was aware of the expansionist pressures that were being generated and dreamed of turning it to his own advantage and to that of his people. In the first years after the Civil War, he saw himself as a Cherokee leader. Had he not served in that capacity as a soldier, delegate to Confederate Congress, and later in two delegations to Washington? This tendency toward public service manifested itself in two ways, the first his attempt to organize a railroad owned and operated by Cherokees and the second his plan for tribal educational and economic reform. Later, as attacks against him from within the Cherokee Nation accelerated, his altruistic tendencies noticeably and probably understandably waned.

There is no doubt, however, that Cornelius was an opportunist, a man obsessed with making a fortune and improving his position. He was driven by the idea of securing his place in an inner circle of wealth and power that he saw himself just outside. He saw that there were fortunes to be made by those who could recognize opportunity and who were willing to take advantage of it. He knew the top players—the railroad men, the politicians, and the corporate executive—and avidly, longingly wished to join them as an equal. From 1865 on, Boudinot saw the hinge swinging and tried to align himself to catch its momentum. During his lifetime, many Cherokees and others castigated him as a traitor to his people, one who sold out the values and principles of his nation for personal gain. Indeed, many historians, in spite of the eyepiece of time and distance to help them focus, have characterized him as a mixed-blood opportunist out of touch with the Indian side of his heritage. But Boudinot did not see his urge for personal wealth and power as incompatible with his desire to serve his people. He rightly saw that one must be in a position to act before effective action may be taken; this is always true, but especially in the war-torn Cherokee Nation of the late 1860s.

In his desire to take advantage of the intensified interest in Cherokee lands and resources after the Civil War, Boudinot was not alone, no matter how he has been portrayed as a lone-wolf lackey for white interests, hoping for a few crumbs from the tables of the railroad builders and politicians. On the contrary, many Cherokees, including some of the most powerful, joined him in championing railroad construction in Indian territory, the private owner-ship of land, and the sale of "surplus" lands and commodities. For example, while the introduction of the railroad into the Cherokee Nation has been portrayed as a struggle of whites against Indians in which, once again, the Indians lost, the situation was a good bit more complicated than that, as Miner points out. The Cherokee legislature in 1866 passed a resolution requesting that railroads be built in the Nation, doubtless bringing joy into the hearts of the white expansionists and confounding the self-styled protectors of the Indians back east. [5] In the negotiations for the 1866 treaties among the Cherokees, Choctaws, Chickasaws, and Seminoles, the delegations submitted proposals for broad provisions for the entry of railroads into Indian Territory, including land grants, autonomy in construction, and schemes for Indians owning stock in the transportation corporations. [6] Many of the Cherokees considered these actions to be astute moves that at once demonstrated their high degree of "civilization," always a point of pride in the Nation, and at the same time shored up their efforts at economic reconstruction after the war's devastation. Other examples abound. Miner reports that in October 1866 the Cherokee

National Council tried to take advantage of the land lost to plains tribes in the 1866 treaty by guaranteeing a half-million-dollar stock subscription by the tribe in the Union Pacific, Southern Branch, Railroad (UPSB). The subscription would be paid for with monies paid by the United States to settle plains tribes on Cherokee lands west of ninety-six degrees. Under the terms of the agreement, the Cherokees would not only become stockholders in the railroad but would have two seats on its board of directors.[7] The council gave itself an option to buy more stock over the next three years. Funds thus raised by the railroad were to be used in construction, and the corporation was allowed to use building materials from Cherokee land to be paid for in stock and cash. The council also authorized the chief to make a similar deal with an east-west railroad when it became feasible.[8] The council action needed ratification by the Department of the Interior, which did not materialize. Within Cornelius's own Ridge-Watie-Boudinot faction, too, there were many standing ready to profit from the whites' expansion into Indian Territory, as we shall see.

When Boudinot cast his lot with the UPSB, then, it was not without precedent and decidedly not the act of a lone wolf preying on his people. The Union Pacific, Southern Branch, Railroad (later to be renamed the Missouri, Kansas, and Texas) held its first stockholders' meeting in Emporia, Kansas, on February 13, 1866, according to V. V. Masterson's history of the enterprise.[9] Some important events followed fast on the heels of this organizational meeting. Just a few days later, on February 23, Congress passed a bill called "An Act Providing for the Sale of Public Lands, to Aid in the Construction of Certain Railroads," which "donated" funds from the sale of half a million acres of public lands to the ten-day-old UPSB and three other upstart railroads. The congressional act was passed during the treaty negotiations between the federal government and the two Cherokee delegations discussed in chapter 4, obviously in anticipation of a provision under debate that would grant railroad right-of-ways through the Cherokee Nation. The day before the 1866 treaty was ratified on July 27, 1866, Congress passed another bill, entitled "An Act Granting Lands to the State of Kansas, to Aid in the Construction of a Southern Branch of the Union Pacific Railway and Telegraph, from Fort Riley, Kansas, to Fort Smith, Arkansas." The act gave the railroad five sections of land per mile of track, but more importantly it granted right-of-way through Indian Territory "with the consent of the Indians."

The granting of railroad right-of-ways through Indian land was a linchpin issue that had a bearing on other important matters. Right-of-way was almost always attached to land grants in the West after the Civil War; while the right-of-way secured a legal passage, the land grants provided the money to finance the railroads and to guarantee a profit to stockholders through sales to settlers and ranchers. Settlers and ranchers, in turn, demanded political domains separate from Indian jurisdiction, that is, territorial governments. The land grants themselves, of course, depended on the extinguishment of Indian title. In practice, a Native American nation checkerboarded with sections of land to which title had been relinquished was a nation destined for extinction.

In October 1867, President N. S. Goss and Secretary P. B. Maxon of the UPSB set out for Tahlequah to secure the consent of the Cherokee National Council for a right-of-way through the Nation. By the end of the month Goss reported that the railroad had reached an agreement with the Cherokees. The National Council had appointed a committee including William Potter Ross (elected principal chief upon the death of John Ross), Lewis Downing, S. H. Benge, Daniel H. Ross, and Redbird Six Killer to negotiate with the railroad representatives. The pact, which pledged the Indians to provide the railroad with $500,000 in exchange for stock with options for more stock when the Cherokee Outlet was sold, passed by a unanimous vote of both branches of the council. The agreement also provided that the Cherokees would have two directors on the railroad's board and that the railroad would have a one-hundred-foot right-of-way. No sections of land along the track were ceded, although this was normally part of such agreements. While the Cherokees had agreed to the plan, it still needed the consent of the commissioner of Indian Affairs. The federal government heard vehement objections from the southern Cherokees, who were concerned that the deal would enrich Ross and his friends, as well as from many in the tribe who were opposed to selling any land. The contract was not approved by the commissioner, and in December 1867 the council declared it void.[10] The affair makes it clear that the Cherokee Nation was anything but adamantine in its opposition to railroads.

Having failed to secure the right-of-way through Cherokee lands, the cash-strapped UPSB cast its bait in other financial waters as it began its desultory way southward toward Indian Territory from Junction City, Kansas. Four Kansas counties along the putative route subscribed $730,000 in thirty-year bonds, but stock sales were slow due to the uncertainty of success. By the fall of 1869 the railroad had laid only five miles of track.

One of the reasons for the difficulty in raising funds lay with the competition. James F. Joy, who had purchased the Neutral Lands for a down payment of $75,000 in a series of shady deals, turned his attention to building a railroad that would connect Kansas City with the Gulf.[11] Joy had been instrumental in the development of a series of railroads that formed a line from New York City through Detroit and Chicago to Kansas City, and he was poised as a key player in the westward explosion. He now turned his eyes southward, gaining control of two railroads in about the same stage of development as the UPSB, the Kansas and Neosho Valley and the Leavenworth, Lawrence and Fort Gibson. UPSB investors grew understandably perturbed at this news. At the annual stockholders' meeting of June 24, 1868, two figures who were to become important to Boudinot's future as well as to that of the entire region emerged: Levi Parsons and Robert S. Stevens.

Parsons was a New Yorker from an old New England family who made his fortune in California during the gold rush as a lawyer, judge, and businessman. After the Civil War he moved back to New York, but sensing the extent of the westward movement that was gathering momentum, he kept his eyes in that direction for any opportunities. On Wall Street he organized the Land Grant Railway and Trust Company, which in 1868, recognizing a chance to connect Kansas with the Gulf, bought controlling shares in the young yet moribund UPSB. Parsons reorganized the officers of the railroad, taking general control himself. As his field commander he appointed Robert S. Stevens. Another New Yorker, Stevens as a young lawyer moved to Lecompton, the early capital of Kansas Territory, and became involved in real estate. He arranged land sales for the areas vacated by Kansas Indians when they moved to the corner of Indian Territory just northwest of the Cherokee Nation. Parsons recognized Stevens as a man who knew the lay of the land and who was hungry to profit from conditions there.

The 1866 treaty provided for two railroads through the Cherokee Nation, one from north to south and one from east to west. It was decided not to grant a right-of-way to any particular railroad, as Goss had tried to secure earlier, but to award the franchise to whichever of the competing roads reached the Nation first. With the arrival on the scene of Joy and the Parsons-Stevens combine, the race began in earnest. Competition was narrowed to Joy's Missouri River, Fort Scott and Gulf (the former Kansas and Neosho Valley Railway) and the Missouri, Kansas, and Texas Railway Company (formerly Union Pacific, Southern Branch). Joy's Border Tier Railroad, as it was commonly known, was working southward along the Missouri border, while the Parsons-Stevens outfit, nicknamed the Katy, was situated to the west and laying track in the same direction. Joy had a second railroad—the Leavenworth, Lawrence and Galveston—also in the race for the land grant, but as the situation developed it pulled out in favor of its sibling.

It was at this point that Boudinot became involved in earnest. As a delegate in both 1866 and 1868, he had helped negotiate many of the points of the treaties and was thus well versed in the fine points of their stipulations. More importantly, he knew the men involved and what their interests were. Like any good negotiator, he was aware of the real desires of all the participants. As we have seen, he recognized the desire on the part of Harlan and others to allot Indian lands in severalty and to extend federal and state jurisdiction to tribal lands. Cornelius understood that the impetus for this was to open up so-called surplus land for settlement and exploitation. He knew as well the extent of the powerful interests arrayed against the Indian nations. Boudinot felt the momentum of change and was determined not to be left in its lurch. His position in 1868 was roughly analogous to that of his father and the Ridges in 1835 back in Georgia: understand the situation and make the best of it. The modus operandi that Cornelius was to follow for the rest of his life took shape at this time. It can be stated simply: take advantage of what you know about where events are leading and make a profit from it.

So at this point, Boudinot reviewed what he knew about the present situation. He saw that the former relative isolation of the Cherokee Nation was over, given the demands of the postwar treaties. It was a matter of either adapting to the larger, more powerful society or death. He knew, too, that very soon one or the other of the railroads would come down into the Cherokee Nation from the north, creating an artery that would, among other things, carry cattle from Texas up to Kansas and beef out to Chicago and points east. Boudinot seized upon that knowledge and determined to place himself in an advantageous position. Accordingly, he and Stand Watie took advantage while they could of Cherokee laws that governed the ownership of improvements on communal land and erected fence on a prime piece of grazing land, well watered by Russell Creek, a few miles south of the Kansas line. The two Cherokees planned to make Russell Creek a great cattle center, a feedlot five miles square, according to the *Southern Kansas Advance*, where they would receive cattle driven from Texas and either buy them or hold them for their owners, wintering the cows or fattening them up before their ride to the packinghouses of Kansas City or Chicago. The editor of the *Advance* deemed the plan a good one—for the nearby town of Chetopa, for the cattlemen, for the packing companies, and for the feedlot operators.[12] Boudinot planned to fence in an area five miles square as his main enclosure, thus taking in around sixteen thousand acres. Within the main enclosure, he could easily build feeding pens or corrals for holding cattle until they could be loaded in railroad cars at a siding along the main track.

It was a good plan. Water was plentiful, the grazing promised to be excellent on the lush prairie grasses, and transportation was on the way. A testimony to Boudinot's foresight is that a visitor to the site today finds hundreds of cows feeding in enclosures beside an impressive array of support structures and, of course, the railroad.

The scheme was possible because of the way the Cherokee law provided for individuals to farm and ranch on land held in communal trust. Cherokee citizens were allowed to stake a ranch or a farm on unoccupied land anywhere in the Nation. Citizens could build on the land, and the "improvements" were their property, which they then could rent out to tenants. But if the site was unoccupied for two years, the improvements reverted to the public domain. Boudinot's improvements at the Russell Creek site, while being perhaps more extensive than usual, followed the Cherokee custom.

Of course, the Russell Creek operation would only be successful if the Katy beat out the Border Tier Railroad to the Cherokee Nation. Cornelius knew that he needed to do whatever he could to make this possible. As part of his intelligence-gathering operation on the progress of the advancing railroads, he had befriended Bob Stevens through one of the Katy agents, Bob Greenwell. Greenwell's job ostensibly was to scout the route the railroad would take along with the engineers. In reality, Greenwell seemed to spend his time keeping an eye on the opposition and conducting a bit of sabotage now and then. But Boudinot and Stevens hit it off, each recognizing in the other a man of talent who would go to great lengths to achieve his ends. Boudinot gained Stevens's confidence, and in return he and Watie, the old ranger and guerrilla fighter, pledged to aid Greenwell in his scouting the Border Tier Railroad. For his part, Stevens promised to do what he could to ensure the success of the Russell Creek operation, in particular, to make sure the Cherokees got the siding they needed between the main line and the enclosure.

When Stevens took over as field supervisor for the Katy, he called in his foreman, John Skullin, a tough Irishman who was an effective leader of the railroad's gandy dancers and navvies, many of whom had emigrated from Skullin's native isle. Stevens told Skullin that he was pulling out all the stops in order to beat Joy to the Cherokee line, even if it meant cutting corners on the quality of the work. Instead of shoulders on the roadbed, he said, where possible lay the bed just to the ends of the ties. "We can come back later and fix it," he said, "after we cross the line." He told Skullin to push the men, double the gangs, work more shifts, promising bonuses and easier going once the goal was reached. For his part, Skullin promised his boss a mile of track a day. Bad weather hampered their efforts for the next weeks, but the Katy crews slogged on. [13] The Border Tier had an easier time of it coming down the former Neutral Lands because there were fewer bridges and culverts to construct. However, their track was headed directly for the Quapaw Nation. Joy expected to be granted right-of-way through the Quapaw lands west to the Cherokee Nation, but he did not know that permission would not be forthcoming.

As the Border Tier neared Baxter Springs on the Quapaw line, Boudinot helped Greenwell scout. As they watched the rival line progress rapidly despite the bad weather, a plan began to form in their minds. When Joy's men got to the line, they were indeed poised to enter Indian Territory, but they were still at least fifteen miles from the Cherokee Nation if the road turned due west, further if it angled southwest down through the Quapaw Nation. The task was to make the Border Tier people believe that they had won the race once they were south of Baxter Springs. Judge Parsons took it upon himself to convince Joy of this, while Boudinot and Greenwell took on the job of spreading the rumor on the construction site. Parsons was able to reach Joy through one of his contacts, Senator S. C. Pomeroy. It was an easy task for Boudinot to talk to the construction gang leaders as Greenwell worked the liquor outlets that trailed the railhead. They knew the ruse had succeeded once the Border Tier track reached south of the town. Joy and his people were convinced they had won the race to the border and would be awarded the franchise for the north-south railway through the Cherokee Nation. However, they were ignoring two important facts: first, they were nearing the line separating Kansas from Quapaw lands, not Cherokee territory; and second, the nearest point to access the Cherokee Nation legally, according to the Land Grant Act, was "in the Valley of the Neosho," seventeen miles away.

The citizens of the little Kansas border town did not realize any of this. Baxter Springs put on the largest festivity in its history to celebrate the event, the coming of the railroad that would connect it, so they thought, with the large metropolises of the East and Midwest as well as with the lands and cities that lay on the Gulf of Mexico. This was a party for all of Kansas, not just the sleepy little town, as dignitaries flooded in to commemorate the event inflated by Pomeroy, Greenwell, Boudinot, and James F. Joy's ego. Invitations were sent to Leavenworth and Lawrence, Kansas City and Topeka, to smaller towns in Kansas and to nearby Missouri. Joy provided a ten-car train for visiting dignitaries including newspaper people and politicians who left Kansas City in the morning headed south, arriving in Baxter Springs early in the evening. The travelers were greeted by local officials and a brass band, blazing bonfires and booming cannons, and were escorted to the town square. There they were regaled by a "war dance" conducted by some Quapaws, Senecas, and Cherokees, doubtless recruited by Boudinot. The Indians having thus expressed their great joy at the coming of the railroad, the rest of the party adjourned to a hall for a "less aboriginal" dance, as the editor of the *Kansas City Commonwealth* put it in his story on the carryings-on.[14] The next day, local citizens, the entourage from Kansas City, and the work crews gathered in a grove a half mile south of town where a speakers' stand had been erected and a barbecue pit dug for the more polite society, while makeshift bars stood in the background to dispense whiskey to the hardworking laborers. As the Border Tier men toasted the occasion with liquor provided by the railroad, the formal ceremonies began. Various dignitaries spoke on the occasion, including the Kansas attorney general, who praised the great transportation that the new railroad had become a part of. As speech followed speech and the day became hotter and longer, the crews drank on. By nightfall most of the men were deliriously drunk, and they drank on with whiskey provided by Boudinot, Watie, and Greenwell, who spent Katy funds lavishly.[15] The party spilled over into the following days, unchecked by the railroad bosses, since in their minds the race had been won, and all that remained was a prosaic trek through Indian country to Texas. Masterson says that "the cow town blew the lid right off, and in the blow Joy's railroad crews were scattered like straws before a Kansas cyclone."[16]

The advantage now was clearly with the Katy. Boudinot advised Stevens to take advantage of the confused state of affairs in the Border Tier camp by buying up that railroad's crews before the construction bosses had a chance to regroup. Hire them, Boudinot urged, whether they were needed or not, and get on with the job. "You are still thirty miles from the Cherokee line. If Joy is able to get his house in order, he may beat you yet." Stevens agreed and ordered Skullin to pick up the pace even more. Furthermore, he announced, he would take command at the end of the track personally.[17] Before that would happen, however, Stevens had to report to the Katy stockholders at their annual meeting in Emporia on May 18. Significantly, Levi Parsons did not attend the gathering.

Stevens's news was well received by the stockholders. However, there was one discordant note, a complaint by Cherokee officials that would have little effect on the railroad's plans but would have a significant impact on Boudinot's. The reason Parsons was not in Kansas at the time was that he was in Washington appearing before Secretary of the Interior Jacob Dolson Cox. The Cherokee delegation in the capital had complained about working parties entering the Nation and grading the line. The secretary of the interior ruled that the Cherokees did not have to recognize the Katy's right to intrude before the land-grant race was won and the award made. Accordingly, Parsons ordered Stevens to remove his men from the Cherokee Nation. Stevens was perplexed because he knew the only men in the Nation were a few ostensibly working over some hard spots just south of the line. Stevens knew that they were really working at Russell Creek to help Boudinot lay out cattle yards and feeder lots. The Cherokee delegation doubtless knew the men's real work assignment, too, otherwise they would not have carried a complaint about a handful of men in a remote area all the way to the secretary of the interior. Stevens explained the situation to Boudinot and ordered his men back north.[18] Boudinot shook his head, perhaps surprised by the depth of animosity for his party and family still harbored by rival Cherokees, and surely stung by the personal turn the hatred had taken.

Feverishly, work continued on the Katy line. Joy finally realized that he was miles from the authorized entry point, but he had reached Indian Territory after all. He made an appeal to Secretary Cox for the franchise on this basis. Cox ruled that the railroad that received the franchise would be the one that entered the Cherokee Nation without "crossing the reservation of any other Indian tribe."[19] When Cox's ruling was brought to President Grant, he approved his secretary's action. So the Border Tier men had no other option but to regroup and head west, hoping to beat their rivals to the crossing. Bad weather hampered both track-laying efforts and particularly slowed building bridges over swollen streams and laying culverts in soggy ground. Stevens supervised his crews' work personally, cajoling, bribing, and threatening. [20] As the railheads came closer together, fights broke out between crews until supervisors ordered their men to stay away from each other. [21] In the end, though, the Katy crews pushed their railhead into the Cherokee Nation first, completing the last twenty-six miles of track and two bridges in twelve days. The railroad reached the town of Chetopa on Saturday, June 4, 1870.

Stevens had his aides telegraph invitations for a ceremony to reporters, legislators, friends of the railroad, and, of course, to the governor, who had to certify that the track was sound. Town officials from Chetopa were determined to outshine Baxter Springs with their celebration, and when the dignitaries rolled into town on Sunday they were greeted with all the fanfare the citizens could muster. But the real celebration was on Monday, during which the rail into the Cherokee Nation would be spiked down. Monday morning the visitors and townspeople boarded the special train for the end of the track some two miles south of town. With flags flying and youngsters hanging onto the cars, the train made the short trip to where Stevens and his workers were waiting with Boudinot, Stand Watie, and a delegation of Cherokees nearby.

The ceremony at the railhead was relatively brief. The master of ceremonies greeted the crowd, then read a poem called "Rivet the Last Neosho Rail," written for the occasion by a Kansas editor. At that point, a forty-five-pound iron rail, manufactured in Sheffield, England, was lowered into place. Stevens then stepped to the rail and was handed a hammer as a workman bent to place the spike. With a few whacks of the hammer, Stevens drove in last spike on the Kansas side. After the applause died down, he delivered a short speech on the rigors of the enterprise, the great rewards to be shared by whites and Indians alike, and the rivers still to be crossed. He ended his oration with a promise to continue until his road crosses the Rio Grande, "till our engine stands panting in the palaces of the Monteczumas and the halls of the Aztecs." With these words, the crowd erupted into shouts of applause.

Then it was Boudinot's turn. Savoring the moment, he stepped up to the rail and received the mallet from Stevens. Then raising it above his head, he brought it forcefully down, driving in the first railroad spike in Indian Territory. Cornelius, too, had a speech to make, short and concise: "My own people, along with the Creeks, Choctaws, Chickasaws and Seminoles have always been pre-eminent to the wild Indians of the plains by virtue of what we have learned by contact with the white man. I stand in no fear or dread of the railroad. It will make my people richer and happier. I feel that my people are bound closer together and to the government by these iron bands."[22] In a way this was a brave speech. Not very far from the spot he stood on was his and Watie's defunct tobacco factory, raided by the authorities months before because of the big-city corporations' greed and jealousy. But in the end it was the old song, the words of his father speaking to the people of Boston and Philadelphia and New York, the anthem of the "civilized" Indian that was to echo for the next hundred years.

His speech over, Boudinot, Watie, and their fellow Cherokees then joined the other dignitaries and boarded the VIP cars behind the new diamond-stacked locomotive for the short trip to Chetopa. Once in town, they all met at the hotel to receive the congratulations of Kansas governor James M. Harvey and the Central and Southern District Indian superintendents, representatives of the federal government.

Now came the task of extending the railroad to the Red River and Texas through the Indian nations. Steel was shipped down the completed road from St. Louis, but ties for the roadbed needed to come from local timber. This was no little item, since it took twenty-six hundred nine-foot ties for each mile of track laid. The Cherokee Nation controlled the natural resources in its territory, including timber not harvested by its citizens for their own use, so a deal needed to be struck with the Nation. The tie business came to be a very lucrative one for many enterprising Cherokees from all parts of the political spectrum. [23] The railroad was very specific about the quality of the ties, describing first-class ties this way: "White, Post, or Burr Oak, Locust, Black Walnut, Red Cherry, or Coffee Beam, ends square, at least 7" thick, bark removed, no scar marks, and piled in perpendicular piles 6–30' from right-of-way." First-class ties fetched forty-five cents, while culls brought only twenty-five. [24]

Tie suppliers were required to post a thousand-dollar bond before they could sell the timber to the railroad, but the bond could be secured by the signature of another citizen of good standing in the Nation. Thus one supplier would sign for another, and the favor was returned. The bond was in place to ensure collection of a five-cent tax that the Cherokee Nation had imposed on each tie. The tie tax was a good source of income for the Nation because of the sheer volume of timber involved. S. H. Mayes, for example, the sheriff of Cooweescoowee District, collected $3,672.80 for the quarter ending June 30, 1882. Some individuals contracted to supply ten thousand ties at a time. From time to time there was difficulty collecting the tax. When it was not paid, the Nation doubled it; if it still was not forthcoming, the contractor's license was not renewed. The Nation's rationale was that since the wood was coming from the common domain, nonpaying contractors were stealing from the people. Soon, tie contracts were drawn up so that the railroads kept back a nickel per tie from the contract price and turned the tax over to the Nation. Boudinot's name appears in the records several times, mostly because a contractor whom he had signed a bond for had not paid the tie tax. There is evidence that Cornelius was involved as a contractor himself, however, and we should be surprised if he were not. But for the most part, his eyes were on bigger prizes.

When the railroad was run through Boudinot's site at Russell Creek, he was still busy with the problems at his tobacco factory. The Russell Creek stockyards and the tobacco enterprise had a direct connection in the person of Augustus C. Larkin, a white citizen of Arkansas and Boudinot's colleague. Boudinot had interested Larkin in his tobacco operation with its promise of high profits. With few assets himself, the Cherokee had turned to Larkin for loans to help finance the purchase of machinery, tobacco, and other raw materials and to cover overhead expenses for the first months. Reluctant to give Larkin an interest in the tobacco firm—he was already beholden to Watie, Polson, and Washbourne—Boudinot offered as collateral a half interest in the Russell Creek stock operation. Larkin had long cast an envious eye across the border at the prime cattle country of the northern Cherokee Nation, at the lush, well-watered prairies and abundant timber for the construction of structures and enclosures. The Russell Creek operation looked like a dream come true to the white man. But how could he take possession of land in the Cherokee Nation without being shot as an intruder?

As usual, Boudinot had figured the angles and had all the answers. Just as he had used the Cherokee customs and laws on improvements to set up Russell Creek in the first place, he now turned to the labor permit laws to accommodate Larkin and, of course, himself. After the Civil War, the Cherokees had evolved a system by which white men were allowed into the Nation to work on farms and ranches. The demand for this labor arose out of the devastation wrought by the war, both in terms of infrastructure that needed to be replaced and in terms of the terrible human loss. A large percentage of the male population had been killed either in the fighting or by disease, causing a labor shortage. Widows and others who needed help in plowing the fields and tending the animals turned to workers from the areas close to the Nation for help. Cherokee officials, already plagued with squatters and intruders, knew that this practice must be regulated in some manner. The result was a system by which citizens applied for permits to hire specific white men (no blacks were eligible) for specific purposes. The citizens paid a nominal fee, and the permit was renewable as long as everyone played by the rules.

According to William McLoughlin, the system was soon abused, mostly by the former slaveholders in the Nation. These people took advantage of the law to build improvements on communal land and then hired sharecroppers or tenants under the permit system, thus building bigger and bigger farming and ranching operations for themselves. The smaller, mostly full-blood farmers who felt that these practices perverted the traditional communal system resented this. [25] The situation was such that it opened old wounds between the Ridge-Watie-Boudinot party and the followers of John Ross; in fact, the permit issue became an integral one in the debate between the factions who favored allotment and a territorial government and those who were against it. Boudinot was not alone in his exploitation of the permit system, but he pushed it beyond the breaking point. This was inevitable, especially given the fact that his and his party's enemies were in control in Tahlequah.

Cornelius secured a permit for Larkin to work for Boudinot as a farmer and cattle herder. However, Larkin in effect became the Cherokee's partner in the enterprise. Both men, it seems, were banking on federal action to open up Indian Territory to white settlement. After all, once the railroad had penetrated, it was logical to expect an influx of farmers and ranchers to occupy the "surplus" lands held by the Indians. Larkin, in fact, was convinced that passage of specific congressional legislation to open the country was imminent. The legislation, which he identified as "the Parker bill," of course never passed, so the Arkansan was in a vulnerable position when, after some years, Boudinot failed to renew the permit. Cornelius knew that resentment in the Nation was growing over abuses in the permit system, and after protesting to the federal government over new, strict rules governing the practice by the Cherokee government, he saw the futility in applying for Larkin's permit.

By that time, he and Larkin were operating separate operations in the same area. Boudinot had become interested in raising sheep on the Russell Creek land, making arrangements to buy the animals from a Kansas shepherd. At one time he had around seven hundred sheep grazing there, with an eye to increasing the flock to a thousand. [26] By this time the Cherokee Nation had passed laws imposing a tax on cattle grazing on Cherokee land not owned by citizens. Larkin now found himself in a vulnerable position, as Boudinot had not renewed his permit. In 1874 Cherokee officials tried to collect five hundred dollars in taxes on Larkin's cattle, and when payment was not forthcoming they confiscated his herd. After some wrangling, Larkin paid the taxes, but his cattle were not returned, since they had been stolen while they were being held for payment. He then made a depredation claim against the Cherokee Nation. Chief William Potter Ross appointed a special committee to investigate the matter, but when the case dragged on, Larkin appealed it to the Department of the Interior. At this point, the almost comical case of one of Boudinot's greedy white colleagues getting his comeuppance became something more serious; because of the appeal to the federal government, the Cherokee Nation's jurisdiction and sovereignty had been called into question. [27] Larkin's case languished in the halls of government until it was thrown out in 1882. By that time Larkin was back in Arkansas, but Boudinot continued over time to ranch the Russell Creek operation, although it never reached the grand extent that he dreamed of.

The theft of Larkin's cattle was eventually traced to Andrew and James

Barker (two white men from Missouri), Boudinot's colleague James M. Bell, and several other men. They were accused of stealing 106 cattle, 3 mules, and 2 horses with a total value of $3,450, but when the case came to a grand jury the indictment handed down said they stole 15 cattle, 6 cows, 20 calves, and 34 hogs, for a total value of $1,074 plus $95 in currency.[28] Larkin apparently tried to implicate Cornelius in the affair, but no indictment was handed down.[29] The trial was a tumultuous one, with the Barkers resisting arrest at one point and various witnesses giving conflicting testimony. In December 1876, Judge Parker's court at Fort Smith found the Barkers guilty, but Bell was acquitted.

Cornelius's difficulties with Larkin and his continuing problems with the tobacco enterprise did not deter him, however. He was convinced that the changing scene in Indian Territory meant financial success for those who could take advantage of the right opportunities. His letters are full of an almost desperate optimism, as if his greatest nightmare was that he might miss a chance and lose a fortune. As it turned out, he missed few chances but still won no fortune. Boudinot's flirtation with the railroad continued as he began to contemplate the southward progress of the Katy and that of its counterpart, the Atlantic and Pacific, as it headed west from Arkansas.

In the 1866 treaty the Cherokees had agreed to two railroads through their land. As we have seen, the Katy had won the race for the north-south route, but nothing like that competition took place for the east-west road. Instead, Congress granted Atlantic and Pacific Central Division 49.5 million acres in public lands from its starting point in Missouri to the Pacific, including a grant in Indian Territory. The Indian Territory grant was especially generous because, for one thing, the Indians had not been consulted, and for another, the grant was twice the usual size. But this was the era of the transcontinental railroad, heralded by white businessmen, settlers, and investors alike, a national desideratum for people of all political persuasions. Congress was certain that the small matter of Indian title could be cleared up with little difficulty. When the Atlantic and Pacific started its survey and applied to the Cherokees to rubberstamp Congress's action, Principal Chief Lewis Downing refused and demanded the immediate withdrawal of the survey crews.[30] Particularly galling to the Cherokees, it seems, was the railroad's request for a loan to help build its track on Indian land. The Atlantic and Pacific officials backed off in the face of this defiance and began negotiations. In December 1870 they reached an accommodation with the Cherokee Nation when its National Council passed an act giving the east-west road the same right-of-way privileges that it had granted the Katy. A little wiser as a result of their dealings with the Katy, the tribe also demanded a $500,000 bond to be posted by the company with the Department of the Interior. This was done to ensure that the railroad would adhere to its contract to construct only one track (it had surveyed several routes) and that it would compensate the Cherokees for raw materials taken from their land. By now the tie business was a lucrative industry for many Cherokees. And so the Atlantic and Pacific began its east-west route through the Cherokee Nation. Actually, it was more a northeast-southwest route as it angled down from Springfield, Missouri, crossing Shawnee and Wyandotte lands before entering Cherokee territory.

Cornelius, of course, was privy to this information, including the railroad's proposed route. Since he knew the route of the Katy, Boudinot could predict where the tracks would cross and where a great railroad center would arise. According to an article written sometime later for the *Indian Chieftain*, he and his partner James Bell, along with Dr. Polson and another member of the Watie faction, Johnson Thompson, fenced in some two miles square at the site, again taking advantage of the Cherokee custom of citizens erecting improvements.[31] The group thus hoped to control the junction and the market for lots in the town that was certain to spring up at this important shipping point. Boudinot planned to name the town Vinita, after his friend Vinnie Ream. He had first met Vinnie in Fort Smith before the Civil War, and now he visited her in Washington DC, where she worked as a sculptor. As the plan developed, however, the Cherokee National Council, controlled by the group's rivals from the old Ross party, passed a law restricting the sale of town lots to the Cherokee national government or to its licensees. This law, passed in 1870, reserved along all railroads passing through the nation an area of a square mile, including all railroad stations. Lots along the railroads were sold under terms previously granted to purchasers of lots in Fort Gibson and Tahlequah. Terms included the provision for occupant title only; that is, mineral rights remained with the Cherokee Nation. In addition, the principal chief was empowered to appoint a town commissioner to sell town lots to citizens of the Cherokee Nation who bid highest in a thirty-day period following a sale notice in the *Cherokee Advocate*.[32] According to the *Chieftain*, supporters of the council tore down Boudinot and company's fences, and the putative town founders' stake in Vinita was ended. Other versions of the story are variants on this one.

Masterson's account of the founding of Vinita, for example, adds a bit more intrigue. According to it, Boudinot had fenced off his townsite in conjunction with the wishes of the Katy officials, setting up where the completed north-south track crossed the survey stacks of the Atlantic and Pacific It was Robert

Stevens's practice to control the southern terminus of his railroad by contracting with overland haulers who would bring freight from Texas to the railhead or unload freight at that point and take it down to the south. Once Boudinot had fenced off Vinita, Stevens hired another contract hauler to transport goods from other areas to the crossing point either to ship on the Katy or to store until the Atlantic and Pacific reached Vinita. Thus, Stevens was collecting shipping and storage charges even before freight was loaded on railcars. Additionally, he was trying to preempt the Atlantic and Pacific, taking away some of its sources of income before the second railroad was built to the crossing point. Boudinot and his partners evidently received a cut for taking over the spot and preventing others from starting competing shipping/storing operations. Then, once the Atlantic and Pacific crossed, Boudinot and friends could sell off town lots. Cornelius and Stevens seemed to have the situation well in hand.

Then, however, Stevens received a telegraph message from one on his men at the crossing to the effect that the Atlantic and Pacific people had begun to erect a passenger and freight house close to the Katy track. When Stevens went up the line to investigate, he found Boudinot's townsite nearly deserted; nearly everyone involved had moved to a new site three miles north, where the Atlantic and Pacific graders had crossed the Katy with the tracklayers just a couple of miles away. It was clear to Stevens that the Atlantic and Pacific management had made an agreement with several Cherokee National Council members to bypass Boudinot's fenced-off townsite and locate the crossing north of the surveyed line. The Cherokees were able to plot with Andrew Pierce, the Atlantic and Pacific chief, to set up the new town, which they named Downingville after the Cherokee principal chief. Steven's freighting and storage facilities were now situated uselessly three miles away. A great gang fight erupted at one point, with Steven's men fighting the Atlantic and Pacific's crews. When the smoke cleared, however, the town remained at the new site.[33] Animosity between the two railroads continued long after the altercation, to the extent that they even refused to synchronize schedules, causing much difficulty for those wishing to use Vinita as a transfer point. Masterson goes on to say that Boudinot cut himself, Bell, and the others in for one-third of the new town lots, but this seems unlikely.

Boudinot did come away with something, however, as the name Vinita was adopted for the new town. He also owned the town's only hotel, but that story deserves its own chapter.

CHAPTER 7

The Hotelier at Vinita

If one episode in Boudinot's life was more bizarre than all the others, it would be his tenure as owner of the Commercial Hotel. While it has its comic side, the situation is worth examining because of the light it casts on the befuddled state of jurisdiction and sovereignty at the time. Whenever the principals in the case sought redress from the governmental entities involved, the Cherokee Nation and the U.S. government, they were met with conflicting claims—or disavowal, depending on the circumstance—of jurisdiction. The case is also worth looking at because of what it demonstrates about the manipulation of the system by individuals for their own purposes, including both government officials and private citizens.

The bare bones of the case may be seen in the following outline of events. In 1873, Boudinot built a hotel at the junction of the Katy line and the Atlantic and Pacific Railroad before either had established a depot there. It was one hundred feet from the Katy tracks, thus at the edge of the right-of-way originally granted by the Nation to the railway.[1] Later the Katy built a depot nearby, putting the hotel in the right-of-way, according to the railroad. The railroad at the same time demanded the removal of all buildings within its bounds but excepted the hotel. Accordingly, it leased Boudinot the land the hotel stood on. Boudinot then leased the hotel for a share of the profits to a white man from Missouri, O. Campbell.

Later, Boudinot contracted with John R. Skinner, another white man, to lease the hotel, but also to cultivate some four hundred acres on Cherokee common land nearby. The contract called for Skinner to pay Boudinot a thousand dollars and half the profits from the hotel and farm. Skinner then leased the hotel to another white man named Edmundson and failed to work the farm, so Boudinot tried to dissolve the contract. Skinner agreed, but demanded his thousand dollars. Boudinot gave Skinner $700 and a note for $365 more to settle the contract.

Boudinot then rented the hotel to another white man named Daniel Ross. Soon the note to Skinner came due, and Boudinot arranged for Ross to pay Skinner $300 in lieu of rent. To settle the remaining $65, Cornelius sent Skinner an order for $85 on a man named Tucker. Ross, then, could not pay Skinner, so Boudinot tried to have James M. Bell take over the hotel and evict Ross for nonpayment of rent. Ross, however, turned the hotel over to Skinner, who promptly turned it over to a Cherokee, Henry Eiffert. At this point, both sides attempted to use the law to make good their conflicting claims. In the middle of the jurisdictional dispute, the hotel was torn down and the lumber diverted to other uses.

Like most of Boudinot's schemes, the hotel affair began with a good idea. Vinita, after all, was at the meeting place of the first two railroads through Indian Territory. The railroads promised to open up the region to increased commerce with the white enclaves surrounding it, thus bringing in travelers in large numbers. Sales agents, cattle buyers, and other merchants could now move back and forth easily into Indian Territory, with no need to hire horses or wagons or coaches from less-than-reliable sources to travel ill-maintained and often impassable roads. Another impasse had been removed, too, at least in the minds of the travelers. If the Indians had allowed the railroads to be built across their lands, they must be ready to welcome strangers and to interact with them. While this reasoning might be logical, it was only partly true; once the railroads had been built, the Indian nations found that they had to bolster their statutes against intruders, squatters, and interlopers in general.

At any rate, Boudinot knew that the travelers were coming and that they would demand accommodations. He knew the travelers' needs firsthand, since he was riding the trains a great deal to St. Louis, Chicago, and Washington DC and also moved around in the region, making a regular circuit around Tahlequah and Vinita in the Cherokee Nation, Parsons and other railroad towns in Kansas, and Fayetteville and Fort Smith in Arkansas. His experience told him that a hotel at Vinita would be useful to many, especially those who planned to take one railroad or the other to that spot, then transfer to the other line. His conversations with railroad men told him that a hotel would be welcomed in that quarter as well; railroad personnel were constantly moving up and down the track for various reasons and needed a comfortable stopping place.

Boudinot introduced the idea to Stevens and his managers on the Katy line and got a positive response. A hotel would make life easier for their employees and would also serve the people involved in the shipping operations Stevens had started. Given this encouragement, Boudinot set out to raise the necessary capital. Perhaps it has become clear by now that Cornelius did few things directly and was involved in few business dealings that were not connected to his other affairs. Other men of commerce and business might have looked for a lending agency to finance his planned operation, then settled the loan over an agreed span of time from hotel receipts. Certainly, the railroad's warm reception for his plan should have indicated that he could count on regular income from that source, enough to convince a bank manager to take on the risk of a startup loan. But for a number of reasons, this orthodox way of doing business was not to be. First, money was tight in Indian Territory and surrounding areas. Big spenders like the railroad itself were financed largely by bonds held by wealthy people from the East and from Europe who were attracted by the promise of huge profits and growth. Local capital was extremely hard to locate at this time as the depressed postwar economy dragged on; money was in short supply, and wages and debts were often settled in kind. Second, much of the available local capital was controlled by those Boudinot whom called his enemies. "Enemy" might be too strong a word, but it is certainly true that many in the Cherokee Nation at this time were unlikely to do Boudinot any favors, let alone wish him well. Third, his financial reputation could not have been strong in the vicinity as a result of the uncertainty brought about by the problems he was having with his tobacco venture. Finally, Boudinot seemed almost pathologically unable to let anyone know his full intentions. He operated by letting people in on small facets of his affairs, rarely letting them see the big picture. This pattern is true even when it involves those closest to him in terms of loyalty, blood, and intention: Stand Watie, his wife, Sallie, and her brother James Bell.

Raising the capital to build the hotel was not a major project, however, since it probably did not cost much to build. In his court testimony and in documents and letters that were part of the case, Boudinot estimated that the hotel cost him six to seven thousand dollars to build and that at the time of its dismantling it was worth twelve thousand dollars owing to improvements made to the structure and the growth of the town. These are almost certainly exaggerated figures, if not wildly inflated ones. At the trial of Henry Eiffert and J. M. Whalen concerning the hotel in 1881, James Barnes, a carpenter from Fayetteville, testified that the lumber in the hotel was worth from $125 to $150.[2] The hotel was not a large structure, measuring sixty by seventy-five feet and consisting of two stories, a total of nine thousand square feet. Once the materials were purchased, it was relatively easy to hire a carpenter and helpers to raise the simple structure. Railroad employees, who often had eclectic building skills, may have been employed, perhaps the very persons who helped Boudinot put up structures at Russell Creek. If these people were not available, it would have been easy for Boudinot to arrange for permits for laborers from Kansas or Arkansas to do the work. Permits usually could be obtained simply by writing a letter to the proper authority (the government agent for each tribe, and later for the agent for the Five Civilized Tribes at Muskogee). At any rate, according to Boudinot, the money for lumber and construction costs—some fifteen hundred dollars—came from the sale of his tobacco machinery. He made this assertion in letters to Sallie Watie and Jim Bell after his opponents called into question the fact that he had built the hotel in the first place.[3]

Incidentally, the hotel was not the first building Cornelius had built in the Vinita area. Before the town was moved three miles north, he had put up a house at the original townsite. After the move he did not abandon that structure but rented it out, usually to whites with permits. As part of the rental agreement, the lessee was obliged to farm, most often raising vegetables that were in high demand up and down the tracks and sharing the profits with his "landlord." The farm was located on Cherokee land near the original townsite that Boudinot, Bell, and company had fenced for the purpose of laying out town lots. Not surprisingly, Cornelius had some difficulties with tenants from time to time, but these problems were nothing compared to the problem tenants at the hotel, or for that matter with the putative rancher at Russell Creek.

Soon after the hotel was built, the Katy built a depot at the junction. Once this was done, the right-of-way was automatically extended from one hundred feet on either side of the track to two hundred feet. The rationale was that the railroad would need extra room at these points for accommodating passengers and freight as well as its own equipment. To clear the right-of-way, the railroad demanded the removal of buildings within the allotted area. Boudinot was not the only opportunist at the site. Many other Cherokee citizens had arrived and erected various business edifices catering to the demands of railroad personnel and anticipating the influx of travelers. These buildings were lined up neatly just outside the one-hundred-foot line, forming a street. All buildings but the hotel were ordered moved. The railroad, desiring a convenient place of accommodation for employees and travelers on the site, agreed to lease the land the hotel sat on to Boudinot. Further, according to his testimony, the railroad promised to treat as its employee anyone he "placed there" and to "protect them from any annoyance under the intercourse laws."[4]

At first the arrangement seemed to work for both landlord and tenants. Cornelius rented to a white man from Missouri named Campbell at first and later to another white man named Johnson, both of whom, he later testified in court, paid him up to one hundred dollars a month. He also testified that both men also made improvements to the premises, thus increasing the value of the property.[5] It was not until "1876 or 1877" that the problems with the hotel began; at this point, Boudinot began his business arrangement with John R. Skinner, yet another white man. With his association with Skinner, Boudinot appreciably raised the stakes both in terms of possible profits and in terms of risks. For the first time, Cornelius offered a part-ownership in the enterprise rather than just tenancy. Skinner saw a chance for profits in the hotel, but he was a speculator rather than an innkeeper, his antennae attuned for quick, large influxes of cash. While he considered the hotel to be a moneymaker, he was probably more interested in the land around Vinita than in the hotel itself.

Skinner, of course, was not alone in gazing covetously at the landscape of Indian Territory. Ranchers and homesteaders from the adjoining states were eager to take up the "surplus" lands they saw lying fallow under communal ownership of the Indian nations. These people caused a continual difficulty for Native governments that was referred to as the "intruder" problem. Dating back to pre-removal days, white intruders had made inroads on Indian lands that varied in scale; sometimes they created minor annoyances, but at other times they brought about disintegration of the tribes' land title. Intruders in the Cherokee Nation in the 1830s contributed greatly to the events that forced the people onto the Trail of Tears. Now, in the years after the Civil War, the intruders were presenting major difficulties again. As much as the cattlemen who grazed their cattle illegally on Indian lands and the squatters who fenced in their illicit farms, speculators added a flammable quality to the volatile mix.

Skinner seems to have been one of these speculators, drawn to the prospect of making a killing through the sale of "surplus" lands. He was encouraged by political events at both the regional and the national level. At the national level it is important to note that from the end of the Civil War on, "territorial bills" were introduced and debated during every session of Congress, adherents hoping to dissolve the tribal governments and Native title to the land, to introduce federal jurisdiction to take the place of that of the Indian nations, to allot the land in severalty to individual Native citizens, and to open the "surplus" lands to white settlement in much the same manner as the Homestead Act of 1862 had opened other areas of the West. Since white speculators like Skinner anticipated passage of one or another of these territorial bills at any time, they felt it was in their best interest to be physically on the land when it happened. The advantages they saw are obvious: they could scout out the best parcels for themselves, including prime agricultural land, potential town sites, and places with mineral deposits or timber resources. They would also know all the local players, the railroaders, other speculators, and the Native citizens who were poised to profit when Indian land became public land. Thus, when Boudinot offered Skinner a deal involving land as well as the hotel, he jumped at the chance.

John Skinner was one of the few on the scene in Indian Territory with money to invest, as Cornelius well knew. Boudinot was dividing his time at this point between Washington DC and Indian Territory, with frequent forays into Arkansas and Kansas. He was angling for a clerkship in Congress and knew that if he got it, he would have little time to supervise his holdings in the Cherokee Nation. [6] So as he began to talk to Skinner, he saw an ideal situation beginning to develop. Boudinot turned once again to the scheme he and other Cherokees were using to introduce white men into the Territory: the exploitation of the permit system. The plan was to fence and farm some four hundred acres just outside the Vinita city limits, with Skinner and Boudinot splitting the proceeds. The farm was to be situated in the quadrant east of the Katy and north of the Atlantic and Pacific. Boudinot would take possession of the land as a Cherokee citizen, then "hire" Skinner under a permit to cultivate the plot. This, of course, was basically the same arrangement he had set up with Larkin earlier at Russell Creek. This time, however, Boudinot did not even bother to construct fences and take physical possession; he left this for Skinner to do, and therein lay the seeds of failure.

For his part, Skinner had only to hand over a thousand dollars to Boudinot, then take control of the hotel and farm. Skinner was obligated to take charge of the hotel and rent it to a suitable proprietor and hire sufficient agricultural workers to till the four hundred acres. He was also to keep accounts on these enterprises and forward one-half of the profits to his partner on a monthly basis. A can't-miss proposition, Cornelius thought, so once he had the money in his pocket he was off to Washington to pursue his clerkship and the social and political life he was beginning to enjoy. He was now assured of a steady flow of income as well as the thousand-dollar fee already collected. Another important consideration was that he had bragging rights to his Vinita "holdings" in the Washington parlors and drawing rooms he frequented in the evenings.

Alas, this happy arrangement did not last. Skinner found his hotel proprietor in the person of one H. H. Edmundson, who with his wife took over the hotel. In his court deposition Boudinot states that he became "dissatisfied with the management" the Edmundsons were providing and notified Skinner of this fact by letter. This dissatisfaction seems misplaced on Boudinot's part given the nature of the agreement, but there was more to it than this. In the same letter, Cornelius complained that Skinner had not begun cultivation of the four hundred acres, a fact that he most likely learned from Jim Bell or Sallie Watie. Skinner probably had no choice in the matter of the farm. First of all, while there was widespread abuse of the permit system, Cherokee officials could not avert their eyes from the sight of a white man brazenly fencing off improvements on land held in common trust. This was especially true of a white man who was in partnership with a Cherokee who was off in Washington trying to bring about the dissolution of the tribal government and open the Nation to white settlement. Even if the Cherokees had allowed this to happen, as a non-Native Skinner would have been hard pressed to get approval for permits for workers to till the land. So the sweet deal began to sour. For his part, Boudinot probably wished Skinner would just go away, minus his thousand dollars, but this was not to be.

In reply to Boudinot's letter, Skinner stated that he was willing to call the whole deal off and surrender his half interest in the enterprise as soon as he got his thousand dollars back.[7] At that point Cornelius left Washington, explaining his sudden departure to friends as one of the inconveniences a man of affairs with widespread holdings must suffer. Upon his arrival in Vinita in March 1877, he met with Skinner and came to a second agreement to settle the matter. Skinner would surrender his half interest in the operation, and Boudinot would refund the thousand dollars. However, Boudinot had only $700 in cash, so he paid Skinner that amount and gave his note for $365 for the remainder, to be paid the following June, four months later. The extra $65, Cornelius later explained in his court deposition, was for "a matter outside the Hotel transaction." Skinner agreed to these terms with the stipulation that if the note were not paid on time, he would resume his interest in the hotel. So far so good.

Now, of course, it was Boudinot's responsibility to find someone to run the hotel. This person was Daniel Ross, a white man from St. Louis, who took over the hotel as Boudinot made his way back to Washington. When the note fell due in June, Cornelius was still short the cash needed, so a third agreement was entered, this one a verbal one involving his tenant. The agreement was that Ross would pay his monthly rent to Skinner instead of to Boudinot until the note was paid. Ross made his payments to Skinner, according to Boudinot, to the extent that $300 was paid off the note. Still owing $65, Boudinot sent Skinner an "order on" a Mr. Tucker, Skinner's father-in-law and a former business associate of Boudinot's, for $85 that Cornelius "supposed he would be willing to accept," according to his later deposition. At the time, however, he wrote to Jim Bell, explaining it this way: "Let Skinner rave . . . if he annoys us too much I shall ask his removal from the Nation. I don't owe him a dollar: I did owe him $290. Balance on my note: he agreed to take Ross for $200. & when Ross tendered him the money, he refused to accept it thinking he would get a half interest in my hotel back; the balance $90." And then a key revelation on Boudinot's part: "I gave him an order on his father-in-law Tucker for that: Tucker owed me on a settlement twice that but I agreed to take that & the fellow went off to Texas & expects to cheat me out of it."[8] The order on Tucker was for a debt Boudinot never expected to collect; he knew that, Tucker knew that, and Skinner knew that. This explains why Skinner chose to ignore the order and to act as if Boudinot had made no attempt to pay him.

Deluding himself that the debt was satisfied in this way, and confident of his legal skills and Washington connections if it was not, Cornelius resumed his life in the capital. He was counting on his monthly rental payments from his Vinita "holdings" to supplement his six-dollar-a-day committee clerk's salary. All seemed well until sometime in the winter of 1877–78, when the rent money failed to arrive. Boudinot questioned Ross about this and was told that the railroad customers, the people whom both men counted on to provide the business base for the hotel, were in arrears. Further, Ross informed his landlord, he did not know when money from that usually trustworthy source would be forthcoming again. Frustrated, Cornelius waited a month. Then, with his own room-and-board bill due in Washington, he wrote to Jim Bell for help, appointing him agent in the hotel matter. He authorized Bell to take possession of the hotel, evicting Ross. But the eviction and possession was not to be so easy.

Late in 1877, Skinner wrote Boudinot asking for his money. Apparently, he had been talking to George Reynolds, who knew what Boudinot's intentions were on the subject. "I think I have waited long enough for money and I believe from the tone of Renolds [sic] that it is intended that I will not get my money on the Hotel. This will be the last time I will write you about the matter," Skinner wrote. Obviously, this was not a real dun letter; Skinner was leaving a paper trail so he could prove he had tried to collect. His real message was in the next paragraph: "I claim that I own ½ in the hotel and I expect to have it soon."[9]

Seeing trouble on the horizon, Boudinot reacted quickly. On February 1, 1878, he made Sallie Watie a partner in the hotel. The affidavit to this effect helps reveal Cornelius's intentions: "This is to certify that Mrs. Sallie Watie, widow of the late Stand Watie, is one half owner of the hotel building at Vinita, Indian Territory, known as the Railroad House; nobody but herself and myself have any interest in said Hotel Building."[10] This was shortly followed by another affidavit transferring title to the four hundred acres and improvements he claimed just outside the town limits to Mrs. Watie and her nephew Aeneas Ridge. Cornelius was trying to muddy the ownership waters on the one hand and to make it clear on the other that he no longer considered Skinner a partner. He could have done the same thing by making Bell or another of his cronies a partner, but in turning to Sallie Watie he played one of his trump cards. The name of Stand Watie was still highly revered in many circles of the Cherokee Nation, and both he and his opponents were well aware of this fact. Boudinot was now throwing down the gauntlet, invoking the memory of Watie and the honor of his widow. The target for this maneuver was not Skinner but rather the two men Cornelius considered to be behind his hotel problem and some of his other troubles, William Penn Adair and Lucien Bell. Adair and Bell had both served as Watie's lieutenants in the Civil War.

William Penn Adair was born in the Cherokee Nation in Georgia in 1830, the son of George Washington and Martha Martin Adair. He was educated in the Cherokee national schools and later studied law. After his service in the Civil War he lived on the Grand River near present-day Adair, Oklahoma, and was prominent in Cherokee affairs. He served as a delegate to Washington, a capacity in which he and Boudinot often found themselves in contention. Later he was a senator, justice of the Cherokee Supreme Court, and assistant principal chief.

Lucien Burr "Hooley" Bell was also born in Georgia before removal, the son of John A. and Jane Martin Bell. A cousin of Jim Bell, he was educated at Ozark Institute and Cane Hill College in Arkansas. After serving in the Civil War he remained in Texas for a time, returning to the Cherokee Nation in 1867. Like Adair, Bell served as a delegate to Washington, and he was also a tax collector for the Nation. Bell later went on to serve as clerk for the Cherokee Senate, member of the Cherokee national board of education, national treasurer, and senator.

At the time the hotel matter was festering, Boudinot had several differences with both men on a variety of issues, but especially with Adair. Despite having served together in Watie's regiment during the Civil War, Adair and Boudinot by now were bitter rivals in Washington as well as in the Nation. Boudinot was involved in nearly every territorial bill that was introduced into Congress, and many that were not, while Adair worked on many Cherokee delegations that were bitterly opposed. At times they were called upon in committee hearings to give direct testimony against each other on the subject. In the same vein, each gave speeches and published pamphlets against the other's position. In addition, as part of his political maneuverings in Washington, Boudinot called for representation in Congress for the Cherokees and other Native groups. As part of advocating this, Boudinot called for an end to the seemingly continual delegations to Washington sent by the various Indian nations, pointing to the large expense of maintaining them. Adair, of course, was one of the delegates Boudinot accused of living high at the expense of Cherokee citizens. At one point, as we shall see, the rivalry between the two came to physical blows.

By the end of 1877, Boudinot saw that he was getting nowhere with Skinner, so he looked around for a plan to get rid of him. It could not be that difficult, he thought. After all, the only reason Skinner was in the Cherokee Nation in the first place was because Boudinot had brought him in. So Cornelius wrote to the U.S. agent as well as to Secretary of War George W. McCrary preferring charges against Skinner, citing his "turbulent and quarrelsome disposition and conduct." Officially, white men had little legal standing in Indian Territory once their employing sponsor withdrew support, and the agent ordered Skinner out of the Territory forthwith.[11] This was not a disaster altogether for Skinner. By this time, seeing the futility of his position, he bought the position of sutler, or fort trader, for the federal garrison at Fort Gibson. Skinner knew that this could be a lucrative job for a man with few scruples, as it involved some wheeling and dealing in commodities and little supervision from Washington. Before he left Vinita for Fort Gibson, though, Skinner plotted revenge against his former partner. He knew that Boudinot's opponents would love to cause him discomfort, especially if they might enrich themselves a little along the way. So he began his discussions with Henry Eiffert, a Cherokee associate of Hooley Bell and a man affiliated with the political group in the Nation who were aligned against the old Ridge-Boudinot-Watie party. Skinner agreed to turn over his share in the hotel to Eiffert for an undisclosed sum. The deal, however, was not consummated until the end of April.

Most likely it was Adair and Hooley Bell who advised Eiffert on the legal aspects of the situation, because it was not long after Eiffert took an interest in the hotel that the jurisdictional disputes that so mark this affair began. Eiffert addressed two questions to the clerk of Cooweescoowee District, the legal division of the Cherokee Nation in which Vinita was found. The hotel dispute had been smoldering for some time now, offering a diversion for Vinita society, but now it heated up. Heretofore the disputes had been between a Cherokee and white men, and it had been almost fun to watch how greed manifested itself in both parties. Now, however, it was to be Cherokee against Cherokee, and the tone became more serious. Clerk C. C. Lipe knew that something was up when Henry Eiffert asked him about a "warrant of ejectment" for the hotel tenant. Lipe knew he was treading on dangerous ground, so on February 12, 1878, he referred Eiffert's questions to the executive of the Cherokee Nation, Principal Chief Charles Thompson. In his letter, Lipe asks if he has the authority to "issue a warrant of ejectment" to persons on the "R. R. stripe," meaning the right-of-way. The clerk identifies Eiffert as the source of the inquiry, further stating that it is Eiffert's intention to take possession of one-half of the hotel. "Please inform me as soon as possible what to do," he asks Thompson, and almost as an afterthought, he adds, "also whether Mr. E. C. Boudinott [sic] is a citizen of this Nation or not."[12]

The first question, touching on the authority of a Cherokee official to take legal action on the right-of-way ceded to the railroad under various treaty agreements, was a weighty one, as Lipe well knew. Caught off guard, Chief Thompson and his advisers were also well aware of the implications, so when Thompson replied to the clerk's letter four days later it was with total obfuscation. "I am not at this moment prepared to furnish the desired information" on the question of authority, he wrote, "but will apprise you as early as may be practicable." That issue deftly sidestepped, Thompson goes on. "As regards the case of Mr. E. C. Boudinot, Sr. citizenship I wish to say, that this Department has no official information touching the subject, and should the question legally arise, as to his rights in this nation as a Cherokee Citizen, I venture to say that the case will then naturally be required to be brought before the judiciary or the Legislative Department of this Nation."[13] Thompson, of course, was perfectly aware of Boudinot's status as a Cherokee citizen, since he had appointed him earlier as a tribal delegate to Washington. But not knowing fully why the question was asked, the chief not only avoided answering but also deflected it away from his branch of Cherokee government. Three weeks later, after the Cherokee executive department had had time to gather information from the field and to consider the matter, Thompson sent another letter. "I desire to state that, since this Department has decided that No person had a legal right to erect, own, or occupy any buildings on said RailRoad land, not strictly used for RailRoad purposes," he says, "it follows that any writ of ejectment in the case you mention, would be deemed illegal and arbitrary at this time."[14] The Cherokee executive had walked a tight line, failing to take sides in the matter. His statement, though, set the stage for the later dismantling of the structure, however inadvertently.

Very quickly, things began to happen on the Vinita right-of-way because of Thompson's letter and from an unexpected second source. When Boudinot got a lease to the land for his hotel, it was for a bit more property than just the sixty by seventy-five feet that the building itself occupied. The railroad had also allowed in the lease another sixty feet on either side of the hotel. Some other Cherokees, including Jim Bell, had put up buildings that were partially on this land. As a result, Boudinot complained to the Katy about non-railroad buildings on the right-of-way and asked that all structures without leases be removed. He wrote to Jim Bell explaining this, adding, "You will not be disturbed, for I shall claim that you built under my direction and with the understanding that it was to be an enlargement of my hotel."[15]

While these events were taking place, Boudinot was in Washington, trying to manage things from a distance. Of concern to him was his other property south of Vinita, which was rented to a man named Timberlake. Specifically, he was afraid that Timberlake might die and that Boudinot's property might be taken to be Timberlake's assets and thus revert to the tribe or to any Chero-kee who might wish to claim them. Accordingly, he directed Bell to get an affidavit from Timberlake explaining the situation, but as of April he had not received the paper. At this point Cornelius found it necessary to reinforce his connection to Bell and his sister and to emphasize the importance of their various holdings in the Vinita area. In a letter to Bell dated April 23, he says that Sallie Watie, "As the heir of General Watie is a ¼ owner anyway in all Vinita, & so far as I am concerned I am willing to divide my interest with you; but all arrangements should be made with me as the agent of all the parties. What I want is that this great property should not pass out of the hands of our family."[16] In closing this letter, Boudinot refers to the hotel, instructing Bell to allow Ross to stay in the business as long as he pays his rent. Make sure, he says, "he does not turn it over to our enemies." Bell accordingly served notice on Ross that he had taken legal possession of the hotel in Boudinot's name. He left Ross as tenant with the same rental agreement as before.[17]

Disaster struck in early May, however, as Boudinot's fears were realized.

Ross, acting under Skinner's orders, turned the hotel property over to Eiffert, sold its furniture for two hundred dollars, and with the proceeds from the sale promptly left the Cherokee Nation. When Boudinot read the telegram from Vinita announcing the takeover, he was furious. His first reaction was self-recrimination. He thought back to the many times he had urged Bell and his sister to take possession of the hotel and move in, thus preempting a move like this. But he knew that he had never pushed the matter far enough, for a couple of reasons. First, he knew that Jim and Sallie saw that the hotel was a trouble spot in a dangerous part of Indian Territory and that they did not consider the personal risk to be worth whatever advantage such a move would give them. Second, Cornelius had to admit to himself that he had not wanted to give up the rent that was coming in, however unreliably, from one of his "holdings."

His self-recriminations did not stop him from venting his anger on his partner back in Vinita, however. "How is it possible that you allowed the God-damned scoundrels to get possession of my Hotel?" The words must have almost shouted off the paper as Bell opened the letter. "Why Jim I would have given my right arm before I would have allowed you to be treated in this way. I begged you to take possession yourself and make all the money you could & I would charge no rent. You could have made $100 a month at least clear." In his anger, Boudinot knew that he needed Bell more than ever and tried to load him with guilt so that Jim might act more forcefully in the next scene of the drama. "You have allowed the thief Skinner to succeed in his conspiracy to ruin me," he continues. But Cornelius knew that all was not lost and made an appeal to Bell: "Now I ask you by hook or crook to get Eiffert out . . . and keep possession yourself. Will you do this? Please answer."[18]

Throughout May 1878 the maneuverings continued, with Jim Bell pressing Eiffert and Hooley Bell for possession of the hotel. Jim attempted to turn the tables on Eiffert and petitioned Clerk Lipe for an ejectment warrant, but Lipe was more wary than ever since the principal chief himself did not seem to want to get involved. Arguments were pressed on both sides and conveyed to Boudinot, who reacted with rage from Washington. "I don't give a damn about explanations, get possession of the House and keep it," he writes to Bell.[19] All the while, however, Boudinot is taking another tack. Knowing it is useless to appeal to the Cherokee Nation authorities, he tries to bring in his friends in Congress, albeit in an indirect way. At this time, Adair was involved in negotiations concerning land in the Cherokee strip purchased by the Osage Nation upon its removal from Kansas. Hooley Bell also had an interest in how these proceedings turned out. Boudinot knew that the negotiations were at a delicate stage and that two of his personal friends and allies in Congress, Senator Daniel Voorhees and Representative Thomas M. Gunter, had something to say in the matter. Following a maneuver typical for him, Boudinot let it be known that the congressmen were not happy about the hotel situation and that their resentment against the perpetrators of the injustice might affect the Osage talks. He went even further, saying that since even Cherokee citizens had no legal protection from their nations, as demonstrated by his case, several key members of Congress saw this as a reason to institute a territorial government. He hoped to spread rumors like these to undermine the support that Eiffert might enjoy in the Nation.[20]

But Boudinot was not one to base his total campaign on such a passive-aggressive foray. When there was an opportunity to make a full frontal attack, the old cavalryman tuned up his bugle. On May 29, from his Washington office, Cornelius directed a letter to Secretary of War McCrary requesting an investigation into the new sutler at Fort Gibson. He makes it clear that he is writing not only in his own interest but on behalf of Sallie Watie. Specifically, he charges Skinner, along with Daniel Ross and Henry Eiffert, with conspiring to seize his and Mrs. Watie's property. Boudinot tell McCrary that he has attempted to bring suit against Eiffert in Cherokee Nation courts, but the Cherokee authorities refused to take jurisdiction because the hotel is on the railroad right-of-way. It appears then, he goes on, that he has no recourse in the courts. This point is made not only for the purpose of convincing the secretary to order the investigation; Boudinot here is going on the record once again for the desirability of a federal court for Indian territory, one of the parts of the Harlan bill in the 1860s and a key part of the package being pushed by the "Territorial Ring," as it was popularly known, in Congress. At this point McCrary may well have asked what the War Department had to do with a civil matter concerning a hotel in the Cherokee Nation. Near the end of the letter, Boudinot provides a reason, saying that Skinner is avoiding answering for his part in the conspiracy by claiming to be under the "special protection" of the War Department. In support of his request, Boudinot included two letters from the U.S. agent and an affidavit from George Reynolds, a man he describes as "personally cognizant" of the situation. Reynolds's statement corroborates Boudinot's, making the point that Skinner had refused payment on the note and had boasted that he would get possession of the hotel for a small amount of money. The first of the two letters from L. W. Marston, U.S. agent for the Union Agency at Muskogee, informs Boudinot that he notified Skinner to remove from Indian Territory, while the second tells him that Skinner has bought out the sutler at Fort Gibson and is on the government reservation there. Apparently, these documents were enough to convince McCrary because he subsequently ordered the post commander at Fort Gibson, Captain C. Rodney Layton, to commence an investigation into the matter.

The proceedings began on July 6, 1878, with Boudinot's brother William acting as his attorney and Hooley Bell as Skinner's. Eiffert, upon the advice of his attorney, W. P. Adair, did not appear, his position being that the military had no jurisdiction over a Cherokee citizen. The lawyers entered twenty-six relevant documents, and witnesses gave testimony. On July 27, 1878, Captain Layton gave his report and recommendation. He ruled that Ross had acted fraudulently in turning over the building to Eiffert. He further ruled that Boudinot had effectively bought back the half interest from Skinner when he paid off the bulk of his note, so Skinner had no right to sell the hotel to Eiffert or anyone else. Substantial justice would be attained, Layton continued in his report, by requiring the complainant to pay to the defendant, or to the holder of the note, the amount due and that upon payment the complainant should be given his property back. Layton does not leave it at that. In the last paragraph he chides both parties, pointing out that if they had gone to the U.S. agent much earlier for arbitration, the affair would have been settled long ago and "many of the complications might have been avoided, as well as the necessity for this investigation."[21] Layton also pointedly declines to consider the conspiracy charge that Boudinot has brought.

After the dust had settled at Fort Gibson, however, the situation had not changed perceptibly. Layton could pronounce judgment, but he had no jurisdiction other than that delineated by his command: the compound at the fort and the government personnel under his direction. He had no authority in the Cherokee Nation. Skinner, who was the one person involved in the affair who was under his command, was not required to do anything until Boudinot paid off the note, and of course Boudinot was not about to do this. Further, even if he had, that would settle things with Skinner, but Eiffert would still be in control of the hotel, well out of reach of Captain Layton. Likewise, Layton's superiors had no jurisdiction in the Cherokee Nation, so they were powerless to help Boudinot get control of the hotel.

To the Cherokee government, the question of jurisdiction over the railroad right-of-way was such an important one that the subject was not dropped with Thompson's March 6 letter to Lipe. More considered opinion was applied to it, and doubtless more information was recovered from the field in the form of opinions from interested parties like Adair and Hooley Bell. The next pronouncement from the chief came in an August letter to Lipe and offered some further points. These were made almost certainly after consultation and with the concurrence of the leaders of the National Council and the Cherokee Supreme Court. First of all, Thompson writes, his full opinions on the matter had not been expressed earlier because of a misunderstanding on the part of his secretary, William F. Rasmus, who "did not comprehend" the chief's instructions when he wrote the February 16 and March 6 letters. The chief goes on to say that he will take the present opportunity to offer his views on the subject more fully.

Early on, Thompson identifies the need for the National Council to "pass some constructive law, on the subject." This comment may be seen as a statement that his views as expressed in his letter to Lipe must serve as the Cherokee position until such laws are passed, but even so he disavows a wish to dictate any. It is easy to conclude that Thompson would have preferred making no pronouncement on the subject at this time; however, since circumstances had forced the issue, he was left with little other choice.

The chief says that the right-of-way enjoyed by the railroad was "reserved" for it by the 1866 treaty and that therefore the Cherokees have no right to occupy it. At the same time, the railroad has no right to use the "stripe" for any purposes other than "railroad" purposes. Even though the stripe is reserved for the railroad, it still "belongs to the Cherokee Nation the same, as the other lands of the Nation," he goes on to say. Legal jurisdiction over the stripe, then, is of a "mixed or dual character." Citing the 1866 treaty and the Indian Intercourse Acts of Congress, Thompson says that the U.S. courts have jurisdiction over the railroads and their employees. But Cherokee authorities have jurisdiction over citizens of the Cherokee Nation who are "not in the employ of the RailRoads," as well as over their property, in both criminal and civil proceedings. Specifically, he goes on, criminal or civil disputes between Cherokees in the right-of-way are under Cherokee Nation jurisdiction. Any other interpretation would violate Cherokee treaty rights and "our rights of self-government." The right-of-way could become "a refuge to escape our law" and the stripe could be "settled up and occupied by citizens of the United States," outcomes clearly not allowed under the terms of the 1866 treaty or the intercourse laws.

Having thus carefully set out the Cherokee position, Thompson goes on to comment on the question of Boudinot's citizenship. Much of the last paragraph of his letter to Lipe is dedicated to this subject.

So far as my knowledge extends, he has always been regarded, by the Cherokee authorities, as a citizen of this Nation by blood, and as such, he has served on our Delegation, before the Government of the United States, and signed one of our treaties, I believe in 1868, as a Cherokee delegate, in reference to the "Neutral" lands—so far as this Department is concerned, he is acknowledged as a Citizen of the Nation and has the very same recourse, before our courts, under our constitution and laws, that any other Cherokee Citizen has, or can have.[22]

It is interesting to note that under Thompson's signature appears that of his new executive secretary, William P. Adair.

At this point, then, Eiffert had control of the hotel property, and according to Thompson, the Cherokee Nation had jurisdiction of any dispute between Cherokee citizens. Boudinot was a Cherokee citizen, as Thompson had just affirmed. This particular Cherokee citizen, however, had his own plan, and it did not include seeking redress in what he considered a hostile Cherokee Nation court. At this point, Boudinot was taking his plan to Vinita and bringing reinforcements. A congressional committee under Senator A. H. Garland was traveling to Indian Territory to assess public opinion on the territorial question. Stops were due throughout Indian Territory, in McAlester, Caddo, Atoka, and Colbert as well as Vinita. While the group was at Vinita, Boudinot planned to press the matter of the ejectment warrant with Lipe in front of some of his congressional allies. In a letter from Terre Haute, Indiana, he tells Jim Bell, "Lipe will be a witness before the committee and let us see if he will refuse to issue a writ. If he does I will get possession. If he doesn't my fight will be in Washington."[23] In the same letter, he asks Bell to get Sallie Watie to assign her interest in the hotel over to Boudinot as part of a new plan to sue "the villains." His plan to embarrass Lipe in November did not produce satisfactory results, so once back in Washington, Cornelius turns to another avenue. In December he tells Bell to "let the Hotel matter stand as is. I am working on a plan."[24] That plan was to ignore the jurisdictional claims of the Cherokee Nation and work through his allies in Washington. At this time the jurisdictional battle began in earnest.

Having gotten nowhere with the War Department, Boudinot approached Secretary of the Interior Carl Schurz and laid before him a presentation of the facts as he saw them early in 1880. Schurz agreed that Eiffert had no claim on the hotel, given the report by Captain Layton. On February 7, 1880, Boudinot wrote to Schurz complaining that Eiffert still occupied the hotel, with William

Kellerman as the tenant, and demanded the department take action. Schurz then notified E. J. Brooks, the acting commissioner of Indian Affairs, that "the Department could not recognize the right of Eiffert to control the property, it being clear from the facts in the case that his assumed title was derived though gross frauds upon Col. Boudinot." The secretary then continued by ordering Brooks to instruct "Agent Tufts of the Union Agency, to forthwith eject Kellerman, and turn over the property to Col. Boudinot, or his properly accredited Agent." [25] On February 9, Brooks wrote to Tufts directing him to evict Kellerman, using as many federal police as he found necessary. On the same date, Price wrote to Boudinot, apprising him of that fact. On February 10, Boudinot requested that once the eviction was carried out, Tufts turn the hotel over to his agent, George W. Fox of Chetopah, Kansas. At the same time, Boudinot wrote to Fox in Chetopa asking him to take possession when the eviction was carried out.

Back in the Cherokee Nation, the news that the federal government was about to move Eiffert's tenant out of the hotel spread like a fire through dry prairie grass. Long before this time the dispute had turned personal, and the intensity of the argument was stoked to a heat level far surpassing the monetary value of the hotel. Eiffert's integrity was called into question, he was sure, and with his friends egging him on he bragged that if the federal people wanted to start a fight with him, they would surely find one. He publicly vowed to resist Tufts and his police. Tufts, perhaps wisely, refrained from acting immediately, thus avoiding a violent confrontation, but his inaction gave time for tempers to rise further and for the Cherokee authorities in Tahlequah to contemplate their next action. Boudinot's people in Vinita kept him apprised of the situation, and as everything seemed to hang motionless, Cornelius decided to set the wheels moving again. Accordingly, he wrote to Schurz, indicating that the secretary's authority had been thwarted once again. Eiffert, Cornelius wrote, had announced his intention of resisting the execution of Schurz's order "by force of arms." Further, Boudinot reported, Eiffert threatened that if Tufts succeeded in evicting Kellerman and in giving Boudinot's agent possession, he would "procure a writ of ejectment from a Cherokee Court, and that the Cherokee Sheriff would summon a posse large enough to put him [Eiffert] in possession." [26]

Schurz's reaction was to direct Brooks to execute the earlier order "with the aid of such police force as might be necessary to place Mr. Boudinot's Agent in possession, having a sufficient force upon the premises to insure a peaceful retention thereof." Fox, the agent whom Boudinot had identified, was waiting in the wings fifty miles up the Katy track at Chetopa. Brooks was further ordered to have his agent notify the Cherokee Nation that "any action by the Cherokee Courts looking to the disturbance of Col. Boudinot's possession would not be approved by the Department, the Cherokee authorities having no jurisdiction in the matter."[27]

A direct confrontation loomed between Eiffert and Tufts, with the Cherokee Nation and the federal government hovering behind each of them. But at this point, Boudinot's opposition took a new tack that defused the pending explosion, thanks to the cooler heads of Adair and William A. Phillips, two of Boudinot's archenemies. Phillips served the Cherokee Nation as legal counsel at various times, bringing him often into confrontation with Boudinot. Later, Boudinot accused Phillips of stealing money from the nation, resulting in a scandal. Adair and Phillips counseled reason, calling for a full investigation of the matter. Tufts carried out his eviction of Kellerman, Eiffert's tenant, and turned the hotel over to Fox. Cornelius, hoping to keep some sort of continuity in the hotel business, promptly instructed Fox to keep Kellerman as tenant. Before relinquishing control over the premises, however, Eiffert wrote to the Interior Department on March 27, complaining that his rights had been interfered with in violation of the law. Operating under Adair and Phillips's advice, he further protested against his removal from the premises, saying that his side of the case had not been heard, and asked for a full investigation. Hoping to present a united front with Eiffert, the Cherokee chief, Dennis W. Bushyhead—there had been a change of administration—wrote endorsing the idea of an investigation. In addition, after prompting all the other principals in the matter, Adair and Phillips finally got into the act directly. At the time they were both part of the Cherokee delegation in Washington, which now filed a written request with Schurz for an investigation to be conducted by Agent Tufts. The object of the inquiry was to be "ascertaining who were the proper parties in interest, and where the jurisdiction of the case properly rested."[28]

So while Boudinot continued to collect rent from Kellerman, an inquiry into the situation began. Tufts's "investigation" consisted of collecting a number of statements by those involved, including Kellerman, Eiffert, Boudinot, Fox, and others, and the forwarding of those documents to his superiors in Washington. Acting Commissioner Brooks received them on June 7. Eiffert's statement pointed out that the two men in contention were both Cherokees and that neither one had been denied the right to legal process in Cherokee courts. Jurisdiction clearly lay with the Cherokee Nation, according to Eiffert. Boudinot's statement reiterated his position concerning Skinner and his "illegal" relinquishment of the hotel to Eiffert in the first place. Thus, he pointed out, the dispute should not be between Eiffert and him, since Eiffert's possession was illegal from the first. Tufts agreed timidly with Eiffert's position, pointing out that the tenants had been white men renting from Cherokees, thus intimating that jurisdiction lay with the Cherokee Nation. However, the Office of Indian Affairs did little or nothing with these "facts" for the next few months, perhaps hoping that now, with Boudinot in control of the hotel, the argument might just die out. But they failed to take into consideration two things: Eiffert's need to be personally vindicated and the importance of the matter of jurisdiction to the Cherokee Nation.

On November 3, 1880, the situation again became inflamed when the sheriff of Cooweescoowee District rode up to the hotel with an armed posse and confronted Kellerman, who had come out to meet him. The Cherokee Nation, the sheriff told Kellerman, had claimed jurisdiction in the case and had found for Eiffert. Accordingly, the sheriff was evicting Kellerman and putting Eiffert in possession of the hotel. Kellerman prudently stepped aside and gave up the premises, whereupon Eiffert motioned him over to the side of the hotel. Eiffert, too, wanted continuity for the business, so he offered Kellerman the tenancy under the same terms as before. Kellerman, having nowhere else to go at the moment, agreed and stepped back into the building. When news of these events was relayed to Boudinot at his office in Washington, his first reaction was to bang his fist on the desk with rage. He soon calmed down, however, and sat down to write a report to Secretary Schurz, who promptly referred the matter to the new acting commissioner of Indian Affairs, H. Price. Price directed Tufts to ascertain by what authority the eviction had taken place and to report any other facts to the Office of Indian Affairs. By January 25, 1881, Tufts transmitted copies of papers he had gathered in connection with the ejectment to Price's office.

Price examined the documents Tufts had forwarded and made his recommendation to S. J. Kirkwood, the new secretary of the interior, on April 14, 1881. Price's report said that the eviction seemed to have been carried out solely against Kellerman, a white man. Since the Cherokee Nation has no jurisdiction over U.S. citizens, "the proceedings are, ab initio, null and void." Price goes on to recommend the removal of Eiffert and the restoration of the property to Boudinot.[29] In his reply to Price's report, Kirkwood cites Schurz's earlier pronouncements on the matter and orders that Boudinot be put back in possession. He insists, however, that Boudinot exercise some prudence this time in his choice of agent.[30] E. L. Stevens, Price's successor as acting commissioner, ordered Agent Tufts to carry out Kirkland's wishes on May 6, notifying Boudinot of this action at the same time.

Boudinot saw the logic in Kirkland's insistence that he exercise prudence in his choice of agents. He assessed the situation carefully on the long train journey from Washington back to Vinita and en route formed a plan. Instead of traveling straight on to take possession of the hotel himself, Cornelius stopped in Fayetteville, Arkansas, and looked up an old acquaintance, George H. Pettigrew. Pettigrew was another in the series of white men who saw golden opportunity in the prairies and woodlands across the border to the west. Cornelius told his story, how the hotel was doing a fine business with a captive base clientele of railroad personnel with further revenues coming in from commercial travelers on the Atlantic and Pacific and the Katy. When Pettigrew questioned him about the difficulties with Eiffert and Skinner, Boudinot admitted that there had been some problems—the facts were well known in every hamlet in that part of the country and would have been impossible to deny—but went on to reassure Pettigrew that the situation was now well under control. The federal government was now holding the premises and waiting for him or his agent to take possession. Pettigrew then made the pitch for a reduction in price, since the hotel had a history of controversy and, despite Cornelius's assertions to the contrary, the title might be challenged again. Reluctantly, Boudinot reduced the price to five thousand dollars and worked out a deal by which Pettigrew would buy the hotel. He signed the hotel over on June 11, 1881.[31]

Cornelius saw obvious advantages to this sale. First of all, he came into some ready cash. Second, he knew that the jurisdiction issue was too big for the Cherokee Nation to give up on. He was certain that Adair and Phillips would keep after Chief Bushyhead to keep the issue alive, thus ensuring turmoil for the foreseeable future. Third, while he was losing a valuable "holding" at Vinita junction, he still had the farm on the northwest quadrant as well as the house and land at the original crossing south of town. It was time to cut his losses. Finally, Boudinot saw the sale as a way around the jurisdictional dispute. The main point the Cherokee Nation had in its favor was that the dispute was between two Cherokees—Boudinot and Eiffert. With Skinner out of the way, they could make an effective case on this issue. If Pettigrew owned the hotel, however, the dispute would become between a white man and a Cherokee, leaving the Nation with no jurisdiction and the federal government in control. The sale would bring Boudinot triumph not only over Eiffert but also over his old enemies Adair, Hooley Bell, and Phillips. Cornelius smiled as he took Pettigrew's money and helped him board the train from Fayetteville to Vinita.

News spread quickly on the frontier, especially when the subject was providing so much entertainment for the area's otherwise bored inhabitants. Before Pettigrew and Boudinot reached Vinita, perhaps even before they boarded the train, Eiffert was told of the sale via the telegraph. The people of Vinita then stood back to see what would happen next, some making bets on whether Boudinot had finally slickered the Eiffert-Adair crowd, others betting that the latter had one more trick up their sleeves. At any rate, the onlookers were not disappointed. Before Boudinot and Pettigrew's train pulled into town, a crew of men approached the hotel with tools and wagons as the tenant watched warily expecting trouble. By this time, Kellerman had realized that whatever future he had, it did not lie with the Commercial Hotel. He had been replaced by a former tenant, H. H. Edmundson, and his wife. Eiffert now explained to the Edmundsons that he was there to make some improvements to the kitchen area and asked them to vacate the premises for a few days. On June 22, before the tenants had moved all of their things out, the workmen moved in under the direction of J. M. Whalen, one of Eiffert's associates. Backing the wagons to the building, they went to work, not improving the kitchen, but tearing the structure down to its foundation, piling the lumber into the wagons. Once this was done, they pulled up the foundation stones as well, loaded them up, and carried the materials away, leaving an empty lot. The Edmundsons stood in the crowd that had gathered and watched, their mouths open in dismay.[32]

Besides having to give the five thousand dollars back, the biggest injury for Boudinot was that he could see where the lumber from the hotel had gone with his own eyes when he looked around Vinita and environs. Charles Johnson built a mechanic's shop from part of the materials, while Sam Collier and Bob Timberlake used stone and lumber around their improvements. Jake "Little Fritz" Fritz, who did most of the hauling, took off a large portion to his place as pay for digging a well on Eiffert's farm.[33] In addition, Mr. Edmundson testified that much of the lumber was used to build Eiffert a new house.[34] But Boudinot was resolved not to let this latest injustice go unpunished. He and Pettigrew left Vinita as soon as they had surveyed the damage and headed for the federal courthouse at Fort Smith, Arkansas. There, in Judge Isaac C. Parker's court on June 30, Boudinot swore out a complaint against Hooley Bell, Eiffert, and Whalen for stealing lumber from Pettigrew. By the time of the trial, the defendants were Eiffert and Whalen, most likely because no one could remember Bell as being in Vinita that day.

The most interesting part of the trial was Eiffert's defense, which was based on Cherokee, not United States, law. He could not very well deny tearing down the structure, since the entire population of Vinita had watched him do it. Adair suggested he use a provision used in the Cherokee Nation when a citizen occupied an improvement on tribal land that had been abandoned. Once the citizen lived there unchallenged for two years, he or she acquired title. Eiffert testified that he had held "quiet and uninterrupted possession" for two years, which gave him title to the hotel under Cherokee law. Thus, all he had done was to tear down his own building. Under cross-examination, Eiffert revealed that he had paid John Skinner five hundred dollars "in money" for his interest in the hotel, but he could not remember the date or the year. He also testified that he may have written to the federal authorities complaining about having been evicted by Tufts but did not remember doing so. Adair, Eiffert testified, was his "authorized attorney" and attended to that kind of business for him. Eiffert also testified about obtaining the writ of ejectment from the Cherokee Nation with which Kellerman was evicted by the sheriff. These comments would, it seems, contradict the "quiet" part of his "uninterrupted possession" and thus negate his claim to title under Cherokee law. Boudinot then took the stand to refute the case for title by possession, outlining his attempts to regain his property and testifying in detail about the periods during the past two years when he had been in possession.

In the end the court found for Boudinot and Pettigrew, but again it was a hollow victory. Judge Parker could hang more than a hundred miscreants from his gallows, but he could not order the hotel at Vinita to be rebuilt. The wood from a structure once meant to be a symbol of the coming prosperity now graced a shed built onto Charles Johnson's shop, provided siding for a chicken coop, and was used as lumber for Henry Eiffert's new house. "Little Fritz" used some of the damaged pieces as palings for his horse corral, and some of it was just burned.

While this is a bizarre story, in many ways it is typical of the unsettled times of postwar Indian Territory. One of its main ingredients is the opportunism— or more plainly, the greed—that drove many of the characters in this tale. The protagonist's greed must have been almost palpable to the men who seemed to flock to the hotel looking for easy money. In the hotel Boudinot was not looking for a place of business, a means to build an estate for himself and provide jobs for others; rather, he was looking for a "holding," an asset he could acquire with minimum investment of capital or time and from which he could extract a profit. His plan for the four-hundred-acre farm just outside the town was a similar undertaking. He did not even plan to help with building the fencing that was the minimum requirement under the Cherokee improvement law. And certainly, both ventures violated the spirit of the traditional use of communal land, which was to take what one needed for self and family, enough land to earn a living from. Further, Boudinot had no intention of living in Vinita, any more than he intended to live at Russell Creek. He had grown accustomed to the city life, to Washington and its society, and it was there he spent most of his time up until five years before his death. The men who must have felt Boudinot's avarice brought a large modicum of that commodity to Vinita themselves. Skinner was an opportunist of the first order, taking all the money he could out of the venture except the last few dollars. These he refused in the hope that he could keep his money and the hotel too, knowing full well it belonged to Boudinot. Eiffert, seeing an opportunity to purchase a thriving business for five hundred dollars, a small fraction of its worth, went along with Skinner's plan to defraud Boudinot. The string of white tenants came to Vinita full of greed as well, and they all carried a full complement of envy for the Cherokee land they hoped someday to occupy.

The story has another subtext as well, one of petty rivalries and personal vendettas. At the heart of it is the animosity between Boudinot and Adair. Theirs was a friendly rivalry at first in the Civil War, but as time went on and the background changed it grew into an intense hatred, each trying to thwart the other for the sake of inflicting pain rather than for any expectation of personal gain. Adair probably saw his opposition of Boudinot at this time as patriotic, since by 1880 his rival was engaged in bringing about the dissolution of the Cherokee Nation. The malice the two men had for one another seemed to be contagious, spreading to many of the other characters in the story.

Finally, the hotel story is but one piece in a much larger drama, that of the Indian nations' struggle for national sovereignty. The issues raised by the battle for ownership of the hotel were too big to be ignored by the Cherokee Nation, which was rightly fearful for the precedent that might be set, or by the U.S. government, ever reluctant to share authority with another political entity within its national borders. In this episode, however, in spite of all the maneuverings and pronouncements, neither side advanced its position in the contest for sovereignty. The struggle was to go on, and Boudinot was to play his part.

CHAPTER 8

The Washingtonian

During the 1870s and 1880s Boudinot spent much of his time in the nation's capital when he was not on the road lecturing or in the Cherokee Nation or nearby. At first his attraction to Washington was the legal maneuverings in his tobacco case and his need to participate fully. Later, his quest for compensation for the loss of his property kept him close, but soon it was a question of being near to the seat of power, to where so many decisions involving Indian Territory were being made. Boudinot had become fully embroiled in a debate in Washington that had been brewing since the end of the Civil War: territorial status for the lands occupied by the Five Civilized Tribes under the removal treaties and for adjacent areas set aside for the settlement of other Native American groups. The treaties forced upon the Indian Territory nations at the end of the war paved the way for this acrimonious debate, so Boudinot was involved in the dispute from the beginning.

Cornelius had first become acquainted with the city in 1866 as a member of the southern delegation of treaty makers, returning in 1868 when Principal Chief Thompson appointed him a delegate of the Cherokee Nation. The appointment was regarded by many, even Boudinot's fellow delegates, as a con-ciliatory gesture to the southern Cherokees, and Cornelius was not welcomed by the group. However, he participated in the delegation's business, the major portion of which was to negotiate the sale of the so-called Neutral Lands—a vast tract in southeastern Kansas to which the Cherokees held title but upon which the tribe had not settled. The area had become valuable because of its attraction to settlers flocking to the West after the Civil War. Under the terms of the 1866 treaty, the secretary of the interior was to sell the land to the highest bidder. However, much intrigue ensued as various interests vied for control of the tract, including the American Emigrant Company, John F. Tremont of the Atlantic and Pacific Railroad, and James F. Joy, a railroad man and entrepreneur. In the end, the land was sold to Joy for a down payment of $75,000, with additional payments at fixed intervals.[1]

Another piece of business for the delegation was the negotiation of a treaty that would settle some matters from the 1866 treaty which were considered unsatisfactory by the Cherokee Nation. The new treaty stipulated that the Cherokees would be paid $3.5 million for land given by the government to other Indian groups plus other amounts for lands in Arkansas and other areas east of the Mississippi. One article, which called for $50,000 for each treaty negotiator, would have appealed greatly to the impecunious Boudinot.[2] While the new treaty was accepted by the commissioner of Indian Affairs, it was never ratified.

Cornelius had kept up his relationship with his old Arkansas political cronies, and when they offered him a seat on the state delegation to the 1868 national Democratic convention, he accepted.[3] This decision did not endear him to his fellow delegates, who had come to regard the Arkansas politicians as those who cast envious eyes over the lands on their western border and who sought to extend their political and economic hegemony over the Cherokees and other Indian nations in Indian Territory. Boudinot left the delegation in Washington just after the new treaty had been hammered out and traveled to New York City, where the convention convened on July 4, 1868. He participated in all the hectic activities that resulted in the nomination of Horatio Seymour, the cannon fodder for Republican Ulysses S. Grant's November guns.[4] This was an important time for the ambitious Cherokee, however, as he was able to network with important men in the states bordering the Cherokee Nation and to set the stage for his tobacco-marketing scheme in those areas. After the convention, he turned his attention to that venture.

During the next two or three years, Boudinot was in Washington arguing his tobacco case and lobbying Congress and various officials in his cause. As his views on territorial issues became known, he was called upon to testify at various congressional hearings. By now many of his old friends from the Confederate South were back in Congress, and he made many new ones among the politicians who favored the opening of Indian Territory. His status as an attorney, too, allowed him to handle cases and claims for clients, although his letters give little indication that he was able to earn a comfortable living from his law practice.

Cornelius subsisted for the most part on the fees he could pick up representing the affairs of clients in various claims against the government, an important industry for lawyers then and now. He and Jim Bell worked together in this regard, with Bell working the Indian Territory end as Boudinot used his knowledge of the ins and outs of the bureaucracy in Washington, often relying on friends and political associates to run interference for him. He was also able to pick up sparse and irregular income from his "interests" in the Cherokee nation—for example, his ranch on Russell Creek, several properties around Vinita, and his hotel. Often accused by his enemies of being on the payroll of the railroads or of other segments of the "Territorial Ring," Boudinot does not mention anything of the kind even in his most private letters to trusted allies like Jim Bell or Sallie Watie. No records have been found to substantiate the charges by his opponents, but of course, there wouldn't be. Any such payments—for favorable testimony before a congressional committee, for instance—would have been under the table and kept very secret by all concerned. His friendship with many politicians suggests that he may have received some largesse at their hands in the form of part-time clerkships, and Lois E. Forde reports in her dissertation on Boudinot that he held at least one committee clerkship per session.[5]

In the late 1870s, Congress abridged its practices concerning clerks attached to various committees. In 1877, regular salaried clerkships existed for only five House committees: Ways and Means, Appropriations, Public Lands, Claims, and War Claims. Other committees employed clerks as well, but on an ad hoc basis at six dollars a day during regular sessions. Boudinot probably was employed in some of these rather tenuous positions after his membership on the Cherokee delegation expired. In 1879, however, the number of committees authorized to employ salaried clerks was increased to forty, as well as a number of assistant clerks. The Clerk of the House office expanded its employees as well.

Now congressmen could select their own clerks, and Boudinot was able to find employment in various clerkships at the Capitol by using his political connections from about 1876 on. He secured one of the more lucrative salaried jobs on the House Committee on Private Land Claims, chaired by Thomas M. Gunter of Fayetteville, Arkansas, an old friend. Boudinot was officially nominated by Representative Adlai E. Stevenson of Illinois, and upon confirmation in April 1879 he drew a salary of just under $4,972.[6] He remained in this capacity until February 1881. Before this windfall, revenues from his law practice and the six-dollar-a-day clerkships barely made ends meet. Later,

Cornelius received fees for his lectures around the country, but these monies were needed to defray travel expenses. While most of the time he was able to secure passes from friendly railroad officials for the journeys, he still needed to pay for his room and board. Many of his letters to Jim Bell complain about his penury.[7]

Cornelius's lack of funds did not seem to greatly affect his social life, however. Every indication is that he was much sought after as a dinner guest and as company for other occasions as well. He had a reputation as a storyteller and reciter of poetry, and many times he found himself literally singing for his supper, his musical skills being regarded as considerable. "Boudinot's outstanding social assets seem to have been his musical and elocutionary talents," writes Forde.[8] He frequently "held whole parties spellbound by singing, and accompanying himself on the piano" with sentimental favorites. In an era in which melodrama was prized, Cornelius gave dramatic readings, presenting a striking figure with his long, flowing hair. Joaquin Miller is reported to have said that he never fully appreciated his own poetry until he heard it read by Boudinot.[9] His talents and flair for the theatrical placed him in high demand in Washington's social life, reports S. W. Harman. His talents were such that "no social function was complete without his presence."[10]

In his musical performances, Cornelius was often joined by Vinnie Ream, a renowned Washington figure. Vinnie, the woman for whom Boudinot named the town of Vinita, was a woman of considerable talent in the social as well as the musical arts. However, she achieved her most public fame as the sculptor chosen to chisel the official bust of Abraham Lincoln. She lived most of her adult life in a swirl of controversy in a world filled with fierce detractors and equally ardent admirers. She and Boudinot had a long and intimate relationship. Born in 1847 near Madison, Wisconsin, according to her biographer O. B. Campbell, she was the daughter of Robert Lee Ream, a draftsman for the surveyor general of the United States, and Lavinia McDonald.[11] Robert Ream's occupation was such that the family moved often during Vinnie's childhood, making it necessary for her to make new friends at each new home. The Reams moved to Kansas and Missouri after Wisconsin, and in 1858 they settled in Fort Smith, Arkansas on the Cherokee Nation border. At Fort Smith, Robert Ream was involved in some unsuccessful real estate ventures as a member of the firm of Carnall and Ream, and it was in the course of business that he met the young Elias Cornelius Boudinot and invited him into his home. Vinnie showed musical and artistic talent as a child, and as a teenager she sketched and painted and learned to play the guitar, harp, and piano. She was an arranger as well, and later in life she set poetry to music. After her elementary education at local schools, she attended Christian College Academy in Columbia, Missouri, where she advanced her study of art and music. The family moved to Washington DC in May 1861, where they came to know members of Congress, including Representative James R. Rollins of Athens, Missouri, who had been a director of Christian College, and Senator Edmund G. Ross of Kansas. Ross roomed with the Reams for a time.[12]

If her birth date was accurately recorded by her biographer, Vinnie began working as a post office clerk at age fourteen in 1861. However, it seems that Vinnie was not always forthcoming about her real age. In the 1860 census, for example, it is given as eighteen, while the 1870 tally, when she had left Arkansas for Washington DC, lists it as twenty-three. Apparently, Congressman Rollins took an interest in the youngster and may have helped secure her postal job. Rollins introduced Vinnie to sculptor Clark Mills at his studio in the basement of the Capitol Rotunda, and a year or so later she became Mills's student. Rollins continued his interest in Vinnie and her career, and by 1864 he decided that she was doing so well that he suggested hat she do a bust of the president. Rollins followed up on his idea by calling on Lincoln to raise the issue along with another congressional figure he had enlisted in the cause, Senator Orville Browning of Illinois. The two men were successful in their petition as Vinnie began a series of half-hour sittings with the president to capture his likeness. The two hit it off, Ream recollects in her diary, because she was "just a poor girl from the West," and she reminded him of his son Willie, who had recently died.[13] Vinnie's diary reveals that she had finished working on the clay model on Good Friday afternoon, April 14, 1865, and did not find out about Lincoln's assassination until her mother returned from the theater that evening.

When Lincoln died, a number of ideas were advanced as how to preserve his memory. One of these was to have a statue made of him to be placed in the Capitol Rotunda. Vinnie was urged by her congressional friends to apply to the commission set up to handle the statue. Her application was accompanied by a petition signed by President Andrew Johnson, General Ulysses S. Grant, 31 senators, and 114 congressmen, headed up by Thaddeus Stevens.[14] In July 1866, Congress voted to award a contract to the precocious young sculptor that called for a $5,000 payment for a plaster model and a like amount for completion and acceptance of a life-size statue in marble. Much criticism of the award broke out in the press. One popular columnist, Jane Grey Swisshelm, who had backed another candidate, described Vinnie as "a young girl of about twenty who has been studying her art for a few months, never made a statue, has some plaster busts on exhibition, including her own, minus clothing to the waist, has a pretty face, long dark curls and plenty of them."[15] Swisshelm misrepresents the statue, either through ignorance or in an attempt to spice up her story; according to Walter Lee Brown, the sculpture is a copy of Martial's ancient bust of Sabrina.[16] The same column goes on to allege that Vinnie "sees members at their lodgings or at the reception room at the Capitol, urges her claims fluently and confidently, sits in the galleries in a conspicuous position in her most bewitching dress." One male editor, at least, did not share Ms. Swisshelm's outrage, and printed her column under the headline, "A Homely Woman's Opinion of a Pretty One." Other women disapproved of the choice as well, reportedly even Mary Todd Lincoln, but the all-male Congress responded to such criticism by providing Vinnie with the room beneath the rotunda as a studio, free of charge.

Vinnie Ream went on to achieve additional fame as a sculptor. She completed a rendering of naval hero David G. Farragut reportedly cast in bronze from his flagship's propeller for Farragut Square in Washington, another commission from the federal government, and did some work on a visit to Europe, reportedly with some major artists. She began work on the statue of Sequoyah, creator of the Cherokee syllabary, which represents the state of Oklahoma in the Capitol Rotunda, but died before it was finished. During her lifetime, though, it is fair to say, she was known as much as a Washington hostess as an artist. Her guest list included General William Tecumseh Sherman, General Albert Pike, Colonel George Armstrong Custer, Horace Greeley, and various senators and congressmen.

To say that Vinnie had many male admirers would be an understatement. When she somehow got mixed up in the vote for Andrew Johnson's impeachment, a fight ensued in Congress over her use of the studio in the basement of the Capitol. Her defenders outnumbered her detractors, however, and she kept her workshop. Before her marriage to Lieutenant Richard L. Hoxie on May 28, 1878, Vinnie collected many affectionate missives from important men in Washington, many of whom seemed to act like love-struck teenagers. A letter from George Caleb Bingham, a portrait and genre painter, written less than a year before her marriage, comments on the situation: "While I was in Washington I discovered that grey haired Senators and Representatives could not muster sufficient self control to resist your charms." He goes on to say, "I have sufficient knowledge of myself to fear that if I were to place myself within the scope of their magnetic power, I would readily fall a victim to them." But Bingham vows to resist and to avoid that "pitiable and hopeless" condition in which the other suitors had placed themselves.[17] Without a doubt, the most pitiful suitor in the whole lot was the venerable Albert Pike, soldier, lawyer, poet, Mason. Time and time again he poured his heart out to her in letters and love poems, even though he was nearly forty years her senior. Even after her marriage, he kept up a correspondence with her, although by the time he reached his seventies his ardor seems to have cooled.[18] She did not have everyone fooled, however. Senator John J. Ingalls, writing to her to assure her that he and General Sherman were working to secure the commission for the Farragut statue, makes this comment: "Vinnie, you are, as I have often told you, the biggest and most delightful fraud I have ever met. Your methods are the most amusing study." He has laughed "a thousand times" at the "wiles and strategems [you use] to accomplish your ends," he adds.[19]

But it was not only the old and gray who were attracted to the young woman. By the time Cornelius Boudinot arrived as part of the southern Cherokee delegation in 1866, his young acquaintance from Fort Smith had already achieved some fame and notoriety in Washington society. The two lost no time in renewing their acquaintanceship, and Boudinot wrote a recommendation for the young sculptor in the form of an endorsement of her good character.[20] When his cousin John Rollin Ridge arrived from California, Boudinot introduced her and the two Cherokees became a part of Vinnie's retinue. According to her biography, Ridge, a poet, novelist, and newspaperman, composed a poem for her entitled "I Love Thee" that Vinnie put to music. The song, along with four Tennyson verses similarly treated, was later published as sheet music, and the lyrics were translated into Cherokee in the Sequoyan syllabary.[21]

Among her other younger admirers she counted Colonel William Penn Adair, who was to become one of Boudinot's primary adversaries in Washington and in the Territory. It is quite possible that some of the personal antagonism between Boudinot and the others arose from the fact that they were all vying for Vinnie's attentions, although no positive proof for this conjecture has surfaced. However, Boudinot—or "Boudy," as Ream called him—seems to have had the longest-lived relationship with her, this being accounted for in no small measure by his musical and declamatory talents. Also, he was close to other members of the Ream family, especially her brother Robert, who married into a Chickasaw family and lived in Indian Territory, and her sister Mary Ream Fuller, with whom Boudinot carried on a correspondence.

"Boudy" soon became a regular at the Ream residence on Pennsylvania Avenue, often joining in with his hostess in the evening's entertainment. These performances, while appearing to be spontaneous, were probably quite well planned and even, perhaps, rehearsed. Ream collected her songs in notebooks, parts of which she later had published.[22] For his part, Boudinot kept a collection of 147 songs and recitations he performed in a notebook copied out in longhand by Mary Fuller.[23] The gala evenings at Vinnie's residence appear to have been works of art in themselves. At other times she held receptions in her studio, which at one point seemed to have been a regular Wednesday-evening event for social Washington. A letter preserved in the Hoxie collection from "J. E. B." to a friend describes such an evening. Guests included "Gens. Sherman and Custer, of national fame, Col's Boudinot and Adair, of the Cherokee Nation, D. W. Voorhees, the tall sycamore of the Wabash," and several others of lesser note, including a gentleman from Germany and an inventor from Rochester, New York. The writer describes being met at the door by Vinnie's mother, then introduced to all by the artist herself, who made him feel like a "specially favored one" as she presented him to her friends. He takes special interest in one of the pieces on display on a rotating pedestal, *Spirit of the Carnival,* described as "the figure of a young female just budding into womanhood. The mask has fallen at her feet, the bust is exposed, and the delicate sensuous face is slighted turned away" as she prepares to throw a wreath of flowers to a waiting, doubtless adoring crowd. The plaster bust is probably the now-famous self-portrait, "minus clothing to the waist," of Ms. Swisshelm's column, which Vinnie would have been sure to make the centerpiece of her displayed art. The star, of course, was Vinnie herself, "small of stature, petite, lithe, active, sparkling, now running over with wit and good humor, now a shade of sadness passing over her face as if some far-off thought or inspiration were working itself out to the surface." Yet, the letter reports, the artist never loses sight of the fact that "she is entertaining friends and admirers on all sides," even when she plays an impromptu song on the harp.[24]

At one point, Vinnie contemplated going on the stage as a professional singer. She was dissuaded in this ambition by friends who pointed out that "popular prejudice" would cast suspicions upon her purity if she were to make such a career choice.[25] Amateur productions were another story, of course, and Vinnie and Cornelius went to elaborate lengths to provide entertainment for friends and acquaintances, especially people Ream was trying to impress. In 1877, she, Boudinot, and a company of assistants put on a theatrical event at Tallmadge Hall, billed as a "Literary and Musical Entertainment and Festival," over two nights, Friday and Saturday, December 6 and 7. Tickets were sold at twenty-five cents each, with proceeds going to the Trinity P. E. Church; the event was advertised in the *Washington Evening Star.*[26] They had competition that weekend, as the newspaper reports, with Dion Boucicault's *Forbidden Fruit* playing at the National Theatre and W. W. Story's lecture on art at Lincoln Hall. Edward C. Townsend gave "Humorous and Pathetic Readings" the night before at Tallmadge Hall, which was located on F Street between Ninth and Tenth. After opening night, Washington was abuzz with tales of Vinnie's appearance playing the harp in a white dress and of her and Boudinot's singing performance, which was so well received that they were called upon to sing encore after encore. With Cornelius's dramatic readings from well-known literary works an additional attraction, the show was a great success. Even the hard-bitten old soldier William Tecumseh Sherman was moved to write a note of appreciation.[27]

No doubt Boudinot carried out as many of his political maneuvers during his evenings with Vinnie as he did during the day on Capitol Hill. Certainly, the contacts he made and friendships he cultivated in his social activities were important to his essentially political life.

For the last fifteen years of his life, E. C. Boudinot was hated among many circles in Indian Territory to the point where he received death threats. For the most part, the animosity arose out of his ardent belief that the old tribal system was obsolete and that Indian Territory should begin a journey toward statehood. His very public and often-expressed view was that the treaties, which had provided at least a semblance of protection for the Indian nations in the past, were by 1870 rendered impotent. For all practical purposes, whatever sovereignty the Indian nations had possessed, in Boudinot's view, was now usurped by the national government. The tobacco case had proven this to his satisfaction: Congress had chosen to ignore the Cherokee treaty, and the U.S. Supreme Court had backed it up. "The Supreme Court has decided the tobacco case against me," he wrote to Stand Watie; "it is the death knell of the Nations."[28] But while his excise tax disagreement with the federal government had been the last nail in sovereignty's coffin for Boudinot, other spikes had been driven previously, some by his own hammer.

Cornelius's experiences with the post–Civil War treaties had given him a fairly accurate look at what the future would hold in U.S.-Indian relations. The federal negotiators had come to the table with an outline for the treaties and were able, for the most part, to include these provisions in the finished documents. Owing to several factors, however, the Native negotiators found themselves in extremely weakened positions. The first of these factors was that the nations themselves were still split into North-South factions by the war, and these wounds remained open and raw; brother still opposed brother. For its part, the federal government treated the Indians as defeated adversaries, ignoring the fact that many of them had fought on the Union side. This was made clear by the very idea that new treaties needed to be negotiated. Further, in the case of the Cherokees, the government held talks with both sides at once, using the old animosity created by the Treaty party–Ross party split, so recently exacerbated by the war, to gain its ends. From his vantage point as a southern Cherokee delegate to the treaty talks, Boudinot was quick to see that the federal government held all the good cards in this important poker game. That vantage point allowed him to see the implications of many of the 1866 treaty provisions—for example, the clauses directing that steps would be taken toward a territorial government, allowing two railroad rights-of-way, and establishing a federal court within the Cherokee Nation. He saw these as steps onto a slippery slope that led to the dissolution of tribal sovereignty. Indeed, sovereignty had already been seriously eroded by other treaty stipulations, namely the forced acceptance of a large group of people (the freedmen) onto the Cherokee citizenship rolls, the opening of tribal lands to other tribes, and the sale of the Neutral Lands in Kansas. Boudinot regarded these treaty elements as damaging to both tribal identity and territorial integrity.

Cornelius was fully aware that since the power of Congress to abrogate treaties was upheld, the Indian nations were at the mercy of a majority in the legislative branch and of those engaged in influencing Congress and manipulating public opinion. His days in Arkansas before and immediately after the war, his tenure in the Confederate Congress, and his dealings with businessmen and politicians from surrounding states gave him insights, too, into the prevailing opinion of the neighbors of Indian Territory. This opinion held that a large expanse of fertile, well-watered land, rich with minerals and other natural resources, lay just beyond their borders. According to this view, parts of this expanse were underutilized by its inhabitants while other vast tracts lay unused. Landless farmers and would-be ranchers cast envious eyes on the rich Indian farming and grazing lands as businessmen and politicians saw almost endless possibilities for profit in timber and mineral wealth as well as townsite and land development. It seemed clear to Boudinot that much of the electorate—at least in the West and Midwest—was clamoring for the opening of Indian lands to white settlement. He decided that it was just a matter of time before Congress passed legislation consolidating the Native nations into a territory and allotting tribal lands in severalty. In addition, he had watched the railroad companies manipulate the political process and saw similar and allied forces at work in the "Territorial Ring," as the group of corporate interests, railroaders, and frontier states lawmakers came to be called. Boudinot understood that many of his fellow Indians desired only to be left alone, to be able to pick up the pieces of their devastated homelands after the war, and to go on with their lives largely as they had before the war's outbreak. But he knew that this wish would never be allowed to materialize, that the war had wrought changes that could not be undone.

Another factor was present in his decision to side with the territorial forces, and it was visceral: he saw the Cherokee Nation being governed by a party opposed to the historic Ridge-Boudinot-Watie party with little relief in sight. The party in power represented the majority of Cherokee citizens, many of them full-bloods who opposed any compromise on the issue of jurisdiction or land cessions, and many of them still harbored grudges against the signers of the 1835 treaty. Boudinot's opposition to this faction was of course rooted in the assassination of his father and the consequent decline in family fortunes. The split of the Nation during the Civil War and the bitter treaty negotiations that followed exacerbated Cornelius's feelings, and nothing, not even brother William's appointment as editor of the *Cherokee Advocate* or his own selection as tribal delegate in the 1868 deliberations, did anything to assuage those sentiments. Maintaining the status quo meant for him that his ambitions for wealth and power would be stillborn, his self-image as the heir to his father and successor to Stand Watie forever doomed.

So for Boudinot, the battle for national sovereignty for Indians could never be won, and to resist was to fight a holding action that was doomed to eventual failure. Perhaps more importantly, for him and his family Cherokee sovereignty was not desirable unless he could somehow rise to power, and that was unlikely. Why not, then, he asked himself, try to manipulate the situation to one's own advantage and to the advantage of one's people? If this thing the whites called Manifest Destiny was going to succeed in the face of all opposition, why not align yourself on the winning side and hitch your wagon to its star? By this time Boudinot had figured this out for himself, but his ideas were reinforced constantly by his white associates in Washington—Senator Daniel Voorhees, Albert Pike, General Sherman, and the myriad officials and politicians who worked for the territorial and railroad interests.

That Boudinot had a pretty clear idea of where the future lay there is little doubt. To call him a prophet for this vision and for his subsequent actions on the part of opening Indian Territory to white settlement and dissolving tribal title to the land, however, would be a mistake. It is abundantly clear from his actions and from his words, public and private, that his primary motivation was to advance his own interests and, secondarily, those of his close family members, the Waties and the Bells. As part of his life's mission, he sought in his own mind to frustrate the Treaty party's old enemies and seek revenge for wrongs perpetrated against the Ridge-Boudinot-Watie clan. This view of him is complicated, though, by the fact that many of his family members, among them loyal followers of the venerated Stand Watie, were among the bitterest of his enemies. Lucien "Hooley" Bell and William Penn Adair, two of Watie's lieutenants in the Cherokee regiment, counted themselves in this number. As he made new enemies, Cornelius opposed them with the old familial fury.

Perhaps it was easy for Cherokees opposed to his ideas to despise him enough to threaten his life. After all, none of Boudinot's proposals were new; most could be found within a bill introduced earlier in the Senate by James Harlan of Iowa, which facilitated the proliferation of railroads in the West and provided for the white settlement of Indian lands on the model of the popular land-grant legislation passed around the same time. Boudinot's adoption of Harlan's proposals were novel, however, to many whites. Adherents of Harlan's ideas could point with glee to the fact that here was a Cherokee citizen, and an educated one at that, who agreed that "surplus" lands should be open to white settlers. It was the fact that Boudinot advertised his Cherokee citizenship and heritage when disseminating his views in speeches and pamphlets that aroused feelings ranging from animosity to hatred in many of his fellow Cherokees.[29] In this light, perhaps the death threats are understandable. Boudinot did not come to these views lightly, however.

The idea of treating Indian Territory like all of the other "federal" territories was not a new one when Boudinot became involved. The unique "dual sovereignty" that governed the Territory stood in the way of many of the entities interested in westward expansion, as many of the Indian nations resisted their efforts. For example, railroads, mining and minerals corporations, and settlers were all eager to extinguish the sovereignty of the tribes and establish a "federal" territory. All these groups had their champions in the halls of government. In 1848, Representative Abraham R. McIlvaine, a member of the House Committee on Indian Affairs, introduced a territorial bill, a major stipulation of which was that whites would eventually be allowed to settle on lands not being "used" by the Indians.[30] One great benefit that would accrue to the Native Americans with federal territorial status, Cherokee agent George Butler reported to the commissioner of Indian Affairs in 1851, was U.S. citizenship. The Cherokees were not impressed by this argument, and even though McIlvaine's bill was not acted upon, they decided to watch for further developments. These were not long in coming, as in 1854, Senator Robert M. Johnson of Arkansas introduced a comprehensive territorial bill for Indian Territory. Johnson's bill, which came after much debate in Congress concerning the opening of new territories and railroad routes in the West, called initially for three territories, Chalohkee (Cherokee), Muscogee (Creek), and Chahta (Choctaw). These would later be organized into the federal territory of Neosho. Chalohkee would have comprised the Cherokee Outlet, the Oklahoma panhandle, and the Seneca-Shawnee, Seneca, and Quapaw lands, and at first the Cherokees would have retained much political control, including determination of citizenship and selection of their own governor and legislature. They would be encouraged to survey their lands—to "sectionalize," as the Cherokees termed it—as a prelude to allotment of the land in severalty and eventual sale of "surplus" lands to white settlers. The Johnson bill was aimed at gradual but inexorable dissolution of tribal sovereignty and the absorption of Indian Territory into the Union. However, the measure did not pass, and the territorial matter was placed on the back burner.[31] As Craig Miner points out, Congress was not "immediately amenable" to the idea. "It was rather a process of slow slippage that finally burst into a tide of promotion."[32] The territorial simmer continued, with the flame often coming from neighboring states. Superintendent Elias Rector from Arkansas, for example, in his reports to the commissioner of Indian Affairs in 1858 and 1860, urged the establishment of a federal territory, and Governor Robert J. Walker of Kansas in his inaugural address saw statehood in the near future.[33]

After the Civil War, congressional efforts to establish a federal territory increased. In 1865, Senator Harlan introduced an unsuccessful territorial bill that nevertheless carried considerable importance; while it did not pass Congress, Commissioner of Indian Affairs Cooley used Harlan's bill as the basis for negotiations over the 1866 treaty.[34] Further, Harlan's constituents, most of whom clamored for the opening of more territory to settlement in the West, saw their cause advanced with Harlan's appointment as secretary of the interior in 1865. Finally, it was the Harlan bill that became Boudinot's guide. Especially after the decision in the tobacco case, he considered Harlan's major tenets—a territorial government, allotment in severalty, federal judicial jurisdiction, and U.S. citizenship—to be his personal gospel.

But Harlan's bill was not the only one; territorial activity was on the boil in Congress. After 1866, four to eight different territorial bills were introduced annually. When one was defeated, another was introduced, often by senators or representatives from western states. [35] The Cherokees, of course, kept a close eye on these proceedings, but it was difficult to keep up. The *Cherokee Advocate* reported with dismay in 1871 that thirty territorial bills would be introduced in the next session of Congress. [36] The territorial bills were not the Cherokees' only concern at the time, either, as a bill was introduced to end treaty making between the federal government and the Indian nations. With these direct threats to their sovereignty, the Cherokees decided that to defend themselves, they would have to seat a delegation in Washington to keep tabs on the almost daily machinations of the Territorial Ring. While support for the delegations that remained in place until the end of the century were expensive, the leaders of the Cherokees and other tribes saw them as necessary. Over the years, the delegations from Indian Territory often slugged it out with Cornelius Boudinot. Time and time again he was brought forward to refute the claims of delegates and they to answer his proposals and assertions. The rivalry between Boudinot and William Penn Adair, a delegation mainstay, became so vehement that on one occasion it resulted in an obstreperous physical set-to in the congressional halls.

Boudinot's first foray into territorial politics was in connection with the international congress held at Okmulgee in 1870. The congress was provided for in the 1866 treaties and allowed for an annual general council to be held among the Indian nations of the Indian Territory. Matters that the council was empowered to act upon included relations and intercourse among the tribes, extradition, justice systems, affairs concerning tribal members other than Indians, and defense and safety. Each tribe was entitled to one delegate plus an added delegate for each thousand Indians in the tribe. The secretary of the interior was to appoint the council's president, and a secretary was to be elected by the members. [37] In July 1870 the federal government appropriated $10,000 to convene such a congress, provided the tribes concerned did not object. Since most of the Indian leaders were interested to see if such a gathering could bring about positive results, the council met at Okmulgee that fall. Representation at this first meeting was sparse—the Choctaws and Chickasaws sent no delegates—mostly because invitations were sent out too late. In this initial gathering, however, delegates had an opportunity to get organized and to arrange for a larger meeting in December. The larger council then set up a twelve-member committee to draft a constitution for a permanent organization; elected G. W. Grayson of the Creek Nation as secretary; and received an invitation from William Potter Ross of the Cherokee Nation to locate a territorial capital at Fort Gibson in the Cherokee Nation.

While Boudinot was not a delegate to the congress, he watched developments intently. One of the important stipulations made in the 1866 treaties provided for a delegate to the U.S. Congress, to be elected by the Congress after provisions for a pan-Indian territorial government were made. Cornelius considered himself a prime candidate for this post, having been the Cherokees' delegate to the Confederate Congress and the friend and confidant of many politicians and bureaucrats in states adjacent to Indian Territory. He began politicking accordingly. His first contact was George W. Reynolds, who would become an important ally in the territorial battles to come. Reynolds was delighted to back a candidate who had the proper Indian credentials yet could be trusted to carry the territorial banner. While Stand Watie was reluctant to get involved, Cornelius and others badgered him to take his place among the Okmulgee delegation, pointing out that without his presence the Ridge-Boudinot-Watie faction would be without effective representation. With Watie monitoring the proceedings at Okmulgee, his nephew turned his attention to Washington, where Senator Harlan was about to introduce legislation to create a congressional delegate for Indian Territory. Cornelius wrote Watie from Chetopa, Kansas, where he had gone to confer with Reynolds, that Harlan's bill had been reported on favorably, but he hoped it would not be voted on until after the holidays. Presumably, this delay would help him to get his votes lined up. But he was confident: "With the help of Maj. Geo. Reynolds & friends among the Creeks and Seminoles, I think I could get a majority of their votes; if you would be in your seat at the time of Election I would not exchange my chances with anyone."[38] The timing, however, had to be exactly right, and he planned to go to Washington to try to stall the vote until January. Secrecy apparently mattered, too, as he added a postscript to his letter, urging Watie to "Destroy this letter after reading for we don't [want] our plans developed prematurely." Cornelius did not want to tip off his enemies, lest they would have time to organize a countermeasure to his plan.

No election took place, however. Instead, the council worked on writing a constitution for the territorial government. On December 16 a constitution describing a republican form of government was introduced to the assemblage. Its provisions were debated at length, but the document was approved by a vote of fifty-two to three.[39] Delegates then agreed to send the constitution to the tribes for their approval and to adjourn for six months. The plan was to meet again in June after the individual tribal councils had ratified the constitution and take the next steps in the process. Boudinot's scheme for a quick coup was thus thwarted.

J. H. Beadle commented that the Okmulgee constitution was popular among three groups in the Cherokee Nation at this time.[40] First, the "territorial" party was in favor of a territory open to white settlement after "considerable acreage" had been set aside for each Indian. Second, a "constitution" party wanted to bring the Indian population under the Okmulgee constitution, with U.S. citizenship, but no white settlement, and no U.S. territorial arrangement. The constitutionalists would give individual Indians land to farm and would provide land grants to railroads, with the rest held in common. The third party, according to Beadle, favored leaving things as they were. Boudinot was a territorialist pure and simple, favoring U.S. territorial status and white settlement. As the Okmulgee convention got set to meet again in June 1871, he found a forum for his views.

With his plans dashed to enter the halls of Congress as a delegate, Boudinot turned against the Cherokee members of the Okmulgee council. As the group was meeting, he addressed "a large number" of Cherokees at Big Cabin, the *New York Times* reported under the headline "A Warning Voice—Common Sense at Last." In the speech he urged a policy on the Cherokees that would sell the Cherokee Outlet, or Strip, and "sectionalize," or survey, their lands. Then, he advised, set aside six hundred acres for each family and sell the remainder, presumably to settlers, the railroads, or to land companies like the American Emigration Society. In ten years, Boudinot calculated, each family holding would be worth $15,000, making the Cherokees "the richest community in the world."[41]

For its part, the Okmulgee Grand Council convened on June 9 to take up its main business, the formation of a government for all the tribes in Indian Territory. This high aim was thwarted, however, when delegates found that only one Indian nation, the Creeks, had ratified the constitution. For one reason or another, other tribes, such as the Chickasaws and the Cherokees, had not been able to bring the matter before their general councils. Many of the smaller tribes, it was found, had taken no action at all, and some did not plan to. Moreover, communication was difficult among the various tribes, with multiple translations to be made and dissimilar traditions in protocol to be observed. Particular problems occurred with regard to the tribes that had arrived more recently in the Territory.[42] Delegates were united on one point, however: their alarm at the decision in the Boudinot tobacco case. The convention adopted a report on the case submitted by the Cherokee delegation, which pointed out that the Supreme Court's decision "commits us wholly to the political department of the Government, and places us entirely at its mercy." The report goes on to say, "In our ignorance we have supposed that treaties were solemn forms, and the most sacred pledges of human faith, that they constituted part of the supreme law of the land, and that they could be abrogated only by mutual consent." It then asks the federal government to remember the promises made to the tribes and to "enact no law that affects our rights without the most careful consideration."[43] These statements, it is fair to say, point up the difference between the delegates' reaction to the case and Boudinot's. On the one hand, the delegates seem to be in a state of denial and to expect the government to respect the spirit, if not the letter, of the treaties. In Boudinot's mind, on the other hand, the purport of the Court's decision was clear: Congress was no longer under any obligation to respect the terms of any treaty, no matter how sacred or inviolable it was held by the other party. The point made by Court's decision in the tobacco case was driven home to Boudinot by the act of Congress passed March 3, 1871, that brought an end to treaty making between the United States and the Indian nations. The specific language of the act's major section was especially poignant to him: "no Indian nation or tribe . . . shall be acknowledged or recognized as an independent nation, tribe, or power, with whom the United States may contract by treaty." Sovereignty was a dead issue as far as Boudinot was concerned.

When Boudinot made his important speech outlining his views on allotment and white settlement in the Cherokee Nation on Thursday, September 21, 1871, his views were already widely known. In fact, by the time he gave his Vinita address, as it came to be called, he had received the first of a series of death threats. One of the leading men of the Cherokee Nation, in fact, had referred to Boudinot as a "traitor."[44] It is no wonder, then, that he referred to those who disagreed with him as "enemies"; some of them very clearly were.[45]

The speech was calculated to establish Cornelius on the winning side, as he saw it. Once again, his idea was to position himself so that when the profits were made he would partake of them along with the movers and shakers of the expansionist movement. The speech was designed, too, to rally support for his position. Boudinot was not alone in his wish to seize opportunity wherever and whenever it presented itself; many prominent men in the Cherokee Nation, especially those among the old Ridge-Boudinot-Watie party, shared his ambition and his views.

Cornelius was well aware that those views were not shared by the majority of Cherokees, however, and he made reference to that fact as he opened his remarks to his fellow citizens. His views are unpopular, he admits, but they are founded upon "truth and good sense," and as such, he predicts confidently,

"they will prevail." Unpopular ideas, he points out, were held by other purveyors of truth, such as Socrates, Galileo, the abolitionists before the Civil War,
and even Jesus, so he feels he is in good company. He refers to the threats of
violence and death that had been levied against him by people who are incensed
by his "simple, honest expression of opinion" on what is the best policy for the
Cherokees in "this grave crisis in their affairs."[46]

In trying to establish his character and authority in this speech, Cornelius
attacks his detractors in straightforward, rough-and-tumble terms, using language he would not use in front of more sophisticated audiences. He asks, for
example, "Who are the persons who are loudest in denunciation of me, because
of my political opinions? In seven cases out of nine they will be found to be
disreputable white men who have been expelled from respectable society in
the States, have found an asylum in the Cherokee Nation and become citizens
by marriage. Col. Vann and a few other blue-eyed fair skinned Cherokees (!)
reinforce this set, and call me a traitor to my people and my nation." He goes
on to identify a "crazy, broken down political hack" and a "skillful obtainer of
money under false pretences" who "has no claim to Indian blood, but talks as
loudly of the wrongs of 'Us Indians' as the jail birds before referred to." Finally,
Cornelius refers his audience to a man in the crowd who attacks Boudinot
while engaging in the illegal whiskey trade. "I do insist," he says, "of this white
man who sets himself up as a judge of who are citizens of this Nation, [who]
continues to introduce whiskey in bags of oats, he shall at least furnish us
with a better article." Of course, Boudinot knew that anyone in a frontier
town like Vinita would expect some supercharged claims and denunciations
of character in a political speech, and he doubtless wanted to get his licks in
early. He knew, too, that this kind of language would appeal to the prejudices
and concerns of his audience. He knew how to pull other emotional strings,
too. In his discussion of the sovereignty of the Cherokee Nation, Boudinot
relates an incident in which the Cherokee chief and his delegation are left
cooling their heels for days until a "sable" clerk to the secretary of the interior
deigns to grant an audience.

Boudinot was not only calling people names here. His remarks were intended to target specific problems in the Cherokee Nation, problems which
he knew were close to the hearts of the people. In the attacks on his detractors,
he is identifying those men with these issues: the white intruder problem in
its various guises; the whiskey trade, on which one Cherokee agent placed the
blame for 90 percent of the crimes committed by Indians;[47] the citizenship

issue; and the problems the Cherokees were having accepting their former slaves as citizens after the Civil War.

Boudinot then goes on to say that his aim is the passage of a "territorial bill for the Indian country," which would bring about the following:

- Allotment in severalty, with each Cherokee receiving 160 acres, "inalienable for twenty years";
- The remaining land to be sold for an average of $1.25 per acre;
- Three million dollars to be set aside as an education fund for Cherokee children;
- Interest on tribal funds to be paid in per capita disbursements annually;
- Creation of U.S. courts in "Indian Country";
- U.S. citizenship for Indians;
- An Indian delegate to Congress.

After setting out the main points of his program, Boudinot goes on to voice his conviction that Congress has the "lawful power, if it thinks best, to abolish every vestige of Indian government and substitute any other it chooses." [48] He goes on to enumerate the many ways in which Cherokee sovereignty and the sanctity of their treaties have been eroded since the early years of the century and concludes with these words: "What folly, then, to talk of the independence of the Cherokee nation! Our government is a mere plaything, allowed to us as toys are given to children for their amusement; we are to hold and enjoy it at the pleasure of the United States."[49] His own experience with the tobacco case is the reality, he declares, and any trust placed in "antiquated and obsolete provision of old treaties" is appearance only, the flimsiest of window dressing. Boudinot then lists the benefits of territorial status for Cherokee citizens; among these is his calculation that the net worth of a Cherokee family of four after the sale of "surplus" land would be much greater than that of families in even the most prosperous states. His conclusions are clear: since the U.S. government can and will in the near future institute the measures that Boudinot is calling for, the Cherokees should negotiate the most advantageous terms while they still can. Stop the wishful thinking, he urges, and see the situation for what it is. The Indian must accept the inevitable and become "educated," or assimilated. The choice is clear: "The Indian must become civilized and learn to live by the sweat of his brow or he will be exterminated."[50]

After his speech in Vinita, Boudinot went to Washington to give the "inevitable" territorial legislation a little shove. His agitation for an Indian delegate to Congress, aside from its self-serving aspects, was in some measure at least aimed at the Cherokee delegations that seemed to be camped constantly in Washington. Officials of the Nation saw a need to have trusted people on the scene, especially when territorial legislation was being pushed by railroads, land companies, settler organizations, and a variety of other lobbies. The delegates appeared and testified at hearings, published pamphlets with the Nation's message spelled out, and buttonholed senators and representatives in the Capitol's corridors. Boudinot and others, however, decried the cost—$60,000 a year, he estimated in the Vinita speech—that came from the Cherokee, and not the federal, coffers. His vehemence against the delegates may be explained by his bitter personal experiences as a member of various delegations—for example, the payment squabble with John Rollin Ridge over the ill-fated Civil War treaty legation and the personal rebuffs received from his fellow envoys to Washington in 1868. The animosity between the Cherokee representatives and Boudinot, in any case, increased as a time went on, and its personal nature was heightened as the territorial battles raged on.

When William Potter Ross, a member of the Cherokee delegation, appeared before the House Committee on Territories early in 1872 to speak against a territory, it is not surprising that Boudinot was standing in the wings prepared to rebut his testimony. The arguments presented in this confrontation were repeated in numerous other testimonies before Congress given by Boudinot and Cherokee officials like Ross. Born at Lookout Mountain in the old Cherokee Nation, Ross acquired an excellent education, beginning in mission schools and culminating with an honors degree from Princeton. He served on the Cherokee National Council and in 1844 became the first editor of the *Cherokee Advocate*. He was elected principal chief of the Cherokees in 1873. When Boudinot's time came to speak, his first words deny that the delegation's views are universal in the Cherokee Nation. A "radical change" has taken place, he says and "nearly everyone, excepting the full bloods" desires a territorial government, or at least a change in the status quo. After this introduction, Boudinot continues the train of thought carried in the Vinita speech by discussing Congress's authority to effect a change, the inevitability of it, the accrual of benefits to the Cherokees by such an act, and the advantages to the country as a whole.[51]

Cornelius attacks the "dead issue—as dead as Lazarus in his tomb" of Indian national sovereignty first, laying out before the committee members legal decisions in the manner of a well-prepared brief, refuting Ross's earlier testimony.

Ross's primary mistake, Boudinot says, is assuming that the Indians have ownership of the lands they occupy. The courts have made it clear that ultimate title to the land resides with the United States; while the Indians have "right of occupancy," this does not supersede the government's claim.[52] In Congress, therefore, resides the power to regulate the uses of the land and its occupants. To bolster his position that the government's position is primary concerning Indians, Boudinot cites the act of Congress passed in March of the previous year in which treaty making with Indian nations was abolished. To top off his case, he cites the Supreme Court decision in his own case, adding that "I did *my* best to uphold the supremacy of Indian treaties" and asking where Ross's eloquence was when that landmark case was being tried.

In answer to the Cherokee delegation's contention that the pending territorial legislation violates treaties, Boudinot then turns to the latest of these, the treaties of 1866, which, he says, call for the establishment of an Oklahoma Territory with a General Assembly made up of delegates from the various tribes in Indian Territory. The General Assembly, he insists, is the same Grand Council meeting in Okmulgee; further, Boudinot quotes from Ross's statements, as reported by the *Cherokee Advocate*, that the proposals emanating from Okmulgee establish a "territorial government in fact."[53] In his endorsement of the Okmulgee Constitution, Ross supports a territorial government for Indian Territory, a position inconsistent with his opposition before the Committee. Boudinot ends his presentation with a recitation of benefits that would accrue to Indian citizens of the new territory as spelled out in his Vinita speech.

Boudinot's remarks caused some stir, as the Cherokee delegation and at least one Washington journalist saw fit to respond to his speech. Cornelius returned to the House of Committee on Territories on March 5 to reply once again to Ross and his delegation.[54] His activities did not go unnoticed back in the Cherokee Nation, either. In a letter to Rev. John B. Jones, longtime Baptist missionary to the Cherokees, Principal Chief Lewis Downing described Boudinot in damning terms: "This man is employed in the interest of Railroads and particularly devoted to the Atlantic and Pacific Railroad Co. With vast schemes, for self-aggrandizement by private speculations in the land which is the common heritage of the Cherokee people, he uses the name of Cherokee for the purpose of robbing and crushing the Cherokee people. He prostitutes his Indian blood to these base purposes for the sake of money."[55] Downing then asks Jones to join the Washington delegation, presumably to strengthen it against Boudinot's onslaughts. Cornelius's efforts drew attention from the Cherokee government's opponents as well. George Reynolds and the other businessmen lobbying Congress to organize the Indian lands into a federal territory must have regarded Boudinot's testimony in the nation's capital as a success; from that point on they clearly saw his presence and his rhetoric as a formidable weapon in their arsenal, bringing him to the front whenever the territorial guns blazed. This is not to say that Boudinot was simply a pawn in the hands of greedy white men eager to carve up Indian lands; he thoroughly enjoyed the attention, the prestige, and the financial support he received through committee clerkships. Too, he saw these appearances as golden public-relations opportunities to flaunt his oratorical and legal skills before powerful people who might prove valuable to his strong, albeit still vague, ambitions. The relationship thus struck continued for the next several years with Boudinot's repeated appearances before legislative bodies in Washington and other audiences elsewhere.[56]

CHAPTER 9

Missionary

If a missionary differs from an adherent or enthusiast in a willingness to spread the word to others, then during the last two decades of his life Boudinot may be described as a territorial missionary. He spent much of this time preaching his gospel on the lecture circuit, in print, and in the halls of government. When he appeared in person, he presented a handsome appearance. As described in Marie Le Baron's "Washington Notables" column in the *Baltimore Sun*, Boudinot "is a grand fellow, above average height, stalwart, well formed. He is slightly lame, having been crippled in childhood, but the halt in his walk does not interfere with his dignity of bearing." Le Baron goes on to describe a look that Boudinot was to cultivate and which is apparent in the few extant photographs of him: "His features are strong, expressive, holding that look of patience which is the facial seal to some fixed, unalterable purpose. His eyes burn and darken with the smile that quickly follows."[1]

At a meeting in Caddo, Choctaw Nation, on October 22, 1875, Boudinot stood before a largely partisan audience and proposed a set of resolutions outlining his policy goals. The *New York Times* stringer covered the meeting, as events in Indian Territory interested many of its readers, especially those in business. "His speech was one of the most impressive and eloquent he ever made," oozed the reporter. His proposal, which came to be known as the Caddo resolutions, comprised the following:

1. Reorganizing the Indian Territory along the lines called for in the Harlan bill, thus effectively diminishing individual governments of the Indian nations and effectively dissolving their sovereignty.

2. Recognizing the Grand Council as the legislative body for the territory. The council was to be made up of delegates from each Indian group.

3. Appointing a delegate to Congress for the new territory.

4. Forbidding any attempts to drive a wedge between full-bloods and other tribal citizens.

5. Settling claims by the Indian nations against the federal government.

6. Barring the resettlement of any additional tribes in the Territory.

This set of principles replaced those pronounced in his 1871 Vinita speech, but the common thread remained as Cornelius made adjustments necessitated by current events.

Reorganization of the Territory into a political entity that undermined Indian national sovereignty remained the core issue for Boudinot and those who would open Indian lands to white settlement, but other topics had become important as well. For example, the resettlement issue had been pushed to the forefront by a government interested in removing certain tribes from their homelands and settling them in Indian Territory, one of the stipulations made in the 1866 treaties. When the government saw fit to remove the troublesome Modocs, they were sent to Indian Territory and assigned a portion of land and an agent. For the Washington bureaucracy, the Modoc subjugation was then complete. Boudinot and his allies, however, saw this process as a threat. Moving in subject tribes would soon use up all the land that they considered "surplus," thus destroying the Territory's attraction to settlers and thus any profits to be made from land sales and exploitation of other resources. Therefore, while Cornelius and others opposed resettlement of tribes like the Modocs on humanitarian grounds in their pronouncements, their real motives were fairly obvious. While Boudinot and his allies used the Caddo resolutions as their credo for a couple of years before circumstances called for further adjustments, Cornelius's ideas were not well received by the Indian inhabitants of the Territory. At its meeting in September 1875, the Grand Council overwhelmingly rejected the resolutions and added a resolution condemning Boudinot as well.

This condemnation was not done hastily but was passed in the light of Boudinot's recent public activities. The Grand Council and its membership were not his main audience, after all. At every opportunity, Cornelius traveled the Midwest and the East spreading his message, telling his willing listeners of the "surplus" lands "not being used" by the Indian nations that owned them. In those heady days of homesteading and Manifest Destiny, Cornelius was preaching to the choir on most nights. The culture of westward expansion was already well established; his job was to fill in the details. From the time of his successful speech at Vinita in 1871, he traveled widely, earning money from collections taken up in the meeting halls where he spoke, his rail fare paid by the railroads. Boudinot always seemed to have a ready supply of rail passes, doling them out as needed to Jim Bell and other supporters. If he was not on a railroad payroll, he certainly received support from them in this way.

His way was paved by an advance pamphlet that he had printed and distributed through the venues where he was booked to speak. An examination of this document says much about Boudinot's methods and intentions. Printed on good stock, the cover carries a bust-size engraving of the speaker, who is dressed in a business suit and vest with a string tie. His handsome face, with its long, black mustache, seems to be gazing into the distance. His shoulder-length hair is black and flowing (Boudinot's hair must have been a trademark feature, as it is mentioned often by both his friends and enemies). Above the engraving, the title "E. C. Boudinot, The Indian Orator and Lecturer" is announced; underneath is his signature and a quote from the *New York Times*: "He is one of the very few speakers who mount a rostrum because they have something to say which the world will be bettered by hearing. He is also one of the few Indians who have had the ability to comprehend the situation of the red man, and manliness to deplore the position of dependence in which the American Government has placed them. He is not only an eloquent speaker, but a thinker candid and unbiased, and actuated by the truest love of his race." Inside the pamphlet, a page is dedicated to a short biography, which begins with the lurid facts surrounding the assassinations of his father, a "Cherokee Chief," and his relatives the Ridges. In the second paragraph he is linked to his illustrious forebears by the mention of death threats that have been leveled at him because of his advanced ideas; the biography closes with another mention of his father's assassination. The "Object" of the lectures follows, outlining Boudinot's plans to use the proceeds from his lectures to establish a newspaper in Indian Territory, "which shall be the fearless champion of Indian rights, and the bold advocate of progress and reform among his people."

The subject of the lectures, "while treating of 'the Indian question' generally, has more especial bearing upon the civilized nations of Indians occupying the Indian Territory. The traditions and customs, advancement in civilization and present condition of these Indians, is treated by Col. Boudinot in a manner, considered by all who have heard him as most interesting and instructive." The promise of both instruction and entertainment is held out to the genteel

Victorian audiences Cornelius intends to cultivate and from which he wishes to solicit support, pecuniary and political. The pamphlet closes with an important endorsement, entitled "From Sherman." An excerpt from a letter of introduction written by General William Tecumseh Sherman at U.S. Army Headquarters in Washington to Peter Cooper in New York City, the piece exhorts Cooper to assist Boudinot "in attracting an audience." Doing so, Sherman goes on, will be an act of service to Indians as well as an "act of courtesy to a most worthy gentleman." The page is filled out by a comment from the *Fort Scott Daily Monitor* to the effect that "the specimens of Indian oratory" found in Boudinot's lecture "are entertaining and eloquent beyond description."[2]

Boudinot spoke in some important venues throughout the 1870s, including the National Geographic Society in 1874 and a series of YMCAs, an organization that engaged speakers with "educational" messages for the public. By this time he had developed a set piece, "The Manners, Customs, Traditions, and Present Condition of the Civilized Indians of the Indian Territory," referred to in the advance pamphlet. The speech was subsequently printed, making up a substantial forty-three-page document. While the text is purportedly educational, it is a persuasive argument for a drastic change in Indian policy. In it, Boudinot advocates doing away with the system of removing the indigenous people from land sought for the use of the white population and placing them on reservations. He also foretells the end of the government policy of treating Indian tribes as sovereign nations, a concept going back to early colonial times. This latter change was already taking place and was evident in Congress's 1871 decision to cease treaty making and in his own tobacco case. Instead of removal, Boudinot advocates assimilation of the Indian cultures into the Euro-American dominant society, a process that the Five Civilized Tribes had already embraced.

Cornelius begins his case by paying homage to Manifest Destiny, a glorious achievement for America. Why, he then asks, separate the Indians from the wonderful fruits of progress that this movement has carried with it? Why not help them to become productive citizens in the mainstream rather than isolated pockets of resistance to modern ideas? He goes on to review the historical accounts from colonial New England to show that the intent of the original white settlers in America was to include the Indians, making them subject to the laws, religious and secular, of each colony. But along the way, he argues, that original purpose had been superseded by a policy of removal and exclusion for the Indian until, of a total population of 235,000, "only 50,000 may be classed as civilized; 20,000 partially so; and the remainder, 165,000, constituting, as will be seen, a large majority of the Indians, are as wild as when Columbus first planted the cross and the standard of Spain upon the shores of this Continent."[3] He maintains that the reason the Five Tribes are civilized while others like the Sioux and Pawnee cling to their old cultures is because the former have been in proximity to whites and have accepted white forms of education. Extend these "privileges" to the other tribes, he argues, and civilization will soon extend to them.

Boudinot then goes on to recount the history of the Natchez and related tribes, connecting them with the ancient Indians of Mexico in blood and beliefs. He treats, in turn, the history of the Choctaws and Chickasaws and the Creeks and Seminoles before turning to that of his own people. His father and the Ridges, along with the Muscogee leader McIntosh, are depicted as martyrs to civilization, done away with by "those who preferred a savage life and clung to their old traditions, manners, and customs, held out to the last against it."[4] Boudinot pays special attention to the high rate of Cherokee literacy and its journalistic tradition, mentioning the Sequoyan syllabary as well as the widely read national newspapers—the *Phoenix*, edited by his father, and the *Advocate*, edited by his brother. Both newspapers, he points out, advocated civilization and education in the American tradition.

After touching on the Senecas and Shawnees, some of whom have moved among the Cherokees, he mentions their great leaders, Red Jacket and Tecumseh, before closing his argument. His final message is to urge not only the civilizing of the untutored bulk of the Indian population but also taking a step beyond that. Boudinot calls for "practical legislation" that "will emancipate the civilized Indian from his dependent condition" so that he can "exclaim as proudly as any other person, 'I too am an American citizen!'"[5] Clearly, there is only one way to make this shift in status possible: by dissolving national sovereignty for the tribes and making them citizens of a reorganized territory.

While Boudinot's oratorical eloquence has been lost in those days before electronic recording, many of his words have been preserved in the form of pamphlets, which, judging by where they turn up today, were distributed widely. Taken down by reporters in shorthand as he spoke, the texts of many of Boudinot's speeches and testimony before Congress were then transcribed into copy that printers could use to reproduce and provide to the speakers and others. In Boudinot's voluminous correspondence with Jim Bell there is mention of procuring "subscriptions" from colleagues and other like-minded individuals to cover the cost of printing and paying the stenographers. The pamphlets would be used in the eastern cities and western white settlements to raise support for the cause. Opponents, of course, were free to print their own pamphlets in rebuttal, and many verbal skirmishes were fought as a result. In Boudinot's case, the audience for his speeches seemed to be the white populations of states surrounding Indian Territory—Kansas, Missouri, Arkansas, and to some extent Iowa, Illinois, and Indiana. He knew he could expect political support from these areas in Washington, and it was important to keep the territorial issue alive and constantly in front of the voting public.

Not just rabble-rousing affairs, Cornelius's speeches were crafted in rather sophisticated ways. One of the most interesting things about these addresses is that they show Boudinot to be a master of classical rhetorical style. He was able to take his education, specifically the teaching of Aristotle and others on the forms of persuasive address, and use it to press his views upon his audiences. These speeches also show that Boudinot knew how to analyze an audience, and while the substance of what he had to say seldom varied, his methods of delivery changed to suit his audience. It may be said that he addressed three types of audiences in speeches designed to promote his political views: first, government, and especially congressional committees; second, the people of Indian Territory; and third, gatherings of whites interested in the "Indian question," and more specifically, the question of opening territories previously reserved for Indian use.

A good example of the government speech is "Oklahoma: Argument of Col. E. C. Boudinot before the Committee on Territories, January 29, 1878." At this time, the committee was considering H.R. bill no. 1596, one to establish a territorial government in Indian Territory to replace the tribal ones. Boudinot begins by making an ethical appeal to his audience, a mode of persuasion in classical rhetoric that establishes the character of the speaker in such a way as to gain their trust and admiration. In his opening remarks, Boudinot says, "Those who are at all acquainted with the condition of affairs in Indian Territory know that such has been the prejudice excited against me on account of the position that I occupy upon this question, that at times my life has been considered to be in danger." Even those who agree with him warn him against speaking out, he says. "They reminded me that too often in that country they who differed with popular prejudices were branded as traitors; and that was sufficient to invite the assassin's knife and the assassin's bullet." He then goes on to establish that his ideas on the subject of territorial government predate the coming of railroads to Indian Territory. "So much," Boudinot says, "for the silly and malicious charge that railroads have anything to do with the views I entertain on this question."

The speaker follows his ethical appeal with an appeal to logic, a sister mode of persuasion in classical rhetoric. At this point he is replying to the delegations from the Indian nations who are arguing against territorial government. In their argument, they cite treaties dating back to 1785 which affirm that lands ceded to the Indians shall be theirs "forever" and that they shall not be removed without their "consent." Boudinot argues with some logical force that the only treaties that should be considered in force are the last ones, the treaties of the Five Civilized Tribes with the United States made in 1866. In these treaties, he argues, the tribes have given their consent for such a government and thus given up their right to the land in perpetuity. As one of his examples, he offers the Creek treaty of 1830.

> [It] designates the country that they shall hereafter occupy in the Indian Territory—six and a half millions of acres of land in round numbers, that shall be theirs "forever." The treaty says it shall be theirs "forever"; but in 1866 what did they do? They sold one-half of it to the United States; is it theirs forever? Where is the three and a half millions of acres of land that is to be yours? In 1866 you sold the three and a half millions of acres of land to the United States Government for thirty cents an acre, and you have got the money for it. Whose land is it today? the government of the United States has purchased it from you. It is not yours forever. You might as well point back to the old treaties and say, "That is our land because the treaties said it should be ours forever." It is not yours; it belongs to the government of the United States because they purchased it by the treaty of 1866.

Boudinot then goes on to apply the same logic to the Seminole treaties and those of the Chickasaws and Choctaws, saving the Cherokee treaties for last.

Later in the same speech, Boudinot argues for the economic sense of establishing a territorial government. Under such an arrangement, he says, the expense of supporting separate national governments for the Indians, as well as the expense of maintaining delegations in Washington, would disappear. This would benefit not the comparatively rich members of the delegations but the poor, ordinary Indian citizen. In a striking appeal to emotion, the third classical mode of persuasion, Boudinot says, "Why gentlemen, the poor Indian who is today shivering in his calico hunting shirt in his little hovel, his pony and two or three pigs around him, constituting his estate—all his property would not bring $100—with his five or six half-naked and half-starved children pays, and each one of those little naked children pays, just as much to support the

Cherokee government and this delegation, as Col. Adair with his $50 or 60 thousand worth of property. These poor Indians pay just as much to support their governments as do the rich."

To some extent, Boudinot changes his tactics when he is speaking back in Indian Territory to an audience very much different from the ones in congressional committee rooms. However, he uses the three persuasive modes of rhetoric with the same effectiveness. In his speech delivered at Vinita, Boudinot begins, as he does in the government speech discussed above, with an ethical appeal to establish his own character and authority: "The views I shall present today are not popular because they are not understood; they are not understood, and disturb your prejudices because the Cherokee people have frowned down all attempts to reason upon them. You are advised by some to appeal to that argument of brutes—force. I trust you will not. Such argument never convinces, but like the boomerang thrown by unskillful hands flies back to the injury of those who use it." Notice, now, however, that emotional language replaces the calm, lawyer-like language of the committee room used in the former speech: "That spirit of proscription which will not tolerate antagonistic sentiments in others has disgraced all periods of the world; it forced the cup of poison to the lips of Socrates; it reviled the Son of Man in His last great agony of Calvary; it imprisoned Galileo; it destroyed the presses, and inflicted violence on the disciples of anti-slavery, but it has never smothered a single great truth, nor extinguished a single sound principle." He then comments on the threats of violence against him, saying that this is the price he pays for differing with those in authority on the best policy for the Cherokee people. Just three paragraphs into his address, he has placed himself in some pretty auspicious company.

In trying to establish his character and authority in the Caddo resolutions speech, he attacks his detractors in straightforward, rough-and-tumble-terms, using language he would not use in the dignified halls of the Capitol. Boudinot knew that this kind of language would appeal to the prejudices and concerns of his audience. He knew how to pull other emotional strings, too. But he knew that he must apply logic as well as ethical and emotional appeals. In the Vinita speech, as in the speech before the House Committee on Territories, Boudinot has come armed with figures. He is able to project in dollars and cents the advantages of a territorial government with charts that would make a modern statistician proud. Finally, Boudinot uses the rhetorical tactic of *confutatio*, or the refutation of opposing arguments, to conclude his address.

Boudinot uses similar rhetorical techniques when he appeals to white audiences in the hinterlands. He advances legal arguments, cites treaties and laws, but adds and emphasizes one key ingredient to those used in Washington: the inherent right of American settlers to occupy "surplus government lands." This issue was in keeping with the spirit of the homestead legislation and of America's expansionist birthright. The speeches he made in Chicago, St. Louis, Boston, and New York as well in many smaller midwestern towns carried this emotionally charged message, accounting for his success with this audience.

Boudinot and others pushing for opening the Indian Territory to white settlement saw the propaganda value of having a Cherokee citizen agitating on the speaker's podium. Having his arguments presented in print, to their way of thinking, was even better, since this method of dissemination reached a wider audience. Thus, when Cornelius proposed establishing a newspaper in the Territory that would broadcast his views, the idea was quickly accepted and some financial backing secured. Boudinot wrote Jim Bell from Chetopa, Kansas, on August 30, 1875, saying, "I have been trying to put the newspaper project on foot: have both the type necessary & am now negotiating for a house here, intending if I succeed to transport it in pieces to Muscogee [sic] & put it up." This method of securing shelter was not unusual on the plains, apparently.[6] In the same letter, Boudinot mentions the difficulty of raising the money needed for the venture and two possible sources: "I am straining every nerve to accomplish this, & if we cant find friends enough to help, I believe I can meet the outlay by lecturing."[7] He had earlier suggested organizing a stock company "of say, about $1500 for the purpose," estimating the costs as a house for $500 and a press and type for $1,000. Cornelius, about to set out on a lecturing tour of Kentucky and Ohio, had high hopes for the success of that endeavor, for he offered to pay in $200 for the venture. The rest would come from "$5, $10, and $20 subscriptions from friends." He promises to canvass Kentucky and Ohio for subscriptions, but he ends his letter asking Bell to write to him in St. Louis care of the Missouri, Kansas, and Texas Railroad.[8] It was probably in St. Louis that he enlisted Reynolds's support. Still, whatever was coming from the railroad was meager. On the eve of publication, he suggested that Bell try to get subscriptions by organizing "Clubs of 5 at $1 a piece."[9]

The plan was to publish from Muskogee in the Creek Nation, a thriving town in 1875, with Cornelius as editor along with E. Poe Harris, a white man. Harris was a physician who came to Indian Territory after the Civil War. He married the daughter of Cherokee Tom Wolfe and for many years tried to establish himself as an intermarried Cherokee citizen, but the tribe rebuffed him. Harris wrote for and edited the newspaper with Boudinot, but he was especially valuable when Cornelius was out of the Territory on business in Washington or on a speaking engagement. After the paper was discontinued, he lived at Tahlequah until 1879, and later at Savanna in the Choctaw Nation. He died at South McAlester in July 1898, at age sixty-seven. [10]

Indian Progress began publication on October 22, 1875, at Muskogee, immediately angering the Creek government. Its prospectus promised to print at least two columns each in the Cherokee, Creek, Choctaw, Chickasaw, and Seminole languages and some twenty in English. The Indian-language issue was a ploy meant to imply a readership and thus support among traditional members of the Five Civilized Tribes, when in truth Boudinot's policies never appealed to these groups. The newspaper likewise boasted that it was owned, edited, and printed by "people of Indian blood," another appeal to white audiences unfamiliar with the real political situation in Indian Territory. This claim also, no doubt, gave impetus to Harris's applications for intermarried status with the Cherokees. Promising to advocate "progress" and "higher civilization" among Indian people, the paper foreshadowed the assimilationist positions of the latter decades of the nineteenth century and first half of the twentieth. In addition, *Indian Progress* promised to promote "faithful observance" of the treaties and "defense of Indian's property against fraud and corruption."

The Creek authorities responded to the newspaper's appearance by sending in the lighthorse police to close it. Before the prospectus for the *Progress* was printed, Boudinot had met with Creek chief Samuel Checote to apprise him of his plans, and Boudinot, at least, felt that he had received the go-ahead from the Creek leader. But before the publishers could print the first number, the Creek National Council passed a resolution banning the paper from the Nation. The reasons listed for their action included the fact that Harris was not an Indian, that Boudinot had put up the building that housed the press without permission, and, most importantly, that the paper intended to publish articles supporting the Caddo resolutions. [11] Accordingly, Boudinot and Harris were given ten days to remove their property from the Creek Nation or face its confiscation. While this could be seen as an act of silencing a political opponent, the situation was a bit more complicated. For some time, the Creek Nation had contemplated supporting a newspaper of its own, and the same National Council that served an eviction notice on the *Progress* passed an act incorporating the International Printing Company, organized to published the *Indian Journal*. The word "International" in the company's title denoted the interest in the company of one William Potter Ross, the old and bitter enemy of Boudinot's, as president, with Joseph P. Folsom, a Choctaw, as secretary, and Samuel Grayson, a Creek, as treasurer. Another stockholder was the Creek principal chief, Samuel Checote.

Boudinot accused an axis of accomplices, including Ross, General John Peter Cleaver Shanks, and Myron P. Roberts, of being behind this action. Shanks had recently arrived in Indian Territory as special U.S. commissioner to settle the question of the "Freedmen" in the Cherokee Nation and had in a brief time brought on Cornelius's wrath. Roberts, born in New York, had been in the wholesale and retail drug business in Chicago and Sheboygan Falls, Wisconsin, before moving to Muskogee in 1874. His association with Ross was enough to put him on the Boudinot enemies list. Boudinot and his allies knew that the trio were about to enter the newspaper business in Muskogee and so had reason beyond a general loathing to wish Cornelius and his newspaper out of the area. The *Oklahoma Star* and other Boudinot friends reported that the *Progress* publishers had until November 15 before their property would be confiscated and sold. The *Star* and *Progress* both filled their columns with cries for the defense of "Freedom of the Press" and free speech. Based at Caddo in the Choctaw Nation, the *Star*'s editor was Granville McPherson, a white man from Little Rock who had married Lizzie P. Folsom, a Choctaw. McPherson had originally come to Indian Territory as a Confederate soldier and as such was an old acquaintance of Boudinot's. As the *Star*'s editor, McPherson followed the Boudinot line so closely that one irate Choctaw citizen physically attacked him. [12] Cornelius appealed the Creek Nation's decision to the Union agent, George W. Ingalls, raising another issue that, he was certain, had figured into the debate. Boudinot's letter to Ingalls denied that the railroads owned any interest in the *Progress* and that he was not employed by any railway as a lawyer. [13] While this assertion may have been technically correct, Cornelius failed to mention that George Reynolds, a Boudinot crony who was a former Seminole agent and presently employed by the Katy Railroad, held a half interest in the *Progress*'s assets. The issue was not dropped with Cornelius's denial to Ingalls; on November 10 the *Vindicator*, a paper published at Atoka in the Choctaw Nation, included the agent in one of its frequent attacks on Boudinot, saying that if Ingalls did not know about Reynolds's interest in the *Progress*, then he was in on the conspiracy and should resign.

With the doors to Muskogee closed to him, Boudinot moved his press and other equipment to Vinita in the Cherokee Nation, from where it resumed publication in December 1875. The paper printed political news and editorials, many written by Boudinot, and despite its vow to be apolitical it was clearly anti-Ross. It supported a territorial government and U.S. citizenship for the citizens of Indian nations of Indian Territory. Similar to other publications that championed the opening of Indian land to white settlement, *Indian Progress* advocated moving the Office of Indian Affairs from the Department of the Interior to the War Department, an issue under debate at the time. Boudinot adhered to the low but entertaining journalistic standards of the time by printing political ridicule and satire, some of which demonstrated his literary talents. "Oklahoma Lyrics," for example, attacked his political enemies in a way that belied his promise to consider courteously the ideas of those holding differing opinions. Nonetheless, it was entertainingly done and added a literary flair to Boudinot's usual fiery invective. In a practice customary for the time, the paper reprinted items that agreed with the editors' views from the national press and from surrounding states.

Indian Progress ceased publication on March 24, 1876. Boudinot blamed its demise on half-owner George Reynolds, whom Boudinot was certain had somehow squandered the paper's assets in spite of a healthy readership. He asserted that when the *Progress* went under, "there were over 700 paid subscribers and six or seven columns of paid up advertisement," a fairly sound footing for the time and place.[14] The press was moved to Caddo, where the *Oklahoma Star* put it to use and also employed Boudinot as a correspondent. The editor put the best face on it, saying in an article that was reprinted without comment in the *Cherokee Advocate*, "we honestly believe the consolidation of the two papers the happiest hit that could be made for the glorious cause we are advocating, and that the friends of each will hail the day the 'twin brothers' are merged into one."[15] Later the press was moved to McAlester, Choctaw Nation, and was used to print the *Star-Vindicator*. Boudinot obviously knew the power of the press, and almost as soon as the *Progress* was defunct he wrote to Charlie Watie from Washington about starting another paper at Vinita. This time, however, he would do it "based on sound business principles." He proposes moving his tobacco building to Vinita, then finding a printer with a suitable press and material as a partner, "who will do the business and take the chances, while you & Jim & I will do the writing for it."[16]

One of the many ironies of Boudinot's life involves the *Indian Progress*. Cornelius set out to establish a proselytizing organ for his ideas in the bosom of his enemies, deep in Indian Territory, intending to convert followers there. But he understood well what his father had tried to do with the *Cherokee Phoenix* decades earlier when he sent the paper to the large cities in the East attempting to influence federal removal policy by soliciting support for the Cherokee position. Attempting to follow in his father's footsteps, Boudinot also sought to use the paper as a propaganda organ outside Indian country, to demonstrate to people in a position to make or influence policy that the Indians were not of one voice in opposing the opening up of the Indian nations to exploitation by railroads, settlers, and commercial interests. In this, of course, he failed, succeeding to put out such a publication for only a few short months. The great irony in this is that his attempt led to the establishment of the *Indian Journal*, the influential newspaper that issued its first number in May 1876 and continued to represent Indian interests until Oklahoma achieved statehood.

Boudinot's enemies, of course, tied him to the Territorial Ring—a group that included land speculators, politicians, and, especially, the railroad interests. Boudinot was accused of being in the employ of various railroads during his career, but there is no hard evidence that he was a "railroad lawyer" or otherwise a permanent member of any railroad payroll. That he accepted favors such as railway passes and funding for his various enterprises, such as printing equipment for his newspaper, there is little doubt. He also benefited from information, such as the locations of future track laying, but his main connection with the Territorial Ring was that he shared its political ideas. In 1871, C. J. Hillyer, an associate of Boudinot's and president of the Atlantic and Pacific Railroad, published a widely read pamphlet that set forth the manifesto of this loosely organized but effective group. The pamphlet said that stipulations made in treaties years ago should not stop westward expansion. Indians needed to come to a mind-set in which they would share in the prosperity brought about by this expansion, it said, and this was exactly the position that Boudinot had developed.[17] There is no doubt that the Territorial Ring was busy. From 1866 to 1876, fifty territorial bills were introduced into Congress. In 1876 alone, the Cherokee delegation fought fourteen territorial bills and several railroad right-of-way bills.[18] No wonder Boudinot had enemies in the Cherokee Nation.

References to assassination abounded in Boudinot's speeches and in private letters to friends, and if he used the threats to his own life to compare with the martyrdom, as some saw it, of his father, this did not diminish their seriousness. At times in the 1870s he had to think twice about where in Indian Territory he could go in safety; at other times he felt it prudent to remain in one of the surrounding states. His longtime colleague Jim Bell was under a similar threat, and several times armed men went out looking for him. Bell's situation was a bit different because he resided in Indian Territory, leaving only occasionally. In addition, he was the active partner in many of their joint schemes, many of which Boudinot had concocted in some far-off place while Jim was expected to put it into effect. Bell handled many of the details of the hotel caper, often making contact with the principals on a daily basis. When tempers ran high, Bell was close at hand, his partner often many miles away, immune from physical contact. Arguments were often settled with guns or knives, especially when law enforcement depended on those who were on the other side of the issue. The threat of danger reached such a level in 1874 that violence was discussed often in the correspondence between Boudinot in Washington and Bell in the Territory. Boudinot once felt compelled to suggest, "I would like for you and Barker to organize quietly a force of say 50 good and true men well armed who will respond for *service* at a moment's call."[19] The force Cornelius was suggesting was to be used in defense against the Keetoowah Society—or "Pin Indians," as they were derisively called—the band of conservative, mostly full-blood Cherokees that had remained opposed to the Watie faction since well before the Civil War. The Keetoowahs had warned Bell to leave the Nation upon at least one occasion.[20]

Bell was Boudinot's partner in many business ventures and was also in a real sense a legal partner. Both men were active lawyers in addition to their other pursuits, and the pair consulted with one another on points of the law all through their careers. For example, in a letter from Washington, Boudinot acknowledges correspondence received from Bell concerning an estate case and gives the following opinion: "In regard to the will matter, I will say that if the verbal will you speak of was made by an Indian on his reservation and in accordance with the customs of his people, it would be considered by the Court good. . . . That is the general law of the case. I cannot give you a more definite statement without knowing all the facts." Then, in his best lawyerly fashion, Cornelius adds, "Send me all the facts & get me a fee of $50, & keep half yourself."[21]

Jim Bell had always lived a political life. As Sarah Watie's younger brother, he could hardly help it, especially after the death of his illustrious brother-in-law. He was elected to the Cherokee Senate from the Canadian District in 1869, but thereafter he found himself in opposition to the Cherokee government, no matter which party was in power. One of the major bones of contention between Bell and the national powers in Tahlequah was over the permit law. It is clear that the split in the Cherokee Nation was in some ways as economic as it was political and ideological. Much of the wealth was concentrated in the hands of the Watie faction minority. While they were not allowed to own land, they could build "improvements" on tribal land and thus lay claim to the acreage as long as they worked it. After the abolition of slavery, farming or ranching large tracts became more difficult for the entrepreneurs like Bell, Boudinot, and others unless they were able to hire laborers. Many did, employing landless white people from neighboring states to work on shares or, in some cases, to lease the improvements. From time to time, the practice resulted in greedy Cherokee citizens exploiting the improvement system grievously. At the same time, the Indian nations of the Territory were plagued with what were termed "intruders," whites who came in to sell illegal whiskey, to steal timber and other resources, or to squat on the land. In order to help prosecute the intruders and regulate the white laborers, the Cherokee government passed a permit law in November 1872 which stipulated that the laborers themselves were to pay a monthly fee of two dollars for a permit that could be issued for a period no longer than a year. Noncompliance carried a heavy fine of five hundred to a thousand dollars. The law thus took control of the laborers away from the farmers and ranchers and gave it to the Cherokee government.

A protest from the Watie faction led by Bell followed the law's passage. In this he had many supporters, some secret, like Ira Williams of Timber Hill, who wrote a letter of support saying, "although not with you I am one of you," [22] but many standing openly beside him, such as William N. West of the Saline District, who expressed disdain for the "Hog and Hominy class" who opposed the entrepreneurs.[23] Another supporter, Samuel H. Payne, suggested to Bell that he lead the fight to organize a "reform" party among the Cherokees. This Bell did zealously, running candidates to oppose the current Cherokee leaders and to oppose their policies in Washington. Bell, like Boudinot, interpreted the 1866 treaty as having given the federal government veto power against any legislation passed by the Cherokee National Council, and thus he carried petitions to Washington asking for overrides of Cherokee law. One such petition was for the allotment of land in severalty, which would settle the improvement and permit issues forever. Bell campaigned actively for allotment and was able to acquire a number of signatures from like-minded Cherokees. In this effort he was joined by George Harkins, active in both Chickasaw and Choctaw polities, who sent Bell a copy of a similar document from the Choctaw Nation. Bell and Sut Beck, a member of the treaty party, took the petition, with "several hundred" signatures, to Secretary of the Interior Columbus Delano. The pair then published a pamphlet of their own, "Address to the Citizens of the Cherokee Nation," that explained their rationale. [24] In the end, Bell's efforts did not generate a groundswell of support, and no real political opposition party arose. Bell himself, however, was arrested twice for treason and lived under threat of death from his more rabid foes for the rest of his life.

Boudinot collected enemies even more rapidly than Bell. One prominent was John Peter Cleaver Shanks, whom Boudinot referred to as "the loudvoiced champion of the Indian." Shanks, a congressman from Indiana, billed himself as an opponent of fraud in the Office of Indian Affairs, embarking on a fact-finding mission to Indian Territory in 1872. From this experience he compiled a report, naming several people as complicit in various schemes to defraud Indian people, including Boudinot ally George Reynolds, an agent to the Seminoles. Later, in January 1876, Shanks pointed his finger again toward Indian Territory, specifically at George W. Ingalls, the Union agent at Musko-gee, accusing him of misconduct. Boudinot came to Ingalls's defense, saying he hoped that Shanks, "the disgusting spectacle of a coarse, ranting, cursing, ignorant Kangaroo," would never again "be witnessed in the fair plains of Oklahoma."[25] Shanks became a frequent subject for Cornelius's barbed tongue, although the two were fairly close in their aspirations for Indian Territory. In January 1876, in an opinion expressed to the *New York Herald*, Shanks, then chair of the House Committee on Indian Affairs, expressed his conviction that no matter what the Indian peoples wanted for themselves, "progress" was coming to Indian Territory, through the medium of the railroad. Whatever the sentiments against it, "EVEN GOVERNMENTS CANNOT STAND IN THE WAY OF PROGRESS." He goes on to say that the process is inevitable, since "the laws of trade are more powerful than Congress."[26] In his belief in economic determinism, Shanks was close to his archenemy, Cornelius Boudinot.

But Cornelius's bitterest enemies were closer to home, on the "fair plains" themselves. William Potter Ross was, of course, near the top of the list. Ever since their heated exchanges at Fort Smith and Washington in the war's aftermath, the pair had locked horns at every opportunity. When he heard that Ross was entering the newspaper business in Muskogee with Myron Roberts, he railed from Vinita, "To what base uses has Billy come at last," ignoring the fact that the Princeton graduate had edited the *Cherokee Advocate* for years. But it was not merely the fact that Ross was reduced to journalism that made Boudinot so gleeful; it was also his choice of business partners. Ross, a former Cherokee principal chief, had fallen mightily, Cornelius boomed, "the lofty aspirations to be a great Sachem of the Cherokee Nation, have dwindled down to ambition to play second fiddle to an ignorant adventurer from some Northern State."[27] The rivalry grew, one of the factors being that Ross was often in a position of opposition to Boudinot while carrying out official duties in the

Cherokee government. Ross was a delegate to Washington to voice opposition to the plethora of territorial bills before Congress, often the very legislation that Boudinot supported and, in some cases, wrote. One of Cornelius's long-standing grievances against the Cherokee government was its support of its delegations to the capital. Time and time again, he fulminated against the sums needed for hotel bills and living expenses. Many times, it is suspected, his own relative poverty caused his protests as he cast an envious eye toward his fellow Cherokees living in posher surroundings than his own. At any rate, the feud between Ross and Boudinot continued for two decades.

Another personal enemy was perhaps a surprising one. William Penn Adair had been an ally of Boudinot's, standing shoulder to shoulder with him in opposition to "Pin" leader Evan Jones in the years before the war. Adair, a fellow officer in the Confederate army, a trusted lieutenant of Watie's during and after the war, and a fellow member of the southern Cherokee delegation in 1866, in time became one of the most hated of Boudinot's adversaries. It is difficult to say why or when this sea change occurred, but it was certainly after the treaty negotiations, as Adair had supported Boudinot against Ridge in their squabble in the aftermath. Both men were Cherokee delegates in 1868, at which time Adair indicated that he and Boudinot were friendly.[28] After this time, however, the two men's careers split, with Adair becoming an important part of the Cherokee establishment, serving as senator, justice of the Cherokee Supreme Court, and assistant principal chief.[29] Most likely the personal animosity came about because of Adair's participation in the protests against the congressional territorial bills. A man as combative as Cornelius himself once he was slighted, Adair was not one to forget, and as time went on their clashes were frequent.

The Boudinot-Adair rivalry reached its climax in March 1880. The two had joined some other men—including Cherokee attorney William A. Phillips, the Cherokee delegation, and some members of Congress—in the office of the commissioner of Indian Affairs to discuss a land matter. As the group was leaving the office, Boudinot reported, Adair grossly insulted him and he responded by striking Adair with his walking stick. The two came to further blows, resulting in Adair's being "badly marked," according to Cornelius, while he "got off without a scratch."[30] The story was carried in the *Washington Star*, which reported that the argument had begun in the commissioner's office, spilled out into the hallway, and deteriorated into "an interchange of blows and the parties clinching fell on the floor." The newspaper reported that once the pair was separated, Boudinot had suffered a small abrasion on his ear and Adair received "a somewhat dilapidated frontpiece."[31] The words between them must have been bitter indeed, for at the time Boudinot was forty-five years old and Adair, at fifty, was in the last year of his life.

One of the most far-reaching acts of Boudinot's life was his publication of a letter in the *Chicago Times*, a newspaper with views similar to his own. This document led to a cascade of events that within a decade led to the opening of Indian Territory to white settlement and its eventual effects: allotment of land in severalty and dissolution of the Indian nations of the territory. The process began with an editorial in the same newspaper on February 11, 1879, which implied that a vast tract of fertile land between Texas and Kansas was going to waste even as a wave of settlers swarmed past it to homestead much less desirable lands in Utah and Colorado. In addition to the lands set aside for the Five Civilized Tribes, the *Times* cited another fifteen million acres "belonging to the United States" yet closed to settlement. The paper went on to advocate allotting a homestead to each Indian family, then opening the "surplus" lands thus made available as well as unsurveyed "United States" lands within Indian Territory to settlement. Following the social Darwinist position popular at the time, the editor writes that the Indians should be "reduced to that test to which our civilization subjects every member of society in the struggle for existence." If they survive, well and good, but if not, "no amount of coddling and government dry-nursing will enable them to survive." The editor ends his piece by urging that laws appropriate to "a civilized state" should be enacted and enforced, courts established, railroads built, and a state ultimately created.[32]

Boudinot responded to the editorial with a letter that in turn elicited a question from a reader. In response to this question, Cornelius furnished an elaboration of his ideas accompanied by a map. It was this subsequently widely disseminated document that gave direction and support to the growing "boomer" movement of white settlers and land speculators waiting on the borders of Indian Territory. While some put the onus for the boomers entirely on Boudinot's shoulders, the fact is that the movement was already formed, if disorganized, when the letter and map were published.[33] There is no denying, however, that they acted as a powerful catalyst, setting in motion a long chain of events. In addition, Boudinot had a personal relationship with one of the leaders of the boomers, David L. Payne, offering him advice and encouragement.

In his reply to the *Times*, Boudinot thanks the editor for his good, sound sense, saying that "there is not an intelligent Indian in the Indian Territory unconnected with the villainous rings which have plundered the Indians for the past ten years, but will heartily indorse your conclusions, 'The time has come when this territory should be opened to civilization.' " [34] He takes his stand against "the sentimentalism of the Quakers and Utopians" as well as the "concentrated power of the corrupt Indian ring." Some Indians, too, have been complicit in their defense of the status quo, standing in the way of progress, trying vainly to push back "the inexorable logic of events." Cornelius rails against the "selfish greed of Indian demagogues who swarm here every session of congress in the capacity of Indian delegations." He singles out his old enemies, Ross and Adair, as being the leaders of a band of "mixed-bloods" who mislead the full-bloods by painting any Cherokee who dares to promote allotment and U.S. citizenship as traitors. As for his own "mixed-blood," Boudinot says, "I am more of an Indian than [Ross and Adair], being one-half." He goes on to decry the cost of maintaining a Cherokee delegation in Washington and the recent permit law for white laborers, seeing these actions of the Cherokee leaders as squandering the full-bloods' money, on the one hand, and keeping them away from the civilizing influence of their white neighbors, on the other.

Having gotten his pet peeves off his chest, Boudinot then moves on to the heart of his letter, first correcting the editor in his estimation of the surveyed lands in the Territory. He states that of the forty-one million acres, fifteen million "belong absolutely to the United States, having been bought and paid for under the treaties of 1866 with the Choctaws, Chickasaws, Creeks and Seminoles." Of this vast tract, some lands have been put aside for the use of "Wichitas, Pottawatomies, Sacs and Foxes," leaving twelve million acres "of excellent soil in the territory, which is to-day 'public land'; the Indian title has been extinguished." Further, he adds, the government has abandoned its policy of removing northern tribes to Indian Territory and has forbidden Indians from Arizona and New Mexico from moving in. "Now what are you going to do with these twelve million acres of rich land—in large in area as the states of Massachusetts and Connecticut, and capable of sustaining as many people?" The answer, Boudinot concludes, lies with "the aggressive white population of this country within the next three years, whether congress legislates or not for the Indian Territory." With this inflammatory remark, Boudinot demonstrates his personal frustration for years of political and bureaucratic maneuverings and his impatience to get Indian Territory open, at least that part of it he called "Oklahoma."

While Cornelius's response to the editorial caused a stir, it was an elaboration of this central message that set the boomer machinery moving. In a letter to Boudinot dated March 25, 1879, Augustus Albert of Baltimore asked the Cherokee for some clarification. He writes of the *Times* letter: "This article has been extensively copied and commented upon by the press east and west, causing great and growing interest on the part of thousands for further and fuller information, to meet which will you please give answer to the following questions." Albert then lists six queries:

1. As to the exact amount purchased.

2. From what tribes bought.

3. Its situation in the Territory.

4. As to the Government's title, if free from restriction; if not, its nature; or was the land so bought purchased with the intention of its use in settling other tribes, to be brought into the Territory, upon it.

5. State the nearest point, reached by rail, to such lands; or if they are on, or near, the surveyed line of the Atlantic and Pacific road; or how far from its present terminus.

6. Where can *accurate* maps of the Territory, showing location and boundaries of said purchased lands, be obtained?

If Boudinot had employed a straight man, he could not have found a better one than Albert. Of course, Colonel Boudinot, as he was now calling himself, was pleased to respond, not only in words but also with a fine map that outlined in red the "U.S. Public Lands" whose existence he was publicizing. His response to Albert largely consists of an answer to each of the six questions. Under the 1866 treaties, the federal government purchased fourteen million acres of land from the Creeks, Seminoles, Choctaws and Chickasaws, he writes in response to the first two, listing the amounts paid to each tribe. He then adds a description of the holdings by other tribes moved into the territory subsequent to the sale, including the Sac and Foxes, Pottowotomies, and the Wichitas, mentioning that certain other "wild" tribes—the Kiowa, Comanche, and Arapahos—have been assigned land by executive order. He then gives his opinion that a portion of the fourteen million acres "has not been appropriated by the United States for the use of other Indians and in all probability never will be." In answer to the third query, Boudinot gives the location of the "unappropriated" lands as west of ninety-seven degrees west longitude and south of the Cherokee Territory. As we shall see, he has plans for the vast area comprising the Cherokee Outlet. He asserts that the federal government has "an absolute and unembarrassed title" to these lands and that they have been designated as "public lands" by the commissioner of the General Land Office, General Williamson, in his annual report for 1878. He does, however, point out an error in the commissioner's designation, saying that it includes all the Cherokee land west of ninety-six degrees and the Chickasaw Nation. "In no sense," he writes, "can these be deemed" public lands.

Boudinot mentions here that the original intention of purchasing the land was to provide land for Indians removed from other parts of the country as well as for African Americans freed after the Civil War. The African Americans, Boudinot says, have all been made U.S. citizens and thus are not eligible for settlement on this territory. In addition, Congress has enacted laws forbidding the removal of tribes into the territory, leaving "several millions of acres of the richest lands on the continent free from Indian title, or occupancy, and an integral part of the public domain." Boudinot then proceeds to pinpoint the various railroad termini leading to the area from several directions, answering the fifth question. At this point he takes up the map question: "To save the time which would be required to answer the many letters I am constantly receiving upon this subject, I have made a plain but accurate map, which I enclose with this letter. I shall be glad to furnish maps and such further information as may be requested." Whether or not Cornelius sent Albert a map is not known, but his letter and map were subsequently reproduced as a handbill and widely circulated, especially in Kansas, where land-hungry settlers agitated for a crack at the vast tracts just over the southern border.[35] The letter and map were like coal oil on a smoldering fire, and a conflagration was not long in coming.

In an April 1, 1879, letter to Bell, Cornelius is clear about his intentions. He describes his answer to Albert as well as the map, saying, "I shall have this letter & my reply lithographed on the map . . . and have several thousand struck off." He then goes on to anticipate the effect: "I tell you it will make a rush; they will pour into the Creek & Seminole ceded lands, and we will be their neighbors on our own soil."[36] He describes the same document to business partner Sallie Watie, calling it "a guide for Jim, & Co., as well as for the Kansans."[37] Boudinot is clearly attempting to incite a run on a part of Indian Territory, knowing full well that if white settlement is allowed in a part, it will be only a matter of time before the rest falls as well. But this was only Plan A. His comments on "neighbors" and "Jim, & Co." references to the Bell-Boudinot plan to begin a colony in the Cherokee Outlet; his map, he says, will show not only the "ceded and unoccupied lands" mentioned in his *Chicago*

Times letter but also "*our* lands [his emphasis]" west of ninety-six degrees. This is Plan B, in which Boudinot and Bell are to plant a colony directly north of the "public lands" in the Cherokee Outlet, positioning themselves for maximum benefit once the area to the south begins to blossom with towns and farms. Once again, Cornelius feels that his dreams of prosperity and power are soon to materialize, his lifetime goal nearly in his grasp. And the pieces begin to fall into place for him.

The white settlers and their leaders reacted predictably. A second circular was issued, this time by the Indian Territory Colonization Society at Chetopa, Kansas. The society, which claimed "branch offices" in Hannibal, Missouri, as well as St. Louis, Chicago, and Quincy, Illinois, was managed by W. H. Kerns, with George W. McFarlin as "superintendent of the colony." Quoted at length in the circular is an interview with Boudinot published in the *New York Graphic* on February 27, 1879, in which Cornelius repeats much of what he has written in the Chicago letter. Chetopa, just across the line from the Cherokee Nation, was a hotbed of activity for boomer activists like McFarlin, C. C. Carpenter, and David L. Payne. Carpenter was an old rabble-rouser, having led settlers into the Black Hills in 1876, and had recently been inciting crowds in Coffeyville, Kansas, another border town filled with eager settlers. By May 1879 he had become enough of a threat that the Cherokee Nation had been placed on alert status and federal troops were dispatched to Vinita. Boomer newspapers fed the flames, with the *Chetopa Advance*, which on April 3 had reprinted Boudinot's *Chicago Times* letter, reporting on May 8 that "the people of Southern Kansas are greatly excited over the movement into the Indian Territory to occupy lands which it is claimed, belong to the government. Hundreds of people in and around Chetopa are preparing to join the grand rush to the Indian Territory." The *Kansas City Journal* predicted on May 15 that "thousands of men in Missouri and Kansas" had made illegal land runs before and says it "would not be surprised if those preparing to overrun the Indian Territory were largely of the same people."

On May 4, John McNeil, an inspector with the Indian Service, reported to Commissioner of Indian Affairs E. A. Hayt from Coffeyville, Kansas, giving his assessment of the situation. While he reported that no sizable group had gone south as yet, "At this season of the year on the frontier will be found hundreds of 'movers,' people who go anywhere to get from where they last lived." Some of these, he opines, have been taken in by the "specious promises" of Carpenter and others. He goes on to describe Carpenter as "the same bragging, lying nuisance that I knew him seventeen years ago when he infested Fremont's quarters." Carpenter was taking advantage of the economic situation in Kansas, in which merchants were desperately trying to attract people to settle in or near their towns in order to increase their trade. The merchants who tempted people to settle in places like Coffeyville, Chetopa, and Sedalia also promoted settlement of Indian Territory, which would bring them more customers. They did not promote only in the abstract, however, but engineered schemes by which they paid Carpenter to deliver parties of settlers to the area. According to McNeil, "The merchants agreed to give him five hundred dollars when his first party came, and a thousand dollars more when a thousand emigrants had been moved to the Territory by him." So far Carpenter had failed, but now he was determined to get the money promised him. His competition in this enterprise was George W. McFarlin, of the Indian Territory Emigration Society. McNeil ends his report by recommending summary ejection of both men and their parties. [38]

With the entire border in a state of agitation, the Indian nations reacted. Principal Chief Ward Coachman of the Creeks wrote to Cherokee chief Thompson saying that troops had been sent to remove settlers and that he had sent warnings to other tribes. Coachman suggested an intertribal council in late May to make plans to confront the problem. Similarly, Chickasaw governor B. C. Burney wrote to Thompson outlining the danger of "the great scheme" by "Rail Road sharpers and land grabbers." Events will ultimately "force the opening up of our country; which will destroy our form of government, and our Nationality as a people." [39] Burney's assessment of this assault on the sovereignty of the Indians nations was accurate, of course, and was shared by the other tribes. The federal government felt compelled to take action. It could not allow the proclamation of a Cherokee opportunist despised by his tribal government to formulate policy in the American West. Accordingly, upon the recommendation of Secretary of the Interior Carl Schurz and other advisers, President Rutherford B. Hayes issued a proclamation on May 15 forbidding white settlement in Indian Territory. Citing "certain evil-disposed persons" who are preparing to enter the Territory, Hayes warns against this action, saying that if they try they will be speedily removed by the U.S. agents there or, if necessary, by the military. With this action, he hoped to slam the door on the boomer movement.

But Hayes's proclamation did not have the intended effect. Boomer papers continued to preach defiance of the law and to invoke the inexorable flow of Manifest Destiny. The *Kansas City Journal* urged the settlers to go forward: "We cannot advise anybody to resist or disregard the authority of the government, on the contrary we hope everybody will obey the law," but "the experience in the Black Hills country points to the fact that the emigrating American, when he makes up his mind to colonize a new country, don't care to be prevented by mere paper declarations." [40] The "immigration societies" continued to draw settlers to the border area, a publication called "The Settler's Guide" was distributed, and the meetings went on. Boudinot was more in demand than ever. A March 6, 1880, report of one such meeting at the Board of Trade rooms in Kansas City was typical. With thirteen hundred persons attending to hear Boudinot speak, the rooms were packed with settlers and "prominent men" who were dismayed to see a U.S. marshal push his way to the podium. The crowd shouted for him to sit down and let Boudinot speak, but the chairman of the event ruled that since the marshal wanted to read a message from the president of the United States, he was recognized. Marshal Allen then proceeded to read Hayes's proclamation, after which the chairman invited him to remain for the rest of the meeting so he could report its character to the president. At that point he introduced Boudinot, who was welcomed with a great roar.

Boudinot gazed around the assembly, thanking the chairman and the marshal. Saying that no one had a higher respect for the words of the president than himself, he went on to add that he believed the reading of the Declaration of Independence or the Emancipation Proclamation would have served the same purpose. Another roar from the crowd. Boudinot then made a reference to the media frenzy that was taking place over the issue, saying that he was greatly surprised by newspaper reports that an armed invasion of Indian Territory was being arranged in Kansas City and that he was to take command of it. Chuckles were heard from some, but a general buzz from the crowd. Boudinot then went on to give his views on how best to open the Territory to settlement. Allotment, U.S. citizenship, the organization of a territorial government were all included in the standard Boudinot litany. He believed that the Fourteenth Amendment had given citizenship to all Indians anyway and asked, if four million slaves could be made citizens, why not the Indians? Make them citizens, give them a plot of land to work or sell, treat them like other Americans, he urged. Sell the "surplus" lands to provide funds for their education and that of their children. Each of his proposals brought cheers from the floor. The meeting then adopted a series of resolutions that followed Boudinot's recommendations, supported territorial bills then in Congress, and supported Secretary Schurz's new policy on the question. [41]

In October 1879, the *Chetopa Advance* had gleefully reported what it saw as the differences in opinion in the administration itself, reporting that U.S. Attorney General Charles Devens had advised President Hayes that it was illegal to send federal troops or marshals to arrest white settlers in Indian Territory. So the proclamation was undercut not only by the boomer forces but also by sources closer to home, including the secretary of the interior. A few months after Hayes's announcement, Schurz appeared at an Indian fair at Muskogee, in the heart of Indian Territory, saying that he doubted that the government could keep the boomers off for very long. "In course of time, immigration will overflow the borders," he said. "I would candidly advise the Indians to take their fate in their own hands, and shape future events so as to protect themselves. I would suggest the dividing of your lands in severalty, with a title in fee simple." He goes on, urging the Indians, ironically, to observe the law and "gain the highest civilization."[42] Schurz seems to be reading a page from Boudinot's book. His comments along these lines were not restricted to Indian Territory audiences. The following month he made it official in Washington, asserting that his visit to the Territory made it clear to him that the present policy, as signified by Hayes's proclamation, was ineffective and doomed to failure. He "expressed the fear that government will not be strong enough to resist the march of empire." As a result, he planned to recommend to Congress the "passage of laws dividing the Indian lands in severalty among them and securing individual titles." This would protect the Indians against "the encroachments of the whites in violation of treaty rights." In the next breath, however, he proposes to "sell the surplus lands of the Indians" thus created by allotment, while puzzlingly proposing "not to open the Indian territory to immigration."[43] With Schurz on board and the boomer newspapers urging the settlers forward, a territorial bill was certain to be put forward in the next session of Congress. In retrospect, of course, what the boomers witnessed was not mutiny on the part of the attorney general and the interior secretary but rather the beginning of a significant shift in Indian policy by the Hayes administration.

If anyone can be called the arch-boomer, it would be David L. Payne, a Boudinot colleague.[44] Cornelius met Payne in Washington when the latter was assistant doorkeeper of the House of Representatives. A native of Indiana, Payne had lived in Kansas, had spent time in Indian Territory while in the Kansas Volunteers during the Civil War, and had later been elected to the Kansas House of Representatives. He was well versed on events in Kansas and the Territory and longed to seek his fortune on the plains of Oklahoma, as Boudinot described them. The pair had several meetings, with Cornelius encouraging Payne's dreams with tales of the expanse and fecundity of the "public lands," or what Boudinot had started to call Oklahoma. In time, Payne left Washington and traveled to Wichita, where he, Boudinot, and M. M. Murdock, editor of the *Wichita Eagle*, discussed how they could take advantage of the situation. Boudinot proposed that the three of them "form a partnership and get the country opened and build a city right where Oklahoma City now stands," Murdock recalled later. "Payne, who took so prominent a part in the opening, got his ideas from Boudinot." [45] Murdock says he demurred in the partnership because he did not want competition for Wichita that a large settlement in Oklahoma would provide. While Boudinot characteristically did not accompany Payne on any of his forays, he did sign on as his lawyer when the boomer was tried in Judge Isaac Parker's federal court at Fort Smith. It was probably Boudinot's idea for Payne to get himself arrested on an alcohol charge in order to use Parker's courtroom as a forum for his and Cornelius's ideas. On August 4, 1884, Payne was charged with the introduction of one gallon of apple brandy into Indian Territory. According to two government witnesses, identified as Blackstone and Rogers, they approached Payne to tell him and others that they had entered the territory illegally and to leave. Payne denied breaking the law and said he would prove it in court. He then produced the brandy and asked the pair to arrest him and bring him to court for a test of the law. [46] This was the sort of legal maneuvering that Boudinot was fond of, so he could not resist signing on as the defense attorney. However, he was replaced as the trial neared. Payne had been tried before Parker in 1881, convicted, and fined one thousand dollars, a defeat for the boomers. In fact, Boudinot and Payne had a falling out after the trial, which is not surprising given the strong tempers both men possessed. But they soon made up, with Cornelius providing whatever support he could to the man he had mentored.

Boudinot gave his blessing to those trying to settle the "unassigned lands" of Oklahoma, but his eye was on the land north of there, the Cherokee Outlet. He had concocted a scheme to colonize the area west of ninety-eight degrees, largely uninhabited but a wonderful resource as grazing land. In fact, the Cherokee Nation had begun to tax white ranchers who had gotten into the habit of running herds there to fatten them on the rich grass. Boudinot knew that his was an entirely different legal situation from that of the boomers; as he put the case to Bell, "We can do this without the authority of the U.S. or anybody else." [47] His reasoning was simple: the Outlet was Cherokee tribal land; they were Cherokee citizens; therefore they were entitled to settle in the outlet. The Cherokee Outlet was created under the 1828 treaty when the

Arkansas Cherokees who had come under the Cherokee removal treaty of 1817 removed again to northeast Oklahoma on seven millions acres and were granted a perpetual outlet, one degree wide, extending west from their lands to the then U.S. border, the one hundredth meridian. The Outlet—or Strip, as it came to me known—was not used by the Cherokees for settlement or pasture. The treaty of 1866 allowed the Cherokees to keep title to the Strip but required them to sell land to "wild" Indians when they were removed from other parts of the country. The Osage, Kaw, Ponca, Otoe and Missouria, and Tonkawa Pawnees had been located on lands ceded by the Creeks, but their reservations extended into the Outlet as well. These reservations were in the eastern part of the Strip, thus separating the main Cherokee Nation from their land further west.

It was this area that Boudinot and Bell had their eye on. The two planned to gather a colonization company made up of Cherokee and white families at a headquarters in border town Caldwell, Kansas, then move into the Outlet and set up a ranching community. Boudinot wrote to Bell in February 1879, saying, "Why not make up a colony West of the Osages; you & I and our friends could control it." He promised to meet Jim in March and discuss it some more. What set Cornelius's wheels turning in this direction was his preoccupation with Hooley Bell and Henry Eiffert's involvement with his hotel. Hooley had been appointed tax collector for the grazers on the Strip, but on January 1, 1879, he had gone a step further. The certificate he issued on that day reads in part, "John T. and Caroline Jones are citizens of the Cherokee Nation and as such are entitled to occupy and hold a claim in the Cherokee Country west of the Arkansas River and to graze cattle." [48] Always one to recognize a legal precedent, however slight, Boudinot saw this as a way to grab some land for himself and his friends. During the spring of 1879 his intention is clear. In April he urges Bell to move into the Outlet: "Go ahead; let Aunt Sally stay to hold our places, & let us do our part west. Just as soon as I can get away from here [Washington], I will be with you but don't wait for me, *go ahead!* & quickly." Boudinot and his partners intend for Sarah Watie to protect their claims to various improvements in the Cherokee Nation while they strike out to claim new land in the Outlet. In the same letter he says, "Let every one oppressed by the infamous laws of our Nation fix up his affairs & go West. We can be independent of the thieves and hold our own too, in the Nation." [49] Boudinot intended, it seems, to establish a Ridge-Watie-Boudinot empire in the Outlet, founding at last a separate Cherokee domain separate from the government at Tahlequah. On June 13 he writes again, saying, "What you want is to settle the question of your right, & the right of every Cherokee citizen to settle & improve the land undisposed of West of 96 degrees; this I am trying to do here."[50]

In April 1879, Bell organized a colony of fifteen to twenty men and left Vinita for the Outlet, where the group settled on the Chickaskia River, a place that he and Cornelius decided was ideal for a colony.[51] Word had gotten out of this venture—not surprisingly in that climate of rumor and turmoil—and a U.S. Army contingent under Sergeant J. M. Warren commanded by Lieutenant W. W. Barrett, stationed at Arkansas City, Kansas, set out to remove the colonists on April 26, 1879. Warren reported that he found Bell's settlement on April 28 on the west side of the Chickaskia River. He reports finding, in addition to Bell, Cherokees George W. Gardenhir, George W. Burnett, George W. Davis, Joshua McLaughlin, and T. J. Jordan and his wife; and several white settlers, including M. Codman, O. M. Codman, the latter's wife and daughter, Houston Hamilton, M. J. Welsh, David Lawler, and William Lawler.[52] Warren arrested Bell and the others, and after waiting for them to round up their stock and secure their belongings he escorted them to Arkansas City. On the way back, Warren reports, they encountered six wagons and families who intended to join Bell at the settlement at Chustee's ranch in Kansas. The sergeant warned these people not to proceed into the Territory and told Chustee to report to the commanding officer at Arkansas City.[53] The other group seems to be one led by Jeff Jordan, who wrote to Bell from Arkansas City in October. He describes his situation and preparedness: he is waiting for the all-clear signal before moving into the Strip. "I am anxious to know our fate as I have . . . a new set of house logs . . . ready to put up," he writes, into a sixteen- by eighteen-foot building. But he fears that the army at Arkansas City will take them back into what he calls the "old" Cherokee Nation, and "We don't want to brought back their [sic] by soldiers." The army's indecision seems to trace all the way back to Washington, where bureaucrats were reviewing the 1866 treaty and the legality of Cherokee citizens moving into the Outlet.

Boudinot was furious, telling Bell to bring suit against Barrett for false imprisonment. "I know all about this fellow Barrett," Boudinot thundered, "and shall ventilate him in the *Kansas City Times*." For its part, the government engaged in dithering, first claiming that the troops who arrested Bell and his party were acting under order of Hayes's proclamation. When it was pointed out that Bell's situation was different because of his status as a Cherokee citizen, the officials looked for some direction. As they searched, Boudinot submitted a brief to the War Department, doubtless advised to do so by his old friend

General William T. Sherman, claiming that Bell's rights as a Cherokee citizen had been violated.[54] As soon as the Cherokee government got wind of this, the Cherokee delegation issued a statement repudiating Boudinot's claims, making clear that it was duly credentialed by the Department of the Interior, thus muddying the jurisdictional waters further. Boudinot waited, sure that the powers in Washington that he thought he knew so well would see the logic of his position. The government's reaction was not long in coming. On July 11, Secretary of War G. W. McCrary queried the U.S. Attorney General Devens as to Bell's status as a trespasser.[55] In September, Acting Commissioner of Indian Affairs E. J. Brooks informed the Cherokees that they were not permitted to settle or reside in the country west of ninety-six degrees, stopping the boomers, but stopping Cherokee citizens as well. The Cherokee Nation, which had been engaged in attempting to tax the white ranchers running cattle in the Outlet, deftly sidestepped the issue by leasing large tracts of the Outlet to a group organized as the Cherokee Strip Live Stock Association. Boudinot screamed, since he could not colonize leased land, and the Cherokee Nation found that dealing with the association opened up a new series of problems.[56]

Boudinot did not give up on the colony idea. What kept him going was news from his friends in the railway business that plans were laid to build new railroads into the Outlet. The St. Louis and San Francisco line wanted to build one hundred miles west of Vinita, crossing the main channel of the Arkansas River about where the Red fork came into it. Further, the Atchison, Topeka, and Santa Fe and the Kansas Pacific expected to build branches to pass close to the colony site. "This of course will make our lands much more valuable," he wrote to Sallie in October.[57] Of course, the partners were disappointed again, and another of Cornelius's plans for recognition and wealth was thwarted.

CHAPTER 10

Lawyer, Rancher, Businessman

Boudinot continued to lecture in the frontier areas around Indian Territory during the early 1880s. He also practiced law in Arkansas and occasionally in Washington DC, but his legal activities were not organized until later in the decade when he settled into a practice at Fort Smith. He continually was involved in Indian politics, however, throwing most of his attention in this direction. One of the major political issues at the time was the Cherokee Outlet, the area in which Boudinot and Bell were interested in establishing their "colony." In 1883, annoyed by the Cherokee Nation's lease of the rich grasslands to white ranchers and by the attempts by intruders to settle there, Congress sought to clarify the murky legal status of the Strip once and for all. The government subsequently offered the Cherokees $300,000 as a final payment for land west of ninety-six degrees. For Cornelius this action was both a blessing and a threat. It would, he knew, give ownership of the land to the federal government, making it similar to the "unassigned lands" he was touting for white settlement. It would diminish the Cherokee Nation's land base and bring the Cherokees a step closer to allotment of tribal lands. The purchase would also halt the leasing scheme he opposed. On the debit side, government ownership of the Outlet would end forever his and Bell's ideas for establishing a ranching empire in the western Cherokee Nation. Additionally, Boudinot found out from his contacts in Washington that the purchase was the brainchild of William A. Phillips, one of his old enemies.[1] From the sidelines, Cornelius watched developments warily, discussing Phillips's possible motives with his confidants and asking Bell to keep him abreast of actions by the Cherokee government in Tahlequah.

When the Cherokee Nation accepted the federal offer, Boudinot and Bell examined the fine print. The National Council, over Principal Chief Dennis W. Bushyhead's veto, enacted a law distributing the proceeds of the sale on a per capita basis, but only to citizens of Cherokee blood. This action excluded the Shawnees and Delawares who had joined the tribe earlier, as well as the former slaves who had become Cherokee citizens under the 1866 treaty. Boudinot saw a double opportunity open up for him in contesting this action: first, he could damage his old political foes in the Cherokee Nation, including Phillips; second, he could become the champion of the freedmen, Delawares, and Shawnees, thus establishing a new political base for himself—and, with luck, some lucrative legal fees. Cornelius threw himself into this new foray with gusto. Phillips and Boudinot had been locking horns for a long time. A Kansan, Phillips as a Union officer had commanded Indian troops in the Cherokee Nation during the Civil War, so the animosity between the men was deeper than just the present unpleasantness. Further, Phillips had attached himself to several Cherokee Nation delegations as an attorney, dating from the treaty deliberations in 1866, and as such he helped the delegates prepare their debates against Boudinot in Congress and before government officials. In his denunciations of the Cherokee delegation's expenses, Boudinot had often railed against the exorbitant, to his mind, fees of its white attorneys.

Cornelius had several people in and out of the Nation on his side, in addition to his usual associates. For example, Robert L. Owen, a prominent Cherokee, wanted to see the lease with the Cherokee Strip Live Stock Association ended and the area opened to Cherokee stockmen, an aim, of course, that he shared with Boudinot. Others were of a similar mind and backed Boudinot in his endeavor. Even within the National Council, some of the Cherokees were distrustful of Phillips, some even calling for an investigation of his dealings with railroads and other economic interests.[2] For their part, Phillips and the Cherokee Nation had provided Cornelius with ample ammunition for the battle ahead.

After the Civil War, the Strip had been partially settled by several tribes, placed there by the government under Article 16 of the 1866 treaty. These tribes occupied 551,732 acres of an area totaling nearly 6.5 million acres. The government arbitrarily assessed the worth of the land at 47.49 cents an acre, making a total amount of more than $3 million. The government proceeded to pay the Cherokees in three installments, beginning with a payment of $313,793 in 1880, one of $48,000 in 1881, and the final payment of $300,000 in 1882. While these payments did not nearly total the amount the government had assessed, the Cherokees were forced to "take it or leave it." Phillips, by now "Special Agent" to the Cherokees, in effect the Nation's chief negotiator, wrung his hands but in the end advised the tribe to accept the offer. At the time the Cherokee Nation and its neighbors were undergoing a severe economic downturn due to widespread crop failures, and the Nation accepted the offer.[3] But it was not only the discrepancy between the assessed value and the payments that provided Boudinot with ammunition against both the deal and Phillips. The special agent had also collected a fee of $22,500 out of the settlement money that was earmarked as "certain obligations."

With the Nation in an uproar over the price of the Outlet sale and suspicions aroused over the "certain obligations" money, Boudinot filed a suit against Phillips for the return of the $22,500. To make sure that the case was tried in the court of public opinion as well as a court of law, Cornelius resorted to a familiar tactic: he issued a pamphlet and made sure it was distributed widely.[4] This document was filled with Cornelius's customary incendiary prose, with the title "The Phillips Steal!" and "Cherokee Nation Frauds!" plastered across the cover. Other statements on the cover, in the style of the day, read, "How he and his tools stole $22,500 of money belonging to the Cherokee people! Humiliating confessions of Dennis W. Bushyhead. He pays $22,500 of the people's money to Wolfe and Ross without taking a receipt and without any idea what they were going to do with it. Clear and convincing testimony of Campbell H. Taylor, showing Phillips' connection with the steal. Self-convicting testimony of Richard M. Wolfe and Robert B. Ross, late Cherokee delegates!" In the text, Boudinot claims (but later was forced to deny) that he had interviewed Principal Chief Bushyhead and got him to admit that he had cashed the draft for the $22,500 which he had drawn on the Nation's account. Bushyhead admitted that he handed the money over to Robert B. Ross and Richard M. Wolfe, members of the Cherokee delegation, in Wolfe's hotel room in Washington, as Phillips looked on. Campbell H. Taylor testified that in a special session in May 1883 the Cherokee Council appropriated 7.5 percent of the federal payment to pay for a contract that Wolfe and Ross said they had signed with some unnamed third parties; the pair failed to produce the contract, Taylor said. Boudinot speculates that one, possibly three, white men are involved. He goes on to demand that Bushyhead, Wolfe, and Ross be fined and imprisoned. Phillips, he goes on, "who everybody knows is the chief criminal, can be punished for aiding and abetting their crime." He ends by stating that Congress will investigate the affair and the guilty will be punished. Jim Bell published a similar pamphlet.[5] Probably both were circulated, Boudinot's mostly in the East and Bell's in Indian Territory.

When Phillips's day in court arrived in 1886, the case was dismissed for lack of evidence.[6] However, Boudinot had opened a criminal case against Phillips as well as his fellows Ross and Wolfe. The three were arrested and charged by the Grand Jury of the District of Columbia in April 1886. When Ross and Wolfe contested their arrest as Cherokee citizens, Judge Isaac C. Parker turned down their motion. The three were convicted on the charge of fraud, but the case was overturned on appeal, and they went free. Boudinot considered an appeal as well but never filed one. In the end, Phillips lost the trust of the Cherokee Nation, which did not pay his salary for 1885 and 1886, the years he was under indictment. In the trial it was intimated by Boudinot that the money had gone to Secretary of the Interior Henry M. Teller and Senator Henry Dawes of Massachusetts. Both Teller and Dawes denied the charge, and it was never proved. Shortly after the court case, Phillips resigned his position as special agent, probably a superfluous act given his ruined reputation in the Nation.[7]

Boudinot had not lost sight of what he considered a new constituency, the Delawares, Shawnees, and freedmen. The Delawares and Shawnees had been incorporated into the Cherokee Nation by mutual consent, more or less, after the Civil War, the Delaware agreement of incorporation made in April 1867 and the Shawnee agreement in June 1869. The Cherokee freedmen, on the other hand, had been granted citizenship in the Nation over the objections of the Cherokees, who argued that no sovereign nation should have the definition of citizenship for itself set by another nation. This, in many Cherokees' eyes, is what the federal government was doing in insisting, in the 1866 treaty, that former slaves be admitted to full citizenship in the Nation. The issue plagued the Cherokees for years. To complicate matters, some of the freedmen, under the leadership of African American attorneys J. Milton Turner and Hannibal C. Carter, had organized the Freedmen's Oklahoma Association with the purpose of settling former slaves on the "unassigned lands" identified by Boudinot in his now famous letter and map. To the chagrin of the Indian Territory nations, Turner and Carter invited to Oklahoma not only the freedmen from the Five Civilized Tribes but also former slaves from all over the United States. Further intensifying the situation was the fact that in January 1879 the Citizenship Court set up by the Cherokee Nation asked Commissioner of Indian Affairs E. A. Hayt to remove two hundred blacks from the Nation as intruders.[8]

Now, with the final payment for the Cherokee Strip about to be distributed to the tribe, the National Council had decreed that the freedmen, Delawares, and Shawnees were to be excluded entirely from sharing the settlement. Boudinot determined to represent this group of aggrieved citizens, hoping to earn a hefty fee. His first move in this direction was to contact J. Milton Turner, who was also interested in the case, naturally, and saw it as another attack on freedmen's rights by the Cherokee Nation. Boudinot and Turner agreed to handle the case jointly and to split the fee. Cornelius's idea was for Turner to work one side of the issue while he worked the Delaware-Shawnee side. The trouble with this strategy is that the two attorneys began to work at cross-purposes. Boudinot, who considered himself a master litigator, was eager to see the issue come to court, while Turner wanted to get federal legislation passed to ensure the freedmen's rights not only in the settlement but in larger issues of citizenship as well. Both men sought to control the situation through the means they saw as most conducive to their personal talents and style. Both, too, were no doubt taking into consideration the contacts they had made in high places.

Turner engaged Washington attorney Henry E. Cuney to help him prepare his litigation. In 1886, Henry Dawes introduced a freedmen's compensation bill in the Senate at Cuney's instigation, but Boudinot was working in another direction. He prevailed upon a friend, Senator John T. Morgan of Alabama, to bring a bill that would have referred the issue to the U.S. Court in the District of Columbia, where Boudinot felt he could get a favorable ruling. When Dawes's bill passed, another of Cornelius's friends, Senator John J. Ingalls of Kansas, moved that the bill be recalled and amended. Ingalls wanted to have the case sent to the U.S. District Court of the Western District of Arkansas, the court, as it just so happened, of another of Boudinot's friends, Isaac Parker. In a further development, probably a parliamentary one, Senator K. Jones of Arkansas introduced a bill that contained Ingalls's amendments. Referred back to the Committee on Indian Affairs, the Ingalls amendment was approved and the Dawes bill defeated. When the amendment got the approval of the whole Senate it was sent to the House, where it died when Congress adjourned before that body could take it up.[9]

Turner had been busy as well. He petitioned President Grover Cleveland to issue an executive order in the case, but Cleveland declined, instead instructing Commissioner Hayt to prepare legislation by which all claimants would be covered, the Shawnees and Delawares as well as the freedmen. This legislation passed in 1888, instructing the Cherokee Nation to make a per capita payment based on the 1880 census in the amount of $75,000. In addition, Congress awarded $15,000 to the claimants' agents as compensation; the next issue was who would get the $15,000, and the judge in the matter was Secretary of the Interior John Noble. Boudinot wrote letters outlining his activities and billable hours and prevailed upon friends to use their influence. In 1890, when Secretary Noble awarded the entire amount to Turner, Boudinot was sure that it was because Noble and Turner were Republicans and Boudinot and his influential friends were not.

It certainly was a political affair when Cornelius's name was bandied about as the next commissioner of Indian Affairs in 1885. Whether or not he was given serious consideration remains a matter for conjecture, as Boudinot himself did not dwell upon it in his letters, and there is little concerning it in the official correspondence. The U.S. attorney general at the time was Augustus H. Garland, Boudinot's longtime colleague, who no doubt had a hand in the nomination. The people of Indian Territory, at least, seemed convinced of his nomination's seriousness. The *Indian Journal* of March 5, 1885, in reporting on Boudinot's comments regarding allotment, wrote that the candidate "stands a very good change of being the next Indian Commissioner." S. S. Stephens, an old Treaty party adherent, wrote to Jim Bell several times during the spring to ask about the appointment, one that he considered a closed matter. "The *Globe* of yesterday's issue speaks of Boudie's chances as nearly sure," he wrote on March 4.[10] In the end, however, John D. C. Atkins, a former congressman from Tennessee, was chosen as commissioner.[11] It is doubtful that Boudinot's selection for the office would have been received with anything other than hostility in Indian Territory, let alone in Indian country anywhere else in the nation. While allotment formally became U.S. policy in 1887, two years earlier it was still being hotly debated.

Over the years, Boudinot was engaged in what some would call business ventures, others moneymaking schemes. In this way he resembled any white man of the period and region—any lawyer, banker, railroad man, or merchant. In this sense, Boudinot lived up to his self-promoted image as a "progressive" citizen. His tobacco venture is famous, his hotel experience notorious, his forays into ranching colorful, but he was engaged in other business activities as well. Some of these never got out of the planning stage. For example, Cornelius and some old associates—E. Poe Harris, for one—joined with James J. McAlester and others to form the Fort Smith and El Paso Railway Company. Boudinot served as the organization's president. This was not his first attempt at starting a railroad. He had suggested to the Cherokee Nation shortly after

LAWYER, RANCHER, BUSINESSMAN

the 1866 treaty that it build a railroad through its land before outsiders did it, but his idea was ignored.[12]

In 1885 Cornelius was one of the organizers of the Pacific and Great Eastern Railway, the idea being to build a track west from Fayetteville, entering the Cherokee Nation at Cincinnati in Washington Country, Arkansas, and running through the Indian Territory to a point on its western border near the thirty-sixth parallel. Ten or twelve miles of track east of Fayetteville have already been laid, the company claimed in 1886.[13] The Pacific and Great Eastern never came to fruition. Congress granted a charter for the new railroad in 1888, recognizing the company's intention to lay track from the Arkansas border at Fort Smith, where connections could be made easily to northern and eastern sections of the country, to the southwestern part of the Indian Territory. There, in the Choctaw Nation, James McAlester already controlled the coal-mining industry, which could not only fuel the railroad's locomotives but also profit from lucrative shipping contracts with the railroad. However, the railroad never became a reality. Perhaps the cost of laying track was prohibitive, though this seems unlikely given McAlester's backing and the relative ease of issuing stocks and bonds at the time. Maybe the company had been formed with the idea of selling the charter to an established road later, a deal that fell through. And maybe Boudinot did not have the time or energy for another venture.

Cornelius was busy at the time. Earlier he had begun another business enterprise that was coming to fruition in 1888: bringing the telephone to northwest Arkansas. In 1884 he met J. Harris in Washington, who had invented a new model telephone that cost only half as much to operate as Alexander Graham Bell's model. Harris was looking for investors, and A. H. Garland among others decided that this was a sure thing for progressive-minded investors. Boudinot agreed, bought in to the new device, and returned to Arkansas to set up a telephone company. He completed a six-mile line between the Arkansas communities of Rogers and Bentonville, the first in that area of the state. The president of the Rogers and Bentonville Telephone Company then reinvested the profits it was receiving and constructed another line between Fayetteville and Farmington, a small community to the west.[14] At the time of his death, Boudinot was also the vice president of the Fort Smith Telephone Company. The telephone interests, along with his ranches and law practice, gave Boudinot more than enough to do in his last half decade. In addition, he owned two ferries, one near Fort Smith that spanned the Arkansas River, the other a "cable ferry" running across the Illinois River east of Tahlequah.[15]

Another event had taken place during this time that gave Boudinot a reason to settle down and consolidate his affairs: his 1885 marriage to Clara Corinth Menear, who was described in Cornelius's *New York Times* obituary five years later as "one of the belles of Washington." [16] Little is known of Clara's past except that she was well accepted in Washington society, that she came from a "good family," and that she was several years younger than Boudinot. Born in 1859 to Ashby Pool and Lucretia Maria Menear in Rainier, Oregon, Clara continued to live in Fort Smith until her death on September 10, 1911. Her grave is in Oak Grove Cemetery in that city. [17] The pair seemed well suited, and Clara must have been an agreeable and somewhat adventurous woman to leave the nation's capital for the little Ozark Mountain town where her new husband took her. Fayetteville was picturesque and a nice enough little town, but even though Cornelius's telephone business was there, the Boudinots moved south after a brief stay. They traveled to Fort Smith, making their way down the tortuous, winding roads to the flatter land of the Arkansas River Valley. There Clara must have been pleased to see more of the bustle she was used to, although the frontier town was a far cry from a large, eastern city.

Fort Smith had been incorporated in 1842, and even before that time it had been the capital city of the Cherokee border. The federal court was there as well as the U.S. Army garrison. The court for a long time served as the seat of the white man's law for western Arkansas as well as Indian Territory. While the Indian nations had their own legal systems, they had jurisdictions only over their own citizens. The area had traditionally drawn outlaws of various sorts, both Indian and white, and the judge, jail, and gallows at Fort Smith were famous for dispensing justice. Judge Isaac Parker, the famous "hanging judge" of western lore, sat on the bench of the ornate courtroom where Boudinot often practiced. By the time Boudinot brought his bride there, the city had grown into a commercial center. Along the wide main street, Garrison Avenue, and its tributaries, one could count 46 grocery stores, 22 dry goods emporiums, 10 pharmacies, and 10 hardware stores, as well as 8 hotels, 37 saloons, 11 barbers, and 2 undertakers. In addition, a number of members of the legal profession hung their shingles there, in the service of justice and the federal court. Boudinot's nameplate joined the others in 1885.

By 1886 Cornelius was joined by R. E. Jackson, doing business in the Halli-well Building in downtown Fort Smith. In the next year the firm had grown, adding D. C. Morgan as a partner. Later this partnership was dissolved, when Boudinot teamed up with Thomas H. Barnes and W. M. Melette, the firm taking up quarters at the corner of Fourth Street and Garrison Avenue, up-stairs. In 1890, with the addition of J. Warren Reed, the firm became Barnes,

Boudinot, and Reed, the lawyers also opening a branch office in Muskogee, where the new U.S. Court was situated.

The practice of law in western Arkansas at that time involved a great many cases with the Indian nations directly to the west. The Cherokee Nation, in particular, was a source of much business for lawyers admitted to practice before the U.S. Court because of the peculiar twist in the law: disputes between Cherokee and Cherokee were decided in one of the courts set up in each of the seven Cherokee districts. However, if a white person was involved, even if the crime was against an Indian, the case had to be tried in Parker's court. This situation was to some extent the result of the rewriting of the Cherokee Code in 1876, largely due to encroachment of U.S. marshals into the Nation. The marshals often disregarded Cherokee jurisdiction and arrested whites and Indians alike in their forays west of Fort Smith. William P. Boudinot played an important part in this process of rewriting the legal code. The result was that a long line formed at the border consisting of whiskey sellers (often women, arrested for peddling their illegal wares in the Nation), accused murderers, rapists, robbers, assaulters, rustlers, and horse thieves as well as squatters and other law violators. Trial in the U.S. Court usually meant defense by one of the Fort Smith lawyers, such as Thomas H. Barnes, W. C. Jackson, or Elias C. Boudinot Sr. (Boudinot had added the "Sr." to his name to distinguish himself from his nephew Elias Cornelius Boudinot Jr., son of William P. and, like his father, a lawyer practicing in Tahlequah).

Sometimes the cases were perfunctory, consisting of a simple plea, a fine, or a jail sentence. However, sometimes the quirky nature of the law caused some interesting dilemmas. The murder case of Henry Eiffert in 1881 is a case in point. Eiffert was accused of murdering an adopted member of the tribe who was white but who had married a Cherokee citizen. He was duly tried in one of the Cherokee district courts and acquitted. Later he was arrested by U.S. marshals, taken to Fort Smith, and indicted for the murder of a white man. The Cherokee Nation, always quick to defend its national sovereignty, appropriated money for Eiffert's defense, maintaining that a Cherokee citizen had killed another Cherokee citizen, albeit adopted, and thus jurisdiction remained with the Nation. The case in U.S. Court was dismissed, and Eiffert was returned to the Cherokee Nation. In any case, the jurisdictional problems became a money machine for Fort Smith lawyers, who were kept busy issuing writs of habeas corpus to Sam Sixkiller, superintendent of the Cherokee penitentiary in Tahlequah, and to sheriffs from the various districts holding white lawbreakers and subsequently defending them in the U.S. Court.[18]

Cornelius took a more important part in the jurisdictional tension when in 1887 he received a letter from his brother in Tahlequah, who at the time was executive secretary to Principal Chief Bushyhead. A Cherokee citizen, Hunter Poorbear, had been convicted, it seems, in U.S. Court for an offense against another Cherokee and sentenced to imprisonment. The Cherokee Nation, citing the jurisdictional importance of the case, asked Boudinot to use his legal expertise and his political connections to secure an unconditional pardon from President Cleveland for Poorbear, and offered a fee of $250.[19] Boudinot accepted and was able to get the pardon, thus paving the way, as it turns out, for further cooperation between the Fort Smith lawyer and the Cherokee Nation.

A new administration was installed in Tahlequah in the new year of 1888, with Joel B. Mayes succeeding Bushyhead as principal chief. One of Mayes's first actions as chief was to appoint Boudinot as "associate counsel in all cases pending in U.S. Court at Fort Smith in which the Cherokee Nation is a party or has an interest."[20] In a report to the Nation, Boudinot says he sees three possible cases in which he might exercise his new authority: a complaint against a white trespasser, action against the Southern Kansas Railroad for using the Nation's timber and other materials without permission or payment, and a case involving the Kansas and Arkansas Railroad, which, according to Boudinot's claim, had built its road illegally on Cherokee land just south of the Arkansas River near Fort Smith. Cornelius saw the third case as most promising, so as his first act representing the Cherokee Nation he set out to sue a railroad company even though he must have smiled at the turn of events. Whatever the irony, however, the circle had closed, and Elias Cornelius Boudinot, long the scourge of the Tahlequah establishment, had now finally joined them, albeit in an "associate" role. He felt accepted by his people in his last years, and it must have brought him peace.

Along with the law practice, the telephone company, and the ferry operations, Boudinot had also returned to ranching. This was apparently an avocation as much as a way to make money. He had purchased the improvements on a ranch in the extreme south Cherokee Nation. Located at Paw Paw, the ranch is situated just north of the Arkansas River, on gently rolling grassland that today is still used for raising cattle and horses. The ranch had a large, rambling house on it, suitable for a man in his position and for his genteel wife. Cornelius made a practice of commuting the few miles to the law office on court days or at other times when business called. The rest of the time he managed his affairs from his comfortable surroundings at Paw Paw. The couple went into town for social occasions, of course, and Clara was welcomed into the higher echelons, such as they were, of Fort Smith society. From every indication, the couple lived a fairly idyllic life as Boudinot's political career wound down in the last few years of his life.

Into the most serene period of life that Boudinot had ever experienced rode a calamity from an unexpected source: a visit from his cousin George Gold from New England. As the story appeared in several contemporary newspapers, Gold had come to visit Boudinot in the late summer of 1890. While the pair reminisced and Cornelius got caught up on family matters, Clara made things as comfortable as possible for the men, glad to have a visitor from the East with the latest news. Suddenly, without warning, Gold fell ill, and it quickly became clear that he had gone insane. With little help in the way of treatment available in the vicinity, Clara and Cornelius decided to take Gold back to New England. The extent and nature of his illness made it clear that he could not travel alone, so Cornelius had to accompany him. Reluctant to leave his wife, Boudinot nevertheless made preparations, and he and Gold set out on the first leg of their journey, to St. Louis. By the time they reached that city, Boudinot himself had fallen ill from dysentery. He found a hotel room and, after making arrangements for Gold to be accompanied east, prepared to rest and make his recuperation. After several days, Cornelius knew he was not improving, so he embarked on the train back to Fort Smith. Arriving at his home on September 16, Boudinot was examined by a physician, who predicted that he would not survive. While Clara frantically tried to nurse him back to health, Cornelius seemed to begin a recovery, but then he lapsed into fever and delirium. On September 27, the man who had been "the very picture of health," according to friends, passed away, attended by his wife, his doctor, and his old friend W. W. Wheeler and Mrs. Wheeler.

The funeral took place at the Wheeler home, the family then removing to Oak Grove Cemetery in Fort Smith, where the body was interred.[21] According to Thomas Colbert, more than a thousand people attended the service at the cemetery, where J. J. Van Hoose, past grand master of the state of Arkansas, performed a Masonic rite. At the graveside with the young widow stood William P. Boudinot and his son Elias C. Boudinot Jr., who had followed his uncle into politics and journalism and who was to survive Cornelius by only a few years. They were comforted by Rev. R. L. Lotz of the Christian Church, who closed the service with a prayer.

Despite the widely attended funeral, the leading citizens decided that it was appropriate to hold another memorial service, this one organized by Cornelius's law partners and business colleagues. This would be a tribute to

Boudinot's "progressive" ideas, Thomas Barnes decided after a consultation with Judge Parker and prominent members of the Fort Smith bar. They decided to hold the tribute on October 9, 1890, in the ornate old courtroom where many of the cases Boudinot had been involved in had been tried. The echoes of the arguments in Bell's colonization case and Payne's apple brandy trial seemed to still ring against the high ceiling as the lawyers and businessmen filed in, followed by the widow, who was escorted to her seat by Mrs. Parker. After Judge Parker's opening remarks, Barnes read a resolution. This document recognized Boudinot's foresight in Indian affairs, pointing out that while his people "rejected with great bitterness" his proposals, "time has vindicated the wisdom of his progressive views as statesmanlike and foresighted." The resolution proclaimed him the "truest and best friend" and the "most eminent citizen and greatest genius of the Indian race." Barnes did not mention Boudinot's service and friendship to white America.

Following the reading of the resolution, several citizens rose to add their testimonials, most keeping to Barnes's theme of Boudinot's foresightedness. [22] Similar tributes were recorded in area newspapers by members of the Indian Territory bar, centered at Muskogee, at a memorial service for Boudinot on December 9. Most commented on his "advanced" positions in Indian affairs, voicing regret that he did not live to be fully vindicated by seeing the policies he advocated being put into practice. His death was widely reported, even in the eastern newspapers, the *New York Times* calling him "the most noted of the Cherokees." [23] Other newspapers carried his obituary prominently, including the *Muskogee Phoenix*, the *Indian Citizen* of Atoka, the *Indian Chieftain* at Vinita, and the *Cherokee Telephone* at Tahlequah. Even the *Cherokee Advocate*, which earlier had been edited by his brother and nephew but was still the official voice of the Cherokee Nation, ended his obituary on a conciliatory note: "Peace, let him rest, / God knoweth best."

Boudinot left his worldly goods to his wife. This turned out to be a goodly share, and according to Colbert, Clara was left in comfortable if not wealthy circumstances. Cornelius had interests in the law firm and the telephone companies as well as his ranch at Paw Paw, which consisted of 215 acres. His holdings at Russell Creek had been diminished over time, but he still held 250 acres there. And, of course, he still doggedly claimed an interest on all the land upon which Vinita stood. Of course, the major portion of Boudinot's legacy was not material.

When Boudinot died in 1890, he had achieved one of his major goals, the respect of his peers, including that of many in the Cherokee national government. This respect, however, was limited. He had lived with one foot in each of two worlds, the Cherokee Nation and white frontier America. A stark example of this is the way he spent the latter years of his life, his evenings at home with his wife on the ranch in Indian Territory, many of his days in his law office in bustling Fort Smith. Perhaps it would have been difficult for anyone to gain high regard from both communities. While his life was honored on the Arkansas side of the boundary dividing it from Cherokee territory, his name, in spite of his acceptance by Cherokee officials, was still anathema to many people living just a few miles away.

By 1890 the days of the Cherokees and the other sovereign Indian nations of the Territory were numbered, and most people knew it. The previous year had seen the great land rush of white settlers on the "unassigned lands," with more promised; the government was busy with its latest shortsighted Indian policy, the allotment of tribal lands into individually owned plots, greatly reducing the Indians' land base and in one fell swoop creating vast tracts of "surplus" lands. Allotment, of course, was popular with the white population, especially homesteaders and the business interests that profited from the movement, so politicians were determined to carry it out. It can be argued that Boudinot had been able to foresee these developments and had merely tried to cash in on the inevitable. This is how white society regarded his career: he had been able to see the inexorable march of history and "progress," the sacred exclusivity of the white American culture, and the hopelessness of his own people's decision to try to arrest the tide. His colleagues in white America, and especially those on the frontier, regarded Boudinot as a curiosity as well as a prophet, a sort of Indian Cassandra whom his countrymen refused to believe. John Hallum, an early biographer, sums it up this way: "Colonel Boudinot, like Belshazzar, sees the handwriting on the wall, and for years has labored with great ability to educate his people up to his own intellectual standard."[24]

On the other side of the border, however, Boudinot was regarded otherwise. "Scoundrel," "traitor," and "robber" were some of the choicer sobriquets showered upon him by his enemies in the Nation, despite what his fellow lawyers at Muskogee might have said. Many of the people uttering these words had good reason; others, like Boudinot himself, were blinded by the hatred engendered by the internecine warfare that erupted with the Treaty of New Echota and had waned but little in the intervening years. What had happened? Why had Cornelius not been able to make his peace with the Ross party in the Cherokee

Nation, as William P. Adair, one of Watie's stoutest allies, had done, and as his own brother William had done so successfully?

Most of Cornelius's early life had been spent far away from the Cherokee Nation. Growing up in the East, what he knew about Cherokee life was filtered through his Yankee relatives, many of whom were not too proud of the child's Indian blood. When discussing his dead parents with the child, these relatives would have focused on their "progressive" qualities, Harriet Gold's wish to educate the aborigines, for example, and Elias Boudinot's attempts to show the world the "civilized" side of the Cherokee Nation. Little of the ancient culture of people would not have been taught to him simply because he lacked proximity to teachers. He would have grown up ignorant of the traditional values of a people he aspired to lead.

Cornelius's education was entirely based in the Euro-American world, and no one would ever claim that he did not learn his lessons well. Once he moved to the West, he settled not in the heart of the Nation, where Adair lived and had been raised, and not in Tahlequah, the Cherokee capital, where his brother William had put down roots. Instead, perhaps because he was more comfortable there, he lived and worked on the border, in western Arkansas, dividing his time between Fayetteville and Fort Smith. Even when he ventured into the tobacco business, the enterprise, though based in the Cherokee Nation, was only a few hundred feet away from Arkansas. He felt more at home in the frontier atmosphere, where the Anglo values and mores that had been instilled in him in New England were practiced in every echelon of society. Furthermore, he flourished there, accepted as a rising young professional man who would someday succeed in a culture that placed material success above all. Cornelius fit in, whether he was in Washington, Little Rock, St. Louis, or on the Cherokee border in Fort Smith. He fit in much better there than he did in the Cherokee Nation, where his father and his relatives were still despised and hated.

It is clear, too, that Boudinot's love-hate relationship with his Cherokee brethren had roots deep in a family history with all its baggage, the alleged treachery and treason followed by the assassinations, the civil unrest during the 1840s, the attempts by the Ridge-Boudinot-Watie faction to split off from the main Cherokee Nation. Cornelius, unlike his brother, could never come to terms with those who had been his father's enemies, or even their offspring. The desire for revenge that he harbored just below the surface was so strong in him that it clouded his judgment in several crucial moments of his life and, in many ways, poisoned his soul.

All of these factors fueled the development of the man Cornelius Boudinot turned out to be, a man obsessed with amassing wealth and success in the white world who at the same time was determined to vanquish the enemies of his father as well as his own, no matter what the cost. These objectives, as we have seen, were often at odds; the effect of trying to achieve both at once most times meant failing to reach either of them. Such was the frustrated life of Elias Cornelius Boudinot, a man on the Cherokee border.

Notes

Abbreviations

CNP   Cherokee Nation Papers, Western History Collections, University of Oklahoma Library, Norman

OR   U.S. Department of War. *War of the Rebellion: A Compilation of the Official Records of the Union and Confederate Armies.* 70 vols. Washington DC: Government Printing Office, 1880–1901

RG   Record Group

WHC   Western History Collections, University of Oklahoma Library, Norman

1. Background and Boyhood

1. Adams, *Elias Cornelius Boudinot*.

2. The *Bartlesville Weekly Examiner* reported on May 2, 1903, that there was a movement to rename the town "Boudinot." Craig County was almost named Boudinot County as Oklahoma neared statehood, according to the *Vinita Daily Chieftain* of March 13, 1906. One of the sites settled by David L. Payne's group was the short-lived Boudinot City.

3. Richard Ellis, interview by author, September 12, 1996, Tahlequah OK.

4. Wilkins, *Cherokee Tragedy*, 125.

5. Gabriel, *Elias Boudinot*, 62.

6. Gabriel, *Elias Boudinot*, 61.

7. Gabriel, *Elias Boudinot*, 65.

8. For an account of this incident see Wilkins, *Cherokee Tragedy*, 150–53.

9. Church, "Elias Boudinot," 212. Elias Boudinot's granddaughter's account of the events surrounding the courtship and marriage is especially valuable for its insights into the family struggle that took place.

10. Church, "Elias Boudinot," 215.

11. Wilkins, *Cherokee Tragedy*, 153.

12. Gold, *Historical Records*, 87.

13. Gold, *Historical Records*, 87.

14. Boudinot, "An Address to the Whites."

15. *Cherokee Phoenix, and Indians' Advocate*, February 18, 1829.

16. Littlefield and Parins, *Indian Newspapers and Periodicals*, 88.

17. For a full discussion of these events see Wilkins, *Cherokee Tragedy*, 235–40.

18. Gabriel, *Elias Boudinot*, 156.

19. Gold, *Historical Records*, 284–92.

20. Gabriel, *Elias Boudinot*, 157–58. Gold and Gabriel give slightly different accounts. Gold has Elias Cornelius's birth in 1834. Nowhere else have I found this date. Gabriel puts Frank's birth in 1835 and records May 1836 as when Harriet delivered a child stillborn.

21. Elias Boudinot to Benjamin and Eleanor Gold, August 16, 1836, in Gaul, *To Marry an Indian*, 183–90.

22. *Cherokee Telephone*, February 26, 1893.

23. Wilkins, *Cherokee Tragedy*, 328.

24. McLoughlin, *After the Trail of Tears*, 15. For a full discussion of the political struggle among the Cherokees in the spring of 1839, see 4–15.

25. Stand Watie Papers, box 151, M943-2-1-E, CNP.

26. 28th Cong., 2d sess., S. Doc. 140, serial 457, 79.

27. For accounts of this period of Cherokee history, see Moulton, *John Ross, Cherokee Chief*; and Franks, *Stand Watie*.

28. Daniel B. Brinsmade to Stand Watie, September 16, 1847, in Dale and Litton, *Cherokee Cavaliers*, 59.

29. Boudinot to Watie, December 16, 1855, Stand Watie Papers, CNP.

30. Dale and Litton, *Cherokee Cavaliers*, 22.

31. Dale and Litton, *Cherokee Cavaliers*, 63.

32. Dale and Litton, *Cherokee Cavaliers*, 23, 63, 47.

33. Dale and Litton, *Cherokee Cavaliers*, 63.

34. Dale and Litton, *Cherokee Cavaliers*, 72.

35. Littlefield and Parins, *Indian Newspapers and Periodicals*, 65.

36. Dale and Litton, *Cherokee Cavaliers*, 59, 47.

37. Dale and Litton, *Cherokee Cavaliers*, 63.

38. Colbert, "Prophet of Progress," 35. Colbert's dissertation is a rich source of information about Boudinot, his family, and the Cherokee Nation.

39. Colbert, "Prophet of Progress," 37.

40. Boudinot to "Dear Aunt," February 25, 1852, CNP, quoted in Colbert, "Prophet of Progress," 37.

41. Dale and Litton, *Cherokee Cavaliers*, 61.

42. Dale and Litton, *Cherokee Cavaliers*, 84n.

43. Hallum, *Biographical and Pictorial History*, 349–59.

44. Quoted in Gaul, *To Marry an Indian*, 198–99.

45. *Cherokee Telephone*, February 26, 1893.

2. The Young Man in Arkansas

1. For a look at Ridge's life and career see Parins, *John Rollin Ridge*.

2. Parins, *John Rollin Ridge*, 32–44.

3. Dale, "Letters of the Two Boudinots," 330.

4. Dale, "Letters of the Two Boudinots," 330.

5. See Dale, "Letters of the Two Boudinots"; and Harman, *Hell on the Border*, 146–47.

Harman goes so far as to include Boudinot's alleged fellow attorneys and to supply a juicy quote from Boudinot concerning the trial. "All the innocent blood and sufferings of my race came in panoramic procession before my mind like the lightning's flash, and determined me to make an effort worthy of my lineage or ruin my brain in the attempt," he reportedly said.

6. Boudinot to Stand Watie, December 16, 1855, Stand Watie Correspondence file, CNP.

7. Huff, *Goodspeed's 1889 History of Washington Country*, reprint of the Washington County section of *Goodspeed's Benton, Washington, Carroll, Madison, Crawford, Franklin, and Sebastian Counties Arkansas History*, 244.

8. Allsopp, *History of the Arkansas Press*, 617.

9. See, e.g., W. P. Boudinot's "Life's Phantom" in the April 2, 1859, issue.

10. *Arkansian*, March 5, 1859, 2.

11. *Arkansian*, April 6, 1860, 2.

12. *Arkansian*, April 27, 1860, p. 2, and May 4, 1860, 2.

13. *Arkansian*, July 2, 1859, 2.

14. *Arkansian*, July 23, 1859, 2.

15. *Arkansian*, September 22, 1859, 2.

16. Moulton, *Papers of Chief John Ross*, 163; Franks, *Stand Watie*, 111–12.

17. *Dictionary of American Biography*, 10:117–18.

18. Wardell, *Political History*, 105.

19. Wardell, *Political History*, 105.

20. Wardell, *Political History*, 107.

21. Huff, *Goodspeed's 1889 History of Washington Country*, 252.

22. Dougan, *Confederate Arkansas*, 12–13.

23. *Dictionary of American Biography*, 9:61–62.

24. Dougan, *Confederate Arkansas*, 17.

25. Dougan, *Confederate Arkansas*, 14.

26. Dougan, *Confederate Arkansas*, 13.

27. Allsopp, *History of the Arkansas Press*, 616–17.

28. See Scroggs, "Arkansas in the Secession Crisis," for an extensive discussion of the situation.

29. Quoted in Dougan, *Confederate Arkansas*, 18.

30. Dougan, *Confederate Arkansas*, 21.

31. Colbert does an excellent job of documenting the editorial exchanges; see "Prophet of Progress," esp. 62–64. See the Arkansas *True Democrat* and the *Old Line Democrat* for May and June 1860.

32. Dougan, *Confederate Arkansas*, 22, 44–45.

33. Scroggs, "Arkansas in the Secession Crisis," 198.

34. Scroggs, "Arkansas in the Secession Crisis," 200–203.

35. Dougan, *Confederate Arkansas*, 49.

36. Wooster, "Arkansas Secession Convention," 176. This article gives significant demographic data on the delegates.

37. Dougan, *Confederate Arkansas*, 54.

38. Colbert, "Prophet of Progress," 70.

3. Soldier and Delegate

1. See Abel, *Slaveholder and Secessionist*, for an extensive discussion of relations between the tribes of Indian Territory and the Confederacy at the beginning of the war.

2. Cunningham, *Watie's Confederate Indians*, 31.

3. Dale and Litton, *Cherokee Cavaliers*, 103–4.

4. Abel, *Slaveholder and Secessionist*, 135.

5. For a full discussion of the Knights see Klement, *Copperheads in the Middle West*, 135–69.

6. William P. Adair to Stand Watie, July 17, 1860, Stand Watie Miscellaneous file, CNP.

7. Parins, *John Rollin Ridge*, 208–10.

8. Wilson and Washbourne to Watie, May 18, 1861, in Dale and Litton, *Cherokee Cavaliers*, 106–7.

9. Franks, *Stand Watie*, 117.

10. Franks, *Stand Watie*, 118.

11. Colbert, "Prophet of Progress," 84.

12. Franks, *Stand Watie*, 118.

13. *OR*, 4th ser., 1:669–86.

14. *OR*, 1st ser., 3:692.

15. Dale and Litton, *Cherokee Cavaliers*, 110–11.

16. Boudinot to Watie, October 5, 1861, in Dale and Litton, *Cherokee Cavaliers*, 110–11.

17. "Compiled Service Records of Confederate Soldiers in Organizations Raised Directly by the Confederate Government," microfilm 258, roll 79, National Archives, Washington DC.

18. Captain W. R. Bradfute to Stand Watie, Stand Watie To/From General Correspondence, box 2E, CNP; McCulloch to Major General Sterling Price, *OR*, 1st ser., 3:721.

19. Franks, *Stand Watie*, 120.

20. *OR*, 1st ser., 8:5–12.

21. Report of Col. Stand Watie, December 28, 1861, and Major Elias C. Boudinot, December 28, 1861, *OR*, 1st ser., 8:32–33; report of Col. James McIntosh, January 1, 1862, *OR*, 1st ser., 8:22–25.

22. Quesenbury to Watie, March 22, 1862, Stand Watie To/From General Correspondence, box 2E, CNP.

23. Pike to Hindman, June 8, 1862, *OR*, 1st ser., 8:939, 956.

24. Pike to Hindman, June 8, 1862, *OR*, 1st ser., 8:286–92.

25. Hindman to Cooper, May 31, 1862, *OR*, 1st ser., 13:40, 183.

26. Marcus J. Wright, "Colonel Elias C. Boudinot," *Southern Bivouac* 2, no. 10 (1884): 434, cited in Colbert, "Prophet of Progress," 94.

27. Franks, *Stand Watie*, 129.

28. Wardell, *Political History*, 160.

29. Wardell, *Political History*, 162–63.

30. Cunningham, *Watie's Confederate Indians*, 87.

31. 58th Cong., 2d sess., S. Doc. 234, vol. 5, p. 502.

32. 58th Cong., 2d sess., S. Doc. 234, vol. 5, p. 514.

33. Boudinot to Watie, January 23, 1863, in Dale and Litton, *Cherokee Cavaliers*, 120.

34. 58th Cong., 2d sess., S. Doc. 234, vol. 6, p. 276.

35. 58th Cong., 2d sess., S. Doc. 234, vol. 6, pp. 280, 494.

36. Dale and Litton, *Cherokee Cavaliers*, 129–30.

37. 58th Cong., 2d sess., S. Doc. 234, vol. 6, p. 529.

38. Watie to Scott, August 8, 1863, in *OR*, 1st ser., 22, pt. 2:1104.

39. Boudinot to Stand Watie, Monroe, Louisiana, November 4, 1863, and Boudinot to Stand Watie, January 23, 1864, in Dale and Litton, *Cherokee Cavaliers*, 143–44, 150.

40. 58th Cong., 2d sess., S. Doc. 234, vol. 6, pp. 542–43.

41. Franks, *Stand Watie*, 145.

42. Franks, *Stand Watie*, 143.

43. James M. Bell Papers, box 170, CNP.

44. Boudinot to Stand Watie, January 24, 1864, in Dale and Litton, *Cherokee Cavaliers*, 150; Boudinot to Davis, December 21, 1863, *OR*, 1st ser., 22, pt. 1:1103.

45. *OR*, 1st ser., 22, pt. 2:810.

46. *OR*, 1st ser., 22, pt. 2:1101.

47. Steele to Watie, April 21, 1864, Stand Watie To/From General Correspondence, box 3F, CNP.

48. 58th Cong., 2d sess., S. Doc. 234, vol. 6, pp. 602, 692, 811.

49. 58th Cong., 2d sess., S. Doc. 234, vol. 6, p. 125.

50. 58th Cong., 2d sess., S. Doc. 234, vol. 7, p. 19.

51. Dale and Litton, *Cherokee Cavaliers*, 153.

52. *OR*, 1st ser., 34, pt. 3:824–25, quoted in Franks, *Stand Watie*, 157.

53. 58th Cong., 2d sess., S. Doc. 234, vol. 7, p. 405.

54. Dale and Litton, *Cherokee Cavaliers*, 157, 159.

55. Dale and Litton, *Cherokee Cavaliers*, 157–59.

56. E. C. Boudinot to William Penn Boudinot, June 2, 1864, in Dale and Litton, *Cherokee Cavaliers*, 166–71.

57. The *London Herald* article has not been found.

58. Boudinot to Watie, July 13, July 25, September 11, October 31, 1864, in Dale and Litton, *Cherokee Cavaliers*, 180, 181, 189, 201.

59. Boudinot to Watie, October 1, 1864, in Dale and Litton, *Cherokee Cavaliers*, 194–94. Sallie Watie complained to her husband that Hooley Bell, one of Stand's officers, did not deliver all the cards in his possession to the refugees, selling some for profit. Sarah C. Watie to Stand Watie, September 4, 1864, Stand Watie Correspondence file, box 147, file 17, CNP.

60. Abel, *Civil War*, 193.

61. For a vivid picture of this period, see especially the letters of Sarah C. Watie and Caroline Bell to their husbands in the Stand Watie Correspondence file and the J. M. Bell

Papers in CNP. Some of the issues were discussed in James W. Parins, "Sallie Watie and Southern Cherokee Women in the Civil War and After," paper presented at the Cherokee History Symposium, Park Hill, Cherokee Nation OK, September 1–3, 1993.

62. Sarah C. Watie to Stand Watie, October 9, 1864, Stand Watie Correspondence file, box 147, file 9, CNP.

63. Boudinot to Watie, October 31, 1864, in Dale and Litton, *Cherokee Cavaliers*, 202.

64. Boudinot to Watie, May 11, 1865, in Dale and Litton, *Cherokee Cavaliers*, 222–23.

65. Maj. Gen. J. J. Reynolds to Adjutant General, May 22, 1865, *OR*, 1st ser., 48, pt. 2:626–27.

66. The first dealt with his own case in challenging the congressional act that barred members of the Confederate government from practicing before the U.S. Supreme Court. See *Ex parte Garland*, 4 Wallace 333–39. Another concerned the validity of contracts for slave sales. See *Osborn v. Nicholson*, 13 Wallace 654–64. Garland and his associates won both cases.

67. *Dictionary of American Biography*, 7:150–51.

68. Franks, *Stand Watie*, 182–83.

4. Peace Negotiator

1. *OR*, 1st ser., 48, pt. 2:631.

2. Franks, *Stand Watie*, 182–83.

3. Wardell, *Political History*, 182–83.

4. Abel, *End of the Confederacy*, 175–77; "Report of the Commissioner of Indian Affairs," in *Report of the Secretary of the Interior*, 39th Cong., 1st sess., H. Exec. Doc. 105½, 480.

5. Parker, or Do-ne-ho-ga-wa, was born in 1828, attended Rensselaer Polytechnic Institute, and represented his tribe, the Senecas, in Washington. He was promoted to brigadier general in 1867 and became commissioner of Indian Affairs in 1869.

6. Wardell, *Political History*, 184.

7. "Report of the Commissioner of Indian Affairs," 480–86.

8. James Harlan to D. N. Cooley and Brig. Gen. W. S. Harney, September 17, 1865, O.I.A., General Files, Cherokee, 1859–1865, vol. 1, p. 1271, National Archives, Washington DC.

9. Despite an extensive search, I have not been able to find this account. Therefore, the information here relies entirely on Abel in *End of the Confederacy*, 204–5n.

10. Abel, *End of the Confederacy*, 177–78.

11. Abel, *End of the Confederacy*, 243.

12. "Report of the Commissioner of Indian Affairs," 491.

13. "Official Report of the Proceedings of the Council," by Charles Mix, secretary, in *Report of the Secretary of the Interior*, 39th Cong., 1st sess., H. Exec. Doc. 106, 527.

14. "Report of the Commissioner of Indian Affairs," 493.

15. "Report of the Commissioner of Indian Affairs," 496.

16. For a good discussion of the 1866 deliberations see Wardell, *Political History*, 194–207.

17. For more on Ridge see Parins, *John Rollin Ridge*.

18. J. W. Washbourne to J. A. Scales, June 1, 1866, quoted in Wardell, *Political History*, 201.

19. J. W. Washbourne to Susan Ridge Washbourne, January 16, 1866, Washburn (Washbourne) Collection, Arkansas History Commission, Little Rock.

20. Wardell, *Political History*, 194n.

21. Wardell, *Political History*, 194.

22. Abel, *End of the Confederacy*, 346.

23. Abel, *End of the Confederacy*, 346.

24. Wardell, *Political History*, 196.

25. Abel, *End of the Confederacy*, 352.

26. Abel, *End of the Confederacy*, 353.

27. Wardell, *Political History*, 198.

28. Washbourne to Scales, June 1, 1866.

29. Forde, "Elias Cornelius Boudinot," 131.

30. Letters Received, Cherokee, 1865–66, M234, roll 100, Bureau of Indian Affairs, National Archives, Washington DC.

31. E. C. Boudinot Papers, CNP.

32. Boudinot to John Rollin Ridge, n.d., Stand Watie Miscellaneous file, CNP.

33. E. C. Boudinot to N. G. Taylor, Commissioner of Indian Affairs, April 13, 1867, Boudinot Papers, CNP.

5. The Tobacco Tycoon

1. Heimann, "Cherokee Tobacco Case," 306.

2. Watie to Bell, April 24, 1869, in Dale and Litton, *Cherokee Cavaliers*, 285.

3. Heimann, "Cherokee Tobacco Case," 301.

4. Boudinot to Watie, Boudyville, Cherokee Nation, November 21, 1868, Stand Watie file, CNP.

5. Boudinot to Watie, January 9, 1868, Stand Watie file, CNP.

6. Heimann, "Cherokee Tobacco Case," 315.

7. *Elias C. Boudinot v. the United States*, U.S. Court of Claims, 12350.

8. Washbourne to Watie, September 27, 1868, quoted in Dale and Litton, *Cherokee Cavaliers*, 267.

9. Boudinot to Watie, November 21, 1868.

10. Affidavit of Joseph C. Henderson, quoted in "Memorial of Elias C. Boudinot, a Cherokee Indian, for Relief against certain proceedings under the internal revenue laws," 42d Cong., 2d sess., H.R. Misc. Doc. 9, 37–38 [hereinafter cited as Boudinot, "Memorial"].

11. Boudinot, "Memorial," 26.

12. Boudinot to Watie, August 15, 1869, Stand Watie file, CNP.

13. Boudinot to Watie, August 15, 1869.

14. Wardell, *Political History*, 292.

15. Boudinot, "Memorial," 2.

16. Quoted in Boudinot, "Memorial," 2.

17. Boudinot, "Memorial," 2.

18. Heimann, "Cherokee Tobacco Case," 313, 315.

19. Quoted in Voorhees, "Boudinot Tobacco Case," 5.

20. Quoted in Boudinot, "Memorial," 3–4.

21. Quoted in Boudinot, "Memorial," 4.

22. Quoted in Boudinot, "Memorial," 6.

23. Quoted in Boudinot, "Memorial," 7–8.

24. Quoted in Boudinot, "Memorial," 9.

25. Boudinot, "Memorial," 10.

26. Quoted in Boudinot, "Memorial," 11.

27. Boudinot, "Memorial," 12.

28. Affidavit of James W. Donnelley, in Boudinot, "Memorial," 34.

29. Boudinot, "Memorial," 36.

30. Boudinot, "Memorial," 12.

31. Boudinot, "Memorial," 15.

32. Voorhees, "Boudinot Tobacco Case," 13.

33. Boudinot, "Memorial," 27–28.

34. Harman, *Hell on the Border*, 97, 150.

35. Albert Pike and Robert Johnson, *Elias C. Boudinot and Stand Watie v. the United States*, Argument for Plaintiffs in Error, Supreme Court U.S., December Term, 1870, no. 253, 1.

36. Heimann, "Cherokee Tobacco Case," 318.

37. Boudinot to Watie, May 10, 1871, Stand Watie file, CNP.

38. Pike and Johnson, *Boudinot and Watie v. the United States*, 81.

39. Benjamin F. Butler, *Elias C. Boudinot et al., Plaintiffs in Error, v. The United States*, Brief for Plaintiffs, Supreme Court U.S., December Term, 1870, no. 253, 4–5.

40. The U.S. Supreme Court at that time consisted of Chief Justice Salmon P. Chase and Associate Justices Noah H. Swayne, Joseph P. Bradley, Samuel F. Miller, Nathan Clifford, Samuel Nelson, David Davis, William Strong, and Stephen J. Field. Chase, Nelson, and Field did not hear the case and did not participate in the decision.

41. *U.S. Supreme Court Reports*, 11 Wallace 616–24.

42. *U.S. Supreme Court Reports*, 4 Howard 567.

43. Boudinot to Watie, May 10, 1871, in Dale and Litton, *Cherokee Cavaliers*, 295.

44. *Cherokee Advocate*, July 8, 1871, 2:1.

45. Quoted in Boudinot, "Memorial," 36.

46. *Cherokee Advocate*, October 21, 1871, 2:2.

47. Quoted in Heimann, "Cherokee Tobacco Case," 317.

48. Boudinot, "Memorial," 7.

49. Elias C. Boudinot to Benjamin L. Duval, Washington DC, December 18, 1871, Duval Family Papers, series 1, box 1, folder 8, Special Collections, University of Arkansas, Fayetteville.

50. *U.S. Supreme Court Reports*, 11 Wallace 624.

51. Sallie Watie to James M. Bell, January 31, 1872, Sarah C. Watie Papers, CNP.

52. J. W. Clarke to Sarah C. Watie, January 18, 1873, Sarah C. Watie Papers, CNP.

6. Railroad Man

1. Miner, *The Corporation and the Indian*, 18.

2. E. C. Boudinot to Stand Watie, January 9, 1868, in Dale and Litton, *Cherokee Cavaliers*, 259–60. See also Self, "Building of the Railroads"; and Hodges, "Col. E. C. Boudinot," 31.

3. Wardell, *Political History*, 217, 219n. The Delawares paid for their land with funds that went into the national treasury. The Delaware people were incorporated into the Nation and had full rights as Cherokee citizens. The Cherokee Treaty of 1828 set out the boundaries of land to be occupied by the tribe in present-day Oklahoma. However, a series of factors, including a lack of geographic information, confusion about Indian cession agreements, and territorial disputes, made boundary lines less than clear. Senecas and Shawnees moved to the extreme northeastern corner of Indian Territory after their removal from Ohio in 1831. The Quapaws, upon their removal from Arkansas in 1834, likewise occupied a part of this area. The government removed several tribes from Kansas into the corner in 1867, including the confederated Peorias, Kaskaskias, Weas, and Piankeshaws, who were joined later by the Miamis.

4. Miner, *The Corporation and the Indian*, 9–10.

5. Miner, *The Corporation and the Indian*, 17.

6. Miner, *The Corporation and the Indian*, 12.

7. McLoughlin, *After the Trail of Tears*, 232.

8. Miner, *The Corporation and the Indian*, 21–22.

9. Masterson, *The Katy Railroad*, 14. Much of Masterson's material concerning Boudinot was reconstructed from company records and the personal correspondence of General Manager Stevens. Most of these records have been lost since Masterson published his book in 1952. According to Mark J. Cedeck, transportation curator of the St. Louis Mercantile Library Association, the Katy's archives were "substantially destroyed" by fire at the Parsons, Kansas, depot (Mark J. Cedeck to James W. Parins, January 11, 1994). This was subsequently confirmed by Don Snoddy of the Union Pacific archives.

10. McLoughlin, *After the Trail of Tears*, 232–33. Also reported in Masterson, *The Katy Railroad*, 16. The abortive agreement was the same as reported by Miner above.

11. Wardell, *Political History*, 214. Other bids for the Neutral Lands were for $800,000 and $1 million.

12. *Southern Kansas Advance*, March 2, 1870.

13. Masterson, *The Katy Railroad*, 49–50.

14. *Kansas City Commonwealth*, May 4, 1870.

15. Self, "Building of the Railroads," 190.

16. Masterson, *The Katy Railroad*, 58.

17. Masterson, *The Katy Railroad*, 60.

18. Stevens certainly knew that Boudinot's enemies were behind Cherokee opposition to the success of the Katy. See Masterson, *The Katy Railroad*, 66n.

19. Quoted in Masterson, *The Katy Railroad*, 68.

20. Masterson, *The Katy Railroad*, 63–65.

21. Masterson, *The Katy Railroad*, 66.

22. Masterson, *The Katy Railroad*, 72.

23. Cherokee records in the Indian Archives at the Oklahoma Historical Society list many familiar names as having dealings in ties. See Special, x-118, Cherokee Railroads 1866–1905, Indian Archives, Oklahoma Historical Society, Oklahoma City.

24. Special, x-118, Cherokee Railroads 1866–1905.

25. McLoughlin, *After the Trail of Tears*, 294.

26. E. C. Boudinot to James M. Bell, August 6, 1875, Boudinot Papers, CNP.

27. Wardell, *Political History*, 279–80.

28. RG 21, jacket 16, box 24, November term, 1875, National Archives, Fort Worth.

29. E. C. Boudinot to James M. Bell, March 11, 1876, Boudinot Papers, CNP.

30. Miner, "Struggle for an East-West Railway," 560–61.

31. *Indian Chieftain*, January 27, 1898. The article was written by D. M. Marrs, editor of the *Vinita Leader*.

32. *Compiled Laws of the Cherokee Nation*, 281–82.

33. Masterson, *The Katy Railroad*, 126–27.

7. The Hotelier at Vinita

1. Later the right-of-way was extended to two hundred feet. Carl Schurz, Secretary of the Interior, to Dennis W. Bushyhead, Principal Chief, November 7, 1879, RG 21, jacket 58, box 98, National Archives, Fort Worth. In 1885, Bushyhead's position was that the right-of-way could be used for railroad purposes only when they need it; it is not title to the land. The land along the railroad, according to Bushyhead, remained in the Cherokee common domain until the railroad makes use of it. Bushyhead to John D. C. Atkin, Commissioner of Indian Affairs, July 11, 1885, RG 21, jacket 58, box 98, National Archives, Fort Worth. See also Principal Chief Charles Thompson's August 15, 1878, letter to C. C. Lipe, note 22 below.

2. RG 21, U.S. District Courts, *U.S. v. Henry Eiffert and J. M. Whalen*, August 4, 1881, U.S. Court, Western District of Arkansas, National Archives, Fort Worth. This is an unpaginated, handwritten record of depositions in the case Boudinot brought against the men he accused of tearing down his hotel.

3. E. C. Boudinot to Sarah C. Watie, June 18, 1878, Sarah C. Watie Papers, CNP; and E. C. Boudinot to James M. Bell, June 17, 1878, Bell Papers, CNP.

4. *U.S. v. Henry Eiffert and J. M. Whalen*.

5. *U.S. v. Henry Eiffert and J. M. Whalen*.

6. Boudinot took the post of clerk for the House Committee on Public Expenditures and Private Land Claims in 1878. He continued in this capacity until 1881, with a five-month hiatus in 1880. Boyd, *Boyd's Directory of the District of Columbia*. See also the U.S. Official Register for 1879 and 46th Cong., 1st, 2d, 3d sess. minutes, H.R.

7. *U.S. v. Henry Eiffert and J. M. Whalen*.

8. Boudinot to Bell, Washington DC, n.d., Bell Papers, CNP.

9. Skinner to Boudinot, —— 22, 1877, Boudinot Papers, CNP.

10. Boudinot to Sarah C. Watie, Washington DC, February 1, 1878, Sarah C. Watie Papers, CNP.

11. Boudinot to George W. McCrary, Secretary of War, Washington, May 29, 1878. Correspondence, and report of investigation, relative to seizure of Hotel, claimed by Elias C. Boudinot, and indebtedness on account thereof of John R. Skinner, Post Trader at Fort Gibson Indian Territory, RG 21, jacket 58, box 98, National Archives, Fort Worth.

12. Lipe to Thompson, February 12, 1878, RG 21, jacket 58, box 98, National Archives, Fort Worth.

13. Thompson to Lipe, February 16, 1878, RG 21, jacket 58, box 98, National Archives, Fort Worth.

14. Thompson to Lipe, March 6, 1878, RG 21, jacket 58, box 98, National Archives, Fort Worth.

15. Boudinot to Bell, March 15, 1878, Bell Papers, CNP.

16. Boudinot to Bell, April 23, 1878, Bell Papers, CNP.

17. Boudinot to Bell, May 22, 1878, Bell Papers, CNP.

18. Boudinot to Bell, May 5, 1878, Bell Papers, CNP.

19. Boudinot to Bell, May 28, 1878, Bell Papers, CNP.

20. E. C. Boudinot to S. C. Watie, May 6, May 24, 1878, Sarah C. Watie Papers, CNP.

21. Correspondence, and report of investigation, relative to seizure of Hotel, claimed by Elias C. Boudinot, and indebtedness on account thereof of John R. Skinner, Post Trader at Fort Gibson Indian Territory, 24.

22. Thompson to Lipe, August 15, 1878, Special, X-118, Cherokee Railroads 1866–1905, Indian Archives.

23. Boudinot to Bell, November 5, 1878, Bell Papers, CNP.

24. Boudinot to Bell, December 6, 1878, Bell Papers, CNP.

25. E. L. Stevens, Secretary of the Interior, to H. Price, Acting Commissioner of Indian Affairs, February 7, 1881, Washington, RG 21, jacket 58, box 98, National Archives, Fort Worth.

26. Boudinot to Schurz, February 25, 1880, RG 21, jacket 58, box 98, National Archives, Fort Worth.

27. E. J. Brooks to John Q. Tufts, March 2, 1880, RG 21, jacket 58, box 98, National Archives, Fort Worth.

28. Price to Kirkwood, April 14, 1881, RG 21, jacket 58, box 98, National Archives, Fort Worth.

29. Price to Kirkwood, April 14, 1881.

30. Kirkwood to Price, April 29, 1881, RG 21, jacket 58, box 98, National Archives, Fort Worth.

31. Affidavit signed by Elias C. Boudinot, notarized by Henry Kaiser, Fayetteville, Arkansas, June 11, 1881, E. C. Boudinot Collection, CNP.

32. Testimony of H. H. Edmundson, *U.S. v. Henry Eiffert and J. M. Whalen.*

33. S. S. Stevens to J. M. Bell, n.d., Bell Papers, CNP.

34. Testimony of H. H. Edmundson, *U.S. v. Henry Eiffert and J. M. Whalen.*

8. The Washingtonian

1. McLoughlin, *After the Trail of Tears*, 233–34.
2. Colbert, "Prophet of Progress," 182.
3. *Arkansas Gazette*, January 30, 1868, 2.
4. Colbert, "Prophet of Progress," 182–83.
5. Forde, "Elias Cornelius Boudinot," 142.
6. 46th Cong., 1st, 2d, 3d sess., Minutes, H.R. Committee on Private Land Claims.
7. See correspondence between Boudinot and Bell at CNP.
8. Forde, "Elias Cornelius Boudinot," 143.
9. Adams, *Elias Cornelius Boudinot*, 55.
10. Harman, *Hell on the Border*, 150.
11. I have serious doubts about Campbell's accuracy in recording Ream's birth year. There is some evidence that Boudinot and his cousin John Rollin Ridge paid her some attention when the family lived in Fort Smith that would not have been appropriate toward an eleven-year-old girl. A date of five or so years earlier is probably more accurate.
12. Campbell, *Vinnie Ream*, 1–4.
13. Campbell, *Vinnie Ream*, 5–6.
14. Campbell, *Vinnie Ream*, 6.
15. Campbell, *Vinnie Ream*, 19.
16. Brown, *Life of Albert Pike*, 455.
17. G. C. Bingham to Vinnie Ream, June 13, 1877, box 2, Vinnie (Ream) and Richard L. Hoxie Collection, Manuscripts Division, Library of Congress, Washington DC.
18. For Pike's voluminous correspondence with Ream see boxes 1 and 2 in the Hoxie Collection, especially for the years 1868–78. See also Brown's comments on their relationship in his *Life of Albert Pike*, 455–56.
19. John J. Ingalls to Vinnie Ream, July 15, 1874, box 2, Hoxie Collection.
20. James S. Rollins to General R. B. Van Valkenburg, February 3, 1866, box 1, Hoxie Collection.
21. See *Cherokee Advocate*, November 14, 1874, 2.
22. "Songs and instrumental pieces for guitar and pianoforte" is one such notebook. It is listed as being in "Miscellaneous Collection of Vinnie Ream" in the catalog of the Performing Arts Collection, Library of Congress, Washington DC, but is missing in the files.
23. As reported in Campbell, *Vinnie Ream*, 21, the notebook is inscribed "Songs of Col. Elias Cornelius Boudinot, Cherokee, Washington DC, 1877, copied by his true friend, Mary Fuller."
24. J. E. B. to friend, April 4, 1876, box 2, Hoxie Collection. The party marked one of the last social appearances for George Armstrong Custer before he left to take command of the Seventh Cavalry in the West.
25. J. S. Cramer to Vinnie Ream, June 4, 1864, box 1, Hoxie Collection.

26. *Washington Evening Star*, December 5, 1877, 4.

27. Sherman to Vinnie Ream, December 7, 1877, box 2, Hoxie Collection.

28. Boudinot to Watie, May 10, 1871, in Dale and Litton, *Cherokee Cavaliers*, 295.

29. The first of the major speeches along these lines, the 1871 Vinita speech, was, in fact, printed as a pamphlet for widespread distribution by associates of Senator Voorhees. The pamphlet's cover identifies the author as a Cherokee.

30. McLoughlin, *After the Trail of Tears*, 117.

31. Wardell, *Political History*, 105–97.

32. Miner, *The Corporation and the Indian*, 77.

33. Wardell, *Political History*, 109.

34. Wardell, *Political History*, 198.

35. McLoughlin, *After the Trail of Tears*, 278.

36. *Cherokee Advocate*, December 9, 1871, 2.

37. Wardell, *Political History*, 293.

38. Boudinot to Watie, December 11, 1870, in Dale and Litton, *Cherokee Cavaliers*, 289–90.

39. Wardell, *Political History*, 295.

40. Beadle, *The Undeveloped West*, 360.

41. *New York Times*, June 23, 1871, 1.

42. *New York Times*, June 20, 1871, 5, June 23, 1871, 1, June 24, 1871, 5–6, and July 5, 1871, 6.

43. *New York Times*, June 26, 1871, 5.

44. Boudinot, "Speech on the Indian Question," 4.

45. Boudinot, "Speech on the Indian Question," 3.

46. Boudinot, "Speech on the Indian Question," 3.

47. The agent was Cherokee Robert L. Owen. Wardell, *Political History*, 264.

48. Boudinot, "Speech on the Indian Question," 4.

49. Boudinot, "Speech on the Indian Question," 6.

50. Boudinot, "Speech on the Indian Question," 9.

51. Boudinot, "Speech before the House Committee on Territories, February 7, 1872," 3.

52. Precedents cited include *Johnson and Graham's Lessee v. William McIntosh* (8 Wheaton 543); *Cherokee Nation v. Georgia* (5 Peters 1); *Worcester v. Georgia* (6 Peters 580); *Clark v. Smith* (13 Peters 195); and *United States v. Rogers* (4 How. 567). Boudinot, "Speech before the House Committee on Territories, February 7, 1872," 3–7.

53. Boudinot, "Speech before the House Committee on Territories, February 7, 1872," 21.

54. Boudinot, "Speech before the House Committee on Territories, March 5, 1872."

55. Downing to Rev. John B. Jones, February 12, 1873, RG 75, Letters Received, Office of Indian Affairs, microfilm 235, roll 105, National Archives, Washington DC.

56. For a discussion of his appearances, see Colbert, "Elias Cornelius Boudinot."

9. Missionary

1. Quoted in Colbert, "Prophet of Progress," 262.

2. Elias Cornelius Boudinot file, Gilcrease Museum, Tulsa OK.

3. Stand Watie to James M. Bell, August 28, 1868, *Western Americana, Frontier History of the Trans-Mississippi West, 1500–1900*, reel 63, no. 617, p. 6.

4. Boudinot, "Manners, Customs, Traditions," 30.

5. Boudinot, "Manners, Customs, Traditions," 43.

6. Boudinot's old tobacco factory, in fact, was dismantled around this time and moved to Vinita, ostensibly for use as a Masonic hall. A certificate giving James M. Bell authority to make the move, dated October 13, 1875, is in the Boudinot Papers, CNP.

7. Boudinot to Bell, August 30, 1875, Boudinot Papers, CNP.

8. Boudinot to Bell, April 3, 1875, Boudinot Papers, CNP.

9. Boudinot to Bell, September 25, 1875, Boudinot Papers, CNP.

10. For a description of this newspaper, see Littlefield and Parins, *Indian Newspapers and Periodicals*, 215.

11. Documents concerning this affair may be viewed in RG 75, Letters Received, Office of Indian Affairs, microfilm 234, roll 235, National Archives, Fort Worth.

12. For a description of this newspaper, see Littlefield and Parins, *Indian Newspapers and Periodicals*, 349–53.

13. Boudinot to Ingalls, October 25, 1875, RG 75, Letters Received, Office of Indian Affairs, microfilm 234, roll 235, National Archives, Washington DC.

14. Boudinot to Charles Watie, May 8, 1876, Boudinot Papers, CNP.

15. *Cherokee Advocate*, April 22, 1876.

16. Boudinot to Watie, May 8, 1876.

17. Hillyer, "Atlantic and Pacific Rail Road."

18. Miner, *The Corporation and the Indian*, 90.

19. Boudinot to Bell, January 4, 1874, Boudinot Papers, CNP.

20. McLoughlin, *After the Trail of Tears*, 308.

21. Boudinot to Bell, May 3, 1876, Boudinot Papers, CNP.

22. Ira Williams to James M. Bell, May 20, 1874, Bell Papers, CNP.

23. McLoughlin, *After the Trail of Tears*, 308.

24. McLoughlin, *After the Trail of Tears*, 310.

25. *Indian Progress*, January 28, 1876.

26. Quoted in Miner, *The Corporation and the Indian*, 84.

27. *Indian Progress*, January 28, 1876.

28. Dale and Litton, *Cherokee Cavaliers*, 261.

29. For accounts of his life, see Moore, "William Penn Adair"; and "Indians Weeping," *Cherokee Advocate*, October 27, 1880.

30. Boudinot to James M. Bell, January 4, 1880, Boudinot Papers, CNP.

31. Reprinted in the *Fayetteville Sentinel*, January 14, 1880.

32. "The Indian Territory," *Chicago Times*, February 11, 1879.

33. Savage says that the boomers were "first attracted to Indian Territory by E. C. Boudinot" ("The Rock Falls Raid," 75).

34. "The Indian Question: The Logic of Events," *Chicago Times*, February 17, 1879.

35. The handbill is found in the Thoburn Collection, box 1, WHC.

36. Boudinot to Bell, April 1, 1879, Boudinot Papers, CNP.

37. Boudinot to Watie, April 23, 1879, Sarah C. Watie Papers, CNP.

38. 46th Cong., 1st sess., S. Exec. Doc. 20, 20–21. This document contains other communications relevant to the issue, including President Hayes's proclamation and Boudinot's letters and map.

39. Coachman's and Burney's comments quoted in Warde, "Fight for Survival," 34–35. Warde's article is an excellent source for the Indian reaction.

40. Reported in the *Chetopa Advance*, May 15, 1879.

41. *Kansas City Commonwealth*, March 6, 1880.

42. *Chetopa Advance*, October 9, 1879.

43. *Chetopa Advance*, November 6, 1879.

44. For more on Payne see Hoig, *David L. Payne*; and Rister, *Land Hunger*. Extensive correspondence is found in RG 48, Special Case 111, "Payne's Oklahoma Colony," passim, National Archives, Fort Worth.

45. *Checotah Enquirer*, June 14, 1901.

46. RG 21, jacket 149, box 272, National Archives, Fort Worth.

47. Boudinot to Bell, February 3, 1879, Boudinot Papers, CNP.

48. See L. B. Bell to D. W. Bushyhead, September 22, 1879, D. W. Bushyhead Papers, CNP, in which he denies giving the Joneses permission to stake a claim. The certificate, however, is in the same file.

49. Boudinot to Bell, April 13, 1879, Boudinot Papers, CNP.

50. Boudinot to Bell, June 13, 1879, Boudinot Papers, CNP.

51. Wardell, *Political History*, 304.

52. Warren got some of the names wrong, resulting in the profusion of George W's.

53. 46th Cong., 1st sess., S. Exec. Doc. 29, 3–4.

54. Boudinot refers to a letter requesting that Sherman order "that no citizens of the Cherokee Nation be molested by the military" in a letter to Bell, May 27, 1879, Boudinot Papers, CNP.

55. 46th Cong., 2d sess., S. Exec. Doc. 6, 5–6.

56. See Dale, "Cherokee Strip Live Stock Association," 97–115.

57. Boudinot to Sarah C. Watie, October 12, 1879, Sarah C. Watie Papers, CNP.

10. Lawyer, Rancher, Businessman

1. Cormier traces Phillips's career in "Land, Currency, Cherokees, and William Addison Phillips: A Study in Contradiction." See also Klema's "The Later Career of William A. Phillips."

2. Miner, *The Corporation and the Indian*, 111–13.

3. Cormier, "Land, Currency, Cherokees," 76–77.

4. "The Phillips Steal!" is in Boudinot Papers, CNP.

5. J. M. Bell, "All About That $300,000 Matter!"

6. *Vinita Indian Chieftain*, March 18, 1886.

7. Cormier, "Land, Currency, Cherokees," 85–89.

8. Wardell, *Political History*, 231–32.

9. Colbert, "Prophet of Progress," 384–87.

10. Stephens to Bell, February 2, March 4, 1885, Bell Papers, CNP.

11. *New York Times*, March 20, 1885.

12. McLoughlin, *After the Trail of Tears*, 269.

13. 49th Cong., 1st sess., H.R. Report no. 1474, April 6, 1886.

14. Colbert, "Prophet of Progress," 359–60.

15. Colbert, "Prophet of Progress," 396.

16. *New York Times*, October 5, 1890.

17. Her last name is sometimes spelled Minear. Helen Davis to James W. Parins, August 10, 2004. Ms. Davis is a descendant of Cornelius Boudinot and a rich source of information on the Boudinot family.

18. For legal activity in the Nation at this time see roll 73, Cherokee National Records, American Native Press Archives, University of Arkansas at Little Rock.

19. William P. Boudinot to Elias Cornelius Boudinot Sr., October 28, 1887, roll 73, Cherokee National Records.

20. Boudinot to Mayes, January 15, 1888, roll 73, Cherokee National Records.

21. This account of the funeral is taken from Colbert, "Prophet of Progress," 417. Colbert cites his source as the Elias C. Boudinot file at the Fort Smith Historical Society, but a search there turned up nothing but an empty folder.

22. Adams, *Elias Cornelius Boudinot*, 3–7.

23. *New York Times*, September 28, 1890.

24. Quoted in Adams, *Elias Cornelius Boudinot*, 23–24.

Bibliography

Abel, Annie H. *The American Indian and the End of the Confederacy, 1863–1866.* Lincoln: University of Nebraska Press, 1993.

———. *The American Indian as Slaveholder and Secessionist.* Lincoln: University of Nebraska Press, 1992.

———. *The American Indian in the Civil War, 1862–1865.* Lincoln: University of Nebraska Press, 1992.

Adams, John D. *Elias Cornelius Boudinot.* Chicago: Rand McNally, 1891.

Allsopp, Frederick William. *History of the Arkansas Press for a Hundred Years and More.* Little Rock: Parke-Harper, 1922.

Baird, David. *A Creek Warrior for the Confederacy: The Autobiography of Chief G. W. Grayson.* Norman: University of Oklahoma Press, 1988.

Beadle, J. H. *The Undeveloped West; or Five Years in the Territories.* Philadelphia and Chicago, 1873.

Bell, George Morrison, Sr. *Genealogy of Old and New Cherokee Families.* Bartlesville: Leonard Printing Co., 1872.

Bell, James M. "All About That $300,000 Matter!" Washington DC: R. A. Waters & Son, 1885.

Benedict, John D. *Muskogee and Northeastern Oklahoma, including the Counties of Muskogee, McIntosh, Wagoner, Cherokee, Sequoyah, Adair, Delaware, Mayes, Rogers, Washington, Nowata, Craig, and Ottawa.* Chicago: S. J. Clarke, 1922.

Berthrong, Donald J. "Cattlemen, etc." *Arizona and the West* 13 (spring 71): 5–32.

Boudinot, Elias C. "An Address to the Whites, Delivered in the First Presbyterian Church on the 26th of May, 1826." Philadelphia, 1826.

———. "Argument of Elias C. Boudinot, Submitted to the Senate Committee on Territories, January 17, 1879. The Committee Having Under Consideration the Resolutions of Hon. D. W. Voorhees, Relating to the Indian Territory." Washington DC: T. McGill & Co., 1879.

———. "Boudinot's Letter, Showing the Status of the United States Lands in the Indian Territory." Baltimore, 1879.

———. "Division of Lands, U.S. Citizens, and a Delegate in Congress for the Civilized Ind[ian]s of the IT. Speech of E. C. Boudinot, of the Cherokee Nation, Delivered at Vinita, IT, Aug. 29, 1874." St. Louis: Barns and Beynon, 1874.

———. "The Indian Territory and Its Inhabitants." *Journal of the American Geographical Society of New York.* N.p., 1874.

———. "Indian Territory: Argument submitted to the Senate Committee on Territories, January 17, 1879, the Committee Having Under Consideration the Resolutions of D. W. Voorhees, Relating to the Indian Territory." Washington DC: T. McGill, 1879.

———. "In the Matter of a Treaty or Treaties between the United States and the People of the Cherokee Nation." Washington DC, 1866.

———. "The Manners, Customs, Traditions, and Present Condition of the Civilized Indians of the Indian Territory." N.p., [1872].

———. "Map of Indian Territory." N.p.: Julius Bien & Co., 1879.

———. "Memorial of E. C. Boudinot, a Cherokee Indian, to the Senate and House of Representatives of the U.S. Can a Bureau or Department Annul the Stipulations of a Treaty? What is the Money Value of the Honor of a Nation Solemnly Pledged?" Washington DC: McGill and Witherow, 1870.

———. "The Memorial of E. C. Boudinot to the Congress of the U.S." Washington DC, 1877.

———. "Oklahoma: An Argument by E. C. Boudinot, of the Cherokee Nation, Delivered before the House Committee on Territories, February 3, 1876." Washington DC: McGill and Witherow, 1876.

———. "Oklahoma: Argument of Col. E. C. Boudinot before the Committee on Territories, January 29, 1878. The Committee Having under Consideration H.R. Bill No. 1596." Alexandria VA: G. H. Ramey and Sons, 1878.

———. "The Phillips Steal! How He and His Tools Stole $22,500 of Money Belonging to the Cherokee People!" N.p., 1884.

———. "Remarks of E. C. Boudinot, of the Cherokee Nation, in Behalf of the Bill to Organize the Territory of Oklahoma, before the House Committee on Territories, May 13, 1874." Washington DC: McGill and Witherow, [1874].

———. "Speech of E. C. Boudinot, a Cherokee Indian, on the Indian Question, Delivered at Vinita, Cherokee Nation, the Junction of the Atlantic & Pacific, and the Missouri, Kansas, and Texas Rail Road, Sept. 21, 1871." Washington DC: McGill and Witherow, 1872.

———. "Speech of E. C. Boudinot, of the Cherokee Nation, Delivered before the House Committee on Territories, March 5, 1872, on the Question of a Territorial Government for the IT, in Reply to the Second Argument of the Indian Delegation in Opposition to Such Proposed Government." Washington DC: McGill and Witherow, 1872.

———. "Speech of Elias C. Boudinot, a Cherokee Indian, Delivered before the House Committee on Territories, February 7, 1872, in Behalf of a Territorial Government for the Indian Territory, in Reply to Wm. P. Ross, A Cherokee Delegate, in His Argument Against any Congressional Action upon the Subject." Washington DC: McGill & Witheroe, 1872.

———. "Speech on the Indian Question, Delivered at Vinita, Cherokee Nation, Sept. 21." Terre Haute IN: Journal Office, 1871.

———. "A Territorial Government for the Civilized Indians of the IT: If They Must Be

Subjected to the Responsibilities of Citizens of the U.S., They Should Have Their Privileges Also." N.p., 1874.

Boudinot, Elias C., with W. P. Adair. "Reply of the Southern Cherokee, etc." Washington DC: McGill and Witherow, 1866.

Boyd, William H. *William H. Boyd's Directory of the District of Columbia.* Washington DC, 1878.

Brown, Walter Lee. *A Life of Albert Pike.* Fayetteville: University of Arkansas Press, 1997.

Campbell, O. Y. *The Story of Vinnie Ream.* Vinita, Indian Territory: Eastern Trails Historical Society, n.d.

Church, Mary Boudinot. "Elias Boudinot." *The Magazine of History, With Notes and Queries* 17 (December 1913): 212–15.

Colbert, Thomas Burnell. "Elias Cornelius Boudinot, 'The Indian Orator and Lecturer.'" *American Indian Quarterly* 1 (summer 1989): 49–59.

———. "Prophet of Progress: The Life and Times of Elias Cornelius Boudinot." Ph.D. diss., Oklahoma State University, 1982.

Compiled Laws of the Cherokee Nation. Tahlequah: Advocate Printing, 1892.

Cormier, Stephen T. "Land, Currency, Cherokees, and William Addison Phillips: A Study in Contradiction." MA thesis, Wichita State University, 1973.

Cunningham, Frank. *General Stand Watie's Confederate Indians.* Norman: University of Oklahoma Press, 1998.

Dale, Edward Everett. "The Cherokee Strip Live Stock Association." *Proceedings of the Fifth Annual Convention of the Southwestern Political and Social Science Association for 1924,* 97–115.

———. *History of the Ranch Cattle Industry in Oklahoma.* Washington DC: Government Printing Office, 1925, 1920.

———. "Letters of the Two Boudinots." *Chronicles of Oklahoma* 6, no. 3 (1928): 328–47.

Dale, Edward Everett, and Gaston Litton. *Cherokee Cavaliers: Forty Years of Cherokee History as Told in the Correspondence of the Ridge-Watie-Boudinot Family.* Norman: University of Oklahoma Press, 1995.

Dictionary of American Biography. 20 vols. New York: Scribner, 1933.

Dougan, Michael B. *Confederate Arkansas: The People and Policies of a Frontier State in Wartime.* University: University of Alabama Press, 1976.

Eaton, Rachel Caroline. "John Ross and the Cherokee Indians." Ph.D. diss., University of Chicago, 1919.

Forde, Lois Elizabeth. "Elias Cornelius Boudinot." Ph.D. diss., Columbia University, 1951.

Foreman, Grant. *A History of Oklahoma.* Norman: University of Oklahoma Press, 1942.

Franks, Kenny. *Stand Watie and the Agony of the Cherokee Nation.* Memphis: Memphis University Press, 1979.

Gabriel, Ralph Henry. *Elias Boudinot, Cherokee, and His America.* Norman: University of Oklahoma Press, 1941.

Gaul, Theresa Strouth. *To Marry an Indian: The Marriage of Harriet Gold and Elias Boudinot in Letters, 1823–39.* Chapel Hill: University of North Carolina Press, 2005.

Gideon, D. C. *Indian Territory, Descriptive, Biographical, and genealogical, including the Landed Estates, Country Seats, Etc., Etc.* New York: Lewis, 1901.

Gittinger, Roy. *The Formation of the State of Oklahoma, 1803–1906.* 1917. Norman: University of Oklahoma Press, 1939.

Gold, Theodore S. *Historical Records of the Town of Cornwall, Litchfield County, Connecticut.* Hartford: Case, Lockwood and Brainard, 1877.

Hallum, John. *Biographical and Pictorial History of Arkansas.* Albany NY, 1887.

Harman, S. W. *Hell on the Border: He Hanged Eighty-eight Men.* Lincoln: University of Nebraska Press, 1992.

Hauptman, Laurence M. *Between Two Fires: American Indians in the Civil War.* New York: The Free Press, 1995.

Heimann, Robert K. "The Cherokee Tobacco Case." *Chronicles of Oklahoma* 41, no. 3 (1963): 299–321.

Hill, L. B. *A History of Oklahoma.* Chicago: Lewis, 1908.

Hillyer, C. J. "The Atlantic and Pacific Rail Road and Indian Territory." Washington DC: McGill & Witheroe, 1875.

Hodges, Dewey Whitsett. "Col. E. C. Boudinot: His Influence on Oklahoma History." MA thesis, University of Oklahoma, 1929.

Hoig, Stan. *David L. Payne: The Oklahoma Boomer.* Oklahoma City: Western Heritage Books, 1980.

Holland, Cullen Joe. "The Cherokee Indian Newspapers, 1828–1906: The Tribal Voice of a People in Transition." Ph.D. diss., University of Minnesota, 1956.

Huff, J. Roger. *Goodspeed's Benton, Washington, Carroll, Madison, Crawford, Franklin and Sebastian Counties Arkansas History.* 1889. Reprint. Siloam Springs AR: J. Roger Huff, 1978.

Klema, Marion. "The Later Career of William A. Phillips." MA thesis, University of Kansas, 1942.

Klement, Frank J. *The Copperheads in the Middle West.* Gloucester MA: Peter Smith, 1972.

Kremer, Gary R. *James Milton Turner and the Promise of America: The Public Life of a Post–Civil War Black Leader.* Columbia: University of Missouri Press, 1991.

Littlefield, Daniel F., Jr., and James W. Parins. *American Indian and Alaska Native Newspapers and Periodicals, 1826–1924.* Westport CT: Greenwood Press, 1984.

Masterson, V. V. *The Katy Railroad and the Last Frontier.* Norman: University of Oklahoma Press, 1852.

McLoughlin, William G. *After the Trail of Tears: The Cherokees' Struggle for Sovereignty, 1829–1880.* Chapel Hill: University of North Carolina Press, 1993.

Miner, Craig. "The Struggle for an East-West Railway into the Indian Territory, 1870–1882." *Chronicles of Oklahoma* 47 (spring 1969): 67–87.

Miner, H. Craig. *The Corporation and the Indian: Tribal Sovereignty and Industrial Civilization in Indian Territory, 1865–1907.* Norman: University of Oklahoma Press, 1976.

———. *The St. Louis-San Francisco Transcontinental Railroad: The Thirty-fifth Parallel Project, 1853, 1890.* Lawrence: University of Kansas Press, 1972.

Monaghan, Jay. *Civil War on the Western Border, 1854–1865*, Lincoln: University of Nebraska Press, 1984.

Moore, Cherrie Adair. "William Penn Adair." *Chronicles of Oklahoma* 29 (spring 1951): 32–41.

Moulton, Gary E. *John Ross, Cherokee Chief.* Athens: University of Georgia Press, 1978.

———, ed. *The Papers of Chief John Ross.* Norman: University of Oklahoma Press, 1985.

O'Bierne, H. F., and E. S. O'Bierne. *The Indian Territory.* St. Louis: C. B. Woodward, 1892.

Parins, James W. *John Rollin Ridge: His Life and Works.* 2nd ed. Lincoln: University of Nebraska Press, 2004.

Rister, Carl Coke, *Land Hunger: David L. Payne and the Oklahoma Boomers.* Norman: University of Oklahoma Press, 1942.

Rock, Marion Tuttle. *Illustrated History of Oklahoma.* Topeka: C. B. Hamilton, 1890.

Ross, Mrs. William P. *The Life and Times of W. P. Ross.* Ft. Smith AR, 1893.

Savage, William W., Jr. *The Cherokee Strip Live Stock Association: Federal Regulation and the Cattleman's Last Frontier.* Columbia: University of Missouri Press, 1973.

———. "The Rock Falls Raid: An Analysis of the Documentary Evidence." *Chronicles of Oklahoma* 49, no. 1 (1971): 75–81.

Schurz, Carl. "Present Aspects of the Indian Problem." *North American Review* 133 (July 1881): 1–24.

Scroggs, Jack B. "Arkansas in the Secession Crisis." *Arkansas Historical Quarterly* 12, no. 3 (1953): 179–224.

Self, Nancy Hope. "The Building of the Railroads in the Cherokee Nation." *Chronicles of Oklahoma* 49 (summer 1971): 180–205.

Shoemaker, Arthur. "The Battle of Chustenahlah." *Chronicles of Oklahoma* 38 (summer 1960): 183–84.

Stephens, S. S. "The Indian Question Discussed by Spencer S. Stephens of the Cherokee Nation." Titusville, Indian Territory, 1882.

Thoburn, Joseph B. "The Cherokee Question." *Chronicles of Oklahoma* 2, no. 2 (1924): 141–242.

———. *A Standard History of Oklahoma.* Chicago: American Historical Society, 1916.

Thomas, David Y. "Elias Cornelius Boudinot." In *Dictionary of American Biography*, ed. Allen Johnson, 2:179. New York: Scribner, 1929.

Thornton, Hurshel Vern. "Oklahoma Municipal History (Indian Territory)." MA thesis, University of Oklahoma, 1929.

Voorhees, Daniel Wolsey. "The Boudinot Tobacco Case." Washington DC: Government Printing Office, 1880.

Warde, Mary Jane. "Fight for Survival: The Indian Response to the Boomer Movement." *Chronicles of Oklahoma* 67, no. 1 (1989): 30–51.

Wardell, Morris L. *A Political History of the Cherokee Nation, 1838–1907.* Norman: Oklahoma University Press, 1938.

Wilkins, Thurman. *Cherokee Tragedy: The Ridge Family and the Decimation of a People.* 2nd rev. ed. Norman: University of Oklahoma Press, 1986.

Woodward, Grace Steele. *The Cherokees*. Norman: University of Oklahoma Press, 1963.

Wooster, Ralph. "The Arkansas Secession Convention." *Arkansas Historical Quarterly* 13 (summer 1954): 172–95.

Wright, Muriel H. "Notes on Col. Elias C. Boudinot." *Chronicles of Oklahoma* 41 (winter 1963–64): 382–407.

Index

Boudinot, Elias Cornelius (*cont.*)
212–14; literary efforts of, 157, 186; marriage
of, 212; promotion to lieutenant colonel,
51; railroad interests of, 19, 24, 27, 210–
11; ranch of, at Paw Paw, 214; ranch of, at
Russell Creek, 116, 122–23; rhetorical skills
of, 170, 179–83; secretary of Arkansans
Secession Convention, 37–39; social life
of, 159–61; speeches of, 168, 169–72, 175–
76, 198; surrender of, at Little Rock, 62,
65; telephone interests of, 211
Boudinot, Elias Cornelius, Jr., 213, 215
Boudinot, Frank Brinsmade, 12, 18, 60
Boudinot, Harriet Gold: death of, 12; marriage
of, 5–7
Boudinot, Mary Harriet, 7, 17–18
Boudinot, Sarah Parkhill, 12; death of, 17
Boudinot, William Penn, 12, 18, 55, 59–60, 103,
143, 213, 215
Boudyville IT: post office at, 89
Boutwell, George S., 99
Bradley, Joseph P., 102–3
Bradley, Thomas H., 37
Brainerd School, 3
Brinsmade, Daniel Bourbon, 6, 16, 17
Bristow, B. H., 102
Britton, William A., 97
Brooks, E. J., 203
Brown, Walter Lee, 158
Brown Academy, 18
Bull Run, First Battle of, 45
Bunce, Isaiah, 5
Burnett, George W., 202
Burney, B. C., 197
Burr Seminary, 18
Bushyhead, Dennis W., 147–48, 206, 207, 214
Butler, Benjamin F., 100–101
Butler, Elizur, 10–11, 14
Butler, George, 164
Byhan, Gottlieb, 3

Caddo Resolutions, 175–76
Caldwell, H. C., 100
Calhoun, John C., 35
Callahan, S. B., 53
Cameron, Simon, 39

Campbell, O., 129
Canadian District: as proposed home for
southern Cherokees, 75
Cape Girardeau, 13
Carpenter, C. C., 196–97
Carter, Hannibal C., 208–10
Case, Lyman W., 18
Cass, Lewis, 10
Central Indian Railroad, 88, 90, 110
Chase, Samuel P., 102
Checote, Samuel, 184, 185
Cherokee Advocate (Tahlequah IT), 103, 126,
179, 186
Cherokee Confederate troops: recruitment of,
45–46
Cherokee Home Guard, 46
Cherokee Light Horse, 43
Cherokee Mounted Rifles, 46
Cherokee Mounted Volunteers, 46
Cherokee Nation: proposed division of, 17, 73,
75, 79; treaty of, with Confederacy, 45–46;
white settlement in, proposed, 52
Cherokee National Council, 4, 100–101, 206,
208; meetings of, banned in Georgia, 10;
Northern, 63, 66; Southern, 52
Cherokee Neutral Lands, 25, 31, 48, 110, 114,
153
Cherokee Outlet, 28, 52; attempted coloniza-
tion of, 195, 200–203; sale of, 78, 168, 205–
7
Cherokee Phoenix (New Echota CN), 8–9, 179,
186
Cherokees, North Carolina, 78
Cherokee Strip Live Stock Association, 203,
206
Cherokee tobacco case, 99–100
Chetopa KS, 120–21, 196
Chicago Times: letter to, 192–93
Chickasaws, 41, 44, 49, 68; Confederate treaty
of, 44, 54
Chickaskia River, 202
Choctaws, 28, 41, 44, 49, 68; Confederate
treaty of, 44, 54
Christie, Smith, 76
Church, Henry, 17
Chustenahlah IT: battle at, 49

citizenship: Cherokee, 1, 66, 162, 170, 208; U.S., of Indians, 85–86, 198

Clarkson, James J., 51

Cleveland, Grover, 63, 209, 214

Clifford, Nathan, 102

Coachman, Ward, 197

coal mining, 211

Codman, M., 202

Codman, O. M., 202

Colbert, Thomas, 38, 215, 216

Comanches, 24

Commissioner of Indian Affairs, 68, 191, 196

Confederate Congress: recruitment of Indian allies by, 41

Confederate States of America: formation of, 42

Connecticut Journal (New Haven), 5

Conway, Elias Nelson, 27

Cooley, Dennis N., 68–74, 77–78

Cooper, Douglas H., 41, 48–49

Cooper, Samuel, 51

Copperhead party, 43

Cornelius, Elias, 4

Cornwall CT: American Board of Commissioners for Foreign Missions school at, 3–7

cotton, 61

Court of Claims, U. S., 107

courts: establishment of in Indian Territory, 54

Cox, Jacob Dolson, 120

Crawford, John, 41

Creeks. *See* Muscogees

Cuney, Henry E., 209

Custer, George Armstrong, 158

Cypert, Jesse, 34

Daggett, Herman, 4

Darcheechee. *See* Steiner, David

Davis, David, 102–3

Davis, George W., 202

Davis, Jefferson, 29, 42, 55, 57

Dawes, Henry, 208

Delano, Columbus, 95–100

Delawares, 206, 208–10

Democratic party: in Arkansas, 28, 154; Arkansas Central Committee of, 30

Devens, Charles, 199, 203

Donnelley, James W., 97, 104

Douglass, J. W., 95

Downing, Lewis, 125, 173

Downingville IT, 127

Drew, John, 46, 50

Edmunds, James M., 68

Edmundson, H. H., 135, 150

education: among the Cherokees, 3

Eiffert, Henry, 130, 138–52, 213

Ewing, Thomas, 75

Farragut, David G.: statue of, 158

Far West Seminary, 22

Fayetteville AR, 15, 21; first city council of, 28–29

Field, Stephen J., 102

Fields, Richard, 73, 75

First Indian Brigade, 58

Folsom, Joseph P., 185

Folsom, Lizzie P., 185

Foote, Henry S., 29

Forfeiture Law, 73

Fort Arbuckle, 16

Fort Scott Daily Monitor (Kansas), 178

Fort Smith AR: description of, 212

Fort Smith and El Paso Railway Company, 210

Fort Smith Peace Conference, 67–74

Fort Sumter: attack on, 39, 42

Fourteenth Amendment, 198

Fox, George W., 146

freedmen, 162, 171, 185, 206, 208–10

Freedmen's Oklahoma Association, 208

Freemasons, 215

Free-Soilers, 24

Frye, M. C., 52

Fuller, Mary Ream, 159–60

Fuller, Perry, 75

Galbreath, Polly, 13

Gallegina. *See* Boudinot, Elias

Gambold, John, 3

Gardenir, George W., 202

Garland, Augustus Hill, 62–63, 65, 100–103, 210, 211

Gold, Benjamin, 5, 7–8, 19

Voorhees, Daniel W., 75, 99–106, 142, 163

Walker, David, 37, 39
Walker, L. P., 46
Walker, Robert J., 29, 165
Wardell, Morris, 28, 68, 76
Warren, J. M., 202
Washbourne, Josiah Woodward, 21, 24, 29, 44, 58, 68, 71, 76, 81, 89
Washburn, Cephas, 21, 22
Washington AR, 62
Washington Star, 160, 191
Watie, Buck. *See* Boudinot, Elias
Watie, David, 3
Watie, Nancy, 18
Watie, Saladin, 75, 83
Watie, Sarah C. (Sallie), 48, 60, 62, 108, 137, 139, 145, 195, 201
Watie, Stand, 3, 11, 16, 21, 22–23, 42, 67–68, 75, 83, 87, 167; in Civil War, 44–63; commission of, 45; death of, 107; election of, as principal chief, 52; promotion to brigadier general, 58; surrender of, 65–66, 73; war responsibilities outlined, 48
Watie, Thomas, 17
Webster, Daniel, 35

Weer, William, 51
Welsh, M. J., 202
West, William N., 189
"western Cherokees." *See* Old Settler Cherokees
Wet Prairie IT, 88
Whalen, J. M., 131, 150
Wheeler, John F., 18
Wheeler, W. W., 215
Whig party, 29
White Catcher, 76
Wichita Eagle, 200
Wilderness, Battle of, 59
Wilkins, Thurman, 13
Williams, Ira, 189
Wilson, A. M., 22, 29, 30, 44
Wilson's Creek, battle at, 45
Wishard, R. W., 95, 98
Wistar, Thomas, 68
Wolfe, Richard M., 207
Worcester, Samuel A., 8–11, 13
Worcester and Butler v. Georgia, 10–11
Wyandots, 68

Yell, James, 36

In the American Indian Lives series